Social Problems:
Constructionist Readings

Social Problems:
Constructionist Readings

editors

**Donileen R. Loseke
&
Joel Best**

ALDINETRANSACTION
A Division of Transaction Publishers
New Brunswick (U.S.A.) and London (U.K.)

Second Printing 2011

Copyright © 2003 by Transaction Publishers, New Brunswick, New Jersey.

All rights reserved under International and Pan-American Copyright Conventions. No part of this book may be reproduced or transmitted in any form or by any means, electronic or mechanical, including photocopy, recording, or any information storage and retrieval system, without prior permission in writing from the publisher. All inquiries should be addressed to AldineTransaction, A Division of Transaction Publishers, Rutgers—The State University of New Jersey, 35 Berrue Circle, Piscataway, New Jersey 08854-8042. www.transactionpub.com

This book is printed on acid-free paper that meets the American National Standard for Permanence of Paper for Printed Library Materials.

Library of Congress Catalog Number: 2002015298
ISBN: 978-0-202-30703-9
Printed in the United States of America

Library of Congress Cataloging-in-Publication Data

Social problems : constructionist readings / editors, Donileen R. Loseke, Joel Best.
        p. cm. — (Social problems and social issues)
    Includes bibliographical references and index.
    ISBN 0-202-30702-6 (alk. paper)
    ISBN 0-202-30703-4 (pbk. : alk. paper)
        1. Social problems. 2. Social perception. I. Loseke, Donileen R., 1947- II. Best, Joel. III. Series.

HN17.5 .S599   2002
361.1—dc21   2002015298

Contents

Preface

It has been 25 years since Malcolm Spector and John Kitsuse published *Constructing Social Problems*, a book calling upon sociologists to adopt a new approach to studying social problems. Offered as an alternative to examining the "objective" characteristics of social problems, constructionist approaches ask how and why particular social problems emerge and become the focus of demonstrations and protests, front-page news stories and television coverage, and new social policies. These approaches also examine how public consciousness of social problems can change the world around us as well as our understandings of this world.

Constructionist perspectives have become the leading theoretical approach for sociologists and others studying social problems. Yet constructionists' impact on the teaching of social problems has been far less dramatic. Undergraduate courses on social problems most often remain a theoretical mish-mash: Just as the first social problems textbooks did almost a century ago, textbooks continue to present a series of unrelated chapters, each devoted to a particular social problem.

We believe that part of the reason why constructionism hasn't had more impact on teaching has been that, until recently, there were no books specifically for students wanting an introduction to the perspective. Rather, books and journal articles exemplifying constructionist perspectives have been written primarily for those who already have done considerable thinking about constructionism, and they are written for academic readers who are interested in subtle and complex theoretical and empirical questions.

Donileen Loseke's *Thinking about Social Problems* was written to fill that gap, to provide an introduction to constructionist approaches that would be accessible to students. However, *Thinking about Social Problems* ought not, ideally, to stand alone as an introduction because, as a short text, it lacks detailed case studies demonstrating how constructionist perspectives actually can be applied to understand particular social problems. This reader is intended to do that; it presents brief, readable examples of constructionist analyses. While these articles can be read alone, we have organized these selections to correspond with the chapter topics in the second edition of *Thinking about Social Problems*. At the same time, some instructors who use this edited collection as a companion to *Thinking About Social Problems* might wish to re-sort some of these selections—many of them make multiple points and so reasonably could be used as examples in chapters other than the ones in which they appear. The notes at the end of every chapter in *Thinking About Social Problems* include some of these possibilities.

We wanted this reader to demonstrate the power of constructionist perspectives to examine the wide variety of claims made by many types of claims-makers. Therefore, some of these readings focus on the construction of problems by scientists and other professionals, others examine the work of social activists, mass media, and social service personnel. We chose our examples to include constructionists' studies of social inequalities as well as of individual deviance, two of the readings compare images of social problems in the United States with those in other countries, and several examine the importance of politics and power in constructing public images of social problems. We also cast a wide net for specific topics so that our articles range from television's portrayal of crime to earthquakes, from prostitutes to gifted children, from fat people to fathers wanting custody of their children, from multicultural education to urine testing for drugs, hate crime legislation and involuntary commitment in mental hospitals. We hope our attempt to include a wide variety of examples will serve to convince readers that constructionist perspectives have the power to examine a wide range of issues and the entire sweep of claims-makers and sites of constructing problems.

Our intent was to compile a reader that is accessible to people who are not already familiar with constructionism or those who are not particularly interested in subtle theoretical and empirical issues of concern to academics studying social problems from constructionist perspectives. While trying to remain true to their authors' intents, all of these pieces have been heavily edited to make them shorter and more readable. In addition to translating dense academic prose into accessible language, we cut out the vast majority of references in these pieces. If you wish to refer to one of these readings in your own work you should examine—and cite—the originals, not our abbreviated versions that often do not do justice to the complex reasoning as well as the theoretical and empirical supports for authors' arguments.

We would like to thank Richard Koffler, Aldine's Executive Editor, and the authors who agreed to let us excerpt their works. Carole Barone at the University of South Florida and Vicky Baynes at the University of Delaware provided expert assistance in scanning the original articles.

I

Examining Social Problems

Introduction to Section I

In daily life, we encounter the world around us as an objective reality: It simply exists, it is real. And it's obvious that our world is littered with *social problems*—a term used to label conditions believed to occur frequently, to be very troublesome in their consequences, and that therefore need to be eliminated. In political speeches, on the nightly news, in newspapers, and in classrooms we hear about multiple conditions called social problems: There are the problems of terrorism, poverty, drugs, and teens who go on killing rampages; we hear about an insolvent Social Security system, unaffordable medical care, pollution, crumbling highways, and drivers on these roads who are drunk or talking on cell phones while driving gas-guzzling SUVs with unsafe tires. There are missing children, abused children, pregnant children, drug-addicted children, and children who can't read. Daily we are bombarded with claims about all the frequent and devastating conditions in our environment that ought to be changed. From this perspective, social problems are objective conditions, elements in our social environment that should be examined to determine their magnitude, causes, consequences, and resolutions. This is the perspective of daily life and, until recently, the most popular perspective among academics studying social problems.

Social constructionist perspectives, the framework for this reader, challenge this commonsense notion that social problems should be studied only as objective conditions assumed to exist in society. Rather, constructionists focus on examining social problems as subjective definitions—how we *think* about social problems is as important as—sometimes more important than—objective characteristics of our world. This focus on examining subjective definitions leads to many questions: Why do we worry about some conditions and don't worry about others that, objectively speaking, are just as devastating in their consequences? What do people say or do to convince others that a troublesome condition exists that must be changed? What are the consequences of the typical ways that social problems attract concern? How do our subjective understandings of

3

social problems change the objective characteristics of our world? Indeed, how do those understandings change how we think about our own lives and the lives of those around us? Constructionist perspectives focus on how people create and respond to conditions, how we categorize and typify, how we subjectively construct the meanings of problems, and how our constructions influence how we act toward those conditions.

The readings in this section alert us to the importance of asking questions about how we define and understand the world around us. We should not assume that we worry about the things we should worry about, or don't worry about things we need not worry about. These readings also demonstrate how attending only to social problems as objective realities can lead us to miss important characteristics of social problems: What we do—and don't—worry about, as well as how we think about social problems, reflect the characteristics of the larger culture around us.

For example, is "spanking" a social problem? Historically, this behavior in the United States was constructed as a form of "parental discipline." It was evaluated by most Americans as something that was necessary—even good—for children. Spanking was a taken-for-granted condition in social life; it wasn't evaluated as troublesome. Yet in "The Changing Meanings of Spanking," Philip W. Davis examines how some people now construct spanking as a form of "child abuse," as a condition that must be eliminated. His exploration of the changing meanings of spanking demonstrates how any particular condition doesn't have a single, necessary meaning. The meaning of a condition can change over time. What is taken for granted in one historical era—spanking, racial discrimination, segregation, smoking cigarettes—can be transformed into a social problem in another era. Likewise, what is a social problem at one time—cohabiting outside marriage, employed mothers—can be considered not a social problem at another. No specific condition has a single, particular meaning. Because meanings are created by people, meanings can change over time.

Similarly, the same condition or behavior can be accorded the status of a social problem in one place but not in another. Consider a major social problem in Great Britain at this particular historical moment: "bullying in the workplace." "Bullying" is an all-purpose term encompassing negative, uncivil behaviors in the workplace. While incivility certainly exists in American workplaces, we do not hear about "bullying" as a social problem. Why not? Why is "bullying" accorded the status of a social problem in Great Britain but not in the United States? Frank Furedi examines "Bullying as a Social Problem in Great Britain," and considers how these two countries differ and how those differences lead to different evaluations of the same condition. What is—and what is not—evaluated as a social problem depends on the characteristics of the larger social, political, and cultural environments in which the condition exists.

Rather than assume Americans worry about what we should worry about and that we don't worry about what we need not worry about, we can ask what *do*—and don't—Americans worry about? We might ask, for example, why don't we worry about the threat of earthquakes? Robert A. Stallings examines "The Problem with the Earthquake Problem." He argues that scientists who study earthquakes believe the earthquake threat is very real yet the public does not seem worried. Textbooks on social problems don't include the earthquake threat, public opinion polls don't ask questions about it, preparing for earthquakes isn't high on political agendas, and so on. Stallings illustrates how our *perception* of risk is more important than any *objective indicators* of risk. Our perception is that earthquakes are "no big deal"; therefore, the earthquake threat is not a social problem even though objective indicators could be used to argue that we should fear them.

As we move from simply assuming that social problems are objective conditions in the social environment to constructionist perspectives examining how we think about social problems, we start to question *how* we know *what* we know. How do we know that homelessness is a social problem? How do we know that we have a social problem of illegal drugs? What is our image of "homelessness" or "drug abuse"? Where do we get these images? Increasingly, we learn about the characteristics of the world around us from the mass media/popular culture. Consider the genre of television called "reality programming," which presents itself simultaneously as fiction and fact. Gray Cavender considers how "Reality Television Constructs Crime." He asks: What do we learn about the social problem of crime when we watch shows such as *America's Most Wanted*, or *Unsolved Mysteries*? He argues that the major themes of television crime reality programs key into larger cultural concerns—what Americans believe and what we fear. He also demonstrates how a sense of "reality" on these programs is a social construction: It is scripted; it is achieved by things *done* by producers and show hosts that give watchers a feeling that "this is reality." Although we might be led to thinking that these shows portray the reality of crime, it is a reality that does not mirror the objective characteristics of crime, it is a reality that is socially constructed by people.

The readings in this section all focus on questions about relationships between objective reality and subjective definitions, between the world existing outside us and our understandings of that world. In various ways, these readings demonstrate how we cannot simply assume that we worry about what we should worry about, that our worries are somehow rational rather than reflecting cultural biases, that our sources of knowledge supply us with facts rather than fiction. These readings set the stage for asking constructionist questions about how people construct reality and make our world meaningful.

1

The Changing Meanings
of Spanking

Phillip W. Davis

Spanking is more than mild physical punishment to make children behave. It is also the focus of competing ideas, beliefs, and vocabularies put forth by critics and advocates in a debate over spanking's definition, appropriateness, and implications. There is a long history of religious and secular justifications for spanking. Beliefs that spanking is natural, normal, and necessary form a "spare the rod ideology" that may perpetuate the practice. Trivializing terms such as "smack," "spank," and "whack" are at the heart of a rhetoric of punishment that presupposes the legitimacy of parental authority and makes assumptions about the impersonality of adult motivation. Spanking is a socially constructed reality; it means what people say it means.

Controversial topics such as spanking cause people to trade competing images and moral vocabularies. They look selectively at certain parts of the "problem" and not at others. My purpose is to compare the traditional defense of spanking with the emergent criticism of spanking, identifying the claims and counterclaims spanking's advocates and critics have made in the popular press since mid-century. I will limit my focus to the debate over spanking by parents, recognizing that there is a parallel debate about spanking in schools. In general I argue that the debate over spanking has become more complex in its themes and vocabularies. New definitions of spanking supplement older ones, and what was once primarily a child-rearing issue has become a child-protection issue as well.

This chapter is excerpted from Davis, Phillip W. (1994). "The Changing Meanings of Spanking." Pp. 133–54 in *Troubling Children: Studies of Children and Social Problems*, edited by Joel Best. Hawthorne, NY: Aldine de Gruyter.

TRADITIONAL DEFENSES OF SPANKING

Spanking's advocates traditionally use a rhetoric and vocabulary that paint spanking as the reasonable reaction of responsible parents to their wayward children. They claim that spanking is (1) the sign of nonpermissiveness, (2) anticipatory socialization, (3) God's will, (4) a morally neutral childrearing tool, and (5) a psychic release.

The Sign of Nonpermissiveness

Advocates often present spanking as an answer to the problem of permissive parents who are responsible for much of the "youth problem." The argument is that parents' lax attitudes result in the "undercontrol" of their children who go on to become delinquents, hippies, political activists, liars, cheaters, and thieves who lack respect for authority. In this view, failure to spank becomes the benchmark of permissiveness. Advocates also argue that character flaws lie behind the permissiveness of parents who do not spank; they lack the courage and responsibility that spanking is said to require. According to these advocates, parents who don't spank have neglected their responsibilities, taken the easy way out, or let themselves be duped by experts into taking a scientifically progressive but unwittingly troubled path.

Anticipatory Socialization

A second claim is that spanking effectively prepares children for the tribulations of life and the vagaries of adulthood. Some advocates argue that children will profit from spankings once they enter the real world, a world that is characteristically more difficult and demanding than family life. One advocate wrote that going "back to the hairbrush" prepares children for life's "booby-traps": ". . . the poor kids, when they eventually break out of the cocoon of an undisciplined childhood, are completely unprepared for the fenced-in and booby-trapped pattern of conventional adult life." This statement appeals to the idea that modernity and nonspanking are an unfortunate combination and that old-fashioned approaches better prepare children for the confinements of adult life.

God's Will

Religious themes appear when authors mention "biblical sanctions" as a traditional argument for spanking. James Dobson, author of *Dare to*

Discipline, writes from the standpoint of Christian fundamentalism and is notorious among critics for his advocacy of spanking and switching: "I think we should not eliminate a biblically sanctioned approach to raising children because it is abused in some cases" (quoted in Neff 1993).

A Morally Neutral Childrearing Tool

Advocates often refer to spanking as a tool, technique, or method, writing about it as if its use were but the impersonal and mechanical application of a morally neutral procedure. The virtues of this technique are said to include speed, efficiency, and efficacy. Spanking creates obedience and respect with minimum effort and without long, "dragged-out" discussions. These claims contend that the good child is an obedient child and that faster techniques are superior to slower ones. Defining spanking as a tool or method suggests that spankers are purposive rather than aimless, and depicts spanking as a logical activity rather than an emotional outburst. The overall image of parents who spank is that their "applications" are part of a method that is reasonable, systematic, and even merciful. The definition of spanking as a childrearing tool or technique is especially clear in the widespread claim that spanking should be used as a last resort, only after other, presumably less harsh, efforts have failed. The rhetoric of "last resorts" implies that spankers possess the knowledge and ability to mete out penalties of varying severity in the proper sequence.

A Psychic Release

Another common contention is that spanking resolves particular conflicts by somehow allowing parents and their children to start over, because it "clears the air." Some authors claim that spanking frees children from guilt by providing them with an opportunity for repentance or offers a cathartic release of the parent's tension and anger. Advocates also contend that parents who don't spank will find other, less healthy, ways of expressing their anger. If they don't become neurotically guilty, insecure, or repressed, parents may erupt later and do greater harm to the child, for all their progressive efforts to conform to the new psychology.

THE CRITICS RESPOND

Critics of spanking claim that these traditional defenses are flawed for a variety of reasons. They argue that, rather than preventing youth problems, spanking creates them. For one thing, spanking makes children untrustworthy because children might cheat or lie in order to avoid spankings. Critics also claim that, although spanking may "work" in the immediate situation, its effects are highly limited because it can cause children's rebellion and resentment. They also argue that, while it may be effective, it is effective for the wrong reason. Instead of complying voluntarily out of respect based on reason, children who are spanked comply out of fear. Critics claim that spankers are irresponsible, because they are avoiding the harder but superior alternatives. Spankers worry too much about teaching the values of respect and authority, oblivious to the fact that spanking really teaches the legitimacy of aggression, brute strength, and revenge. Critics also contend that spanking can easily escalate. Critics argue that the true meaning of discipline involves teaching children the lesson of self-control, whereas "physical discipline" only teaches them "might makes right."

In sum, since mid-century advocates and critics in the popular press have been invoking several different meanings of spanking. Advocates for spanking claim that children are "underdisciplined," that they need to be spanked, that parents who do not spank are mollycoddling their children, that being spanked doesn't harm children, and that nonspanking parents are irresponsible. Critics respond that spanking is futile at best and counterproductive at worst. In this traditional debate, advocates emphasize the drawbacks of permissiveness as a cause of delinquency and rebellion, and critics argue that discipline should involve teaching and self-control.

EMERGENT MEANINGS

The traditional claims about spanking persist. But spanking's critics bring newer, supplementary meanings to the debate, meanings that coincide with changing concerns and arguments borrowed from debates over other issues.

Spanking Is Compulsive

The critics' first new claim is that spanking is compulsive, habit-forming, or addictive. This claim depicts parents as people who have lost their autonomy by becoming dependent on a highly satisfying behavior that they can abandon only with considerable difficulty. Critics compare spanking to smoking, because both practices are legal, harmful, and habitual, and given the widespread criticisms of each, they are increasingly secretive practices. Responding to a report that time out is more popular with parents than spanking, for example, one pediatrician was skeptical, saying that "spankers today are like closet smokers."

Spanking Is a Demeaning, Violent Act

Critics routinely echo the view of most family violence researchers that spanking is a form of violence. They describe spanking as an act of violence that models violent behavior for the child and teaches children that violence is socially acceptable. Critics argue that spanking humiliates and devalues the child and demonstrates that physical violence is a good way to solve problems. For critics, spanking is a prime example of minor violence that later causes adult violence, especially by those who experience frequent, severe spankings as children. With increasing frequency, newspaper and magazine articles interweave references to spanking and abuse and some emphasize that a "fine line" separates spanking and abuse, a line that is too easily crossed.

The Advocates Respond

Advocates have had little say about the idea that spanking is a compulsion, but they take issue with critics who claim it is violent or abusive. Some claim that critics are less concerned about raising children than they are about social appearances. Some writers make increasingly sharp distinctions between spanking and abuse, between "an occasional swat" and spankings, or between rare swats and corporal punishment. Some advocates tell parents just what to do so that they will not be considered abusive:

> Spank only for a few specific offenses, such as blatant disrespect and defiance. . . . John Rosemond, in his Knight News Service newspaper column "Parent and Child," gives these guidelines: "With no threats or warnings, spank with your hand, not a wooden spoon, paddle, belt or switch. A spanking is not more than three swats to the child's rear end. A swat to any other part of the child's body is abuse. (Oliver 1987)

DISCUSSION

"Spanking" remains a fighting word, and what people are fighting about is both complex and changing. Over time, a topic traditionally approached as a childrearing issue in a debate over "what works" has also become a child-protection issue in a debate over whether spanking is violent and abusive.

Advocates of spanking extol its virtues in the name of tradition, effectiveness, efficiency, and responsibility, defining it essentially as a tool, technique, or method for making children behave. Spanking is said to offer an antidote to the youth problem, release tension for both parent and child, and prepare children for life's hardships. Advocates generally ignore or trivialize children's suffering, portray nonspankers as irresponsible, and cite their own positive personal histories as spanked children. Critics counter that spanking promotes, rather than deters, misbehavior. They contend that it is usually an expression of the parent's anger and frustration and teaches children that violence and aggression are acceptable. More recent critics also define spanking as a bad habit, an act of violence, and a form of abuse. All too often, they argue, spanking leads to abuse later in life or is closely linked to the abuse of the spanked child.

In the context of increasingly broad definitions of child abuse, some advocates argue for narrow definitions of spanking (spank only on the bottom). Narrow definitions, as well as distinctions between planned spankings and the occasional smack, are ways of maintaining a "place" for spanking on the list of what parents can rightfully do to their children without lapsing into a category of "child abuser."

Activities in wider professional, scientific, religious, and political contexts have no doubt prompted and shaped these changing meanings for spanking. Psychological research and popular writings on aggression in the 1950s and 1960s challenged behaviorist assumptions about the role of punishment. Some well-publicized studies provided dramatic ironies such as physical punishment for aggressive behavior is associated with more, not less, aggression by children. Many of these scholarly ideas and facts made their way into articles and stories in the popular press.

Moreover, in the 1960s and early 1970s, the development of a modern child-protection movement, the discovery of child abuse, and the continuing emergence of violence as a major policy issue led to a series of controversies associated with the idea that children are increasingly "at risk." As these issues developed, spanking was mentioned, and sometimes its importance was highlighted.

There has also been a convergence of interests and activities among anticorporal punishment and antiabuse organizations. Organizations such as the National Coalition to Abolish Corporal Punishment in Schools, the National Center for the Study of Corporal Punishment and Alternatives, and End Violence against the Next Generation, although they focus on educational settings, regularly point to spanking and physical punishment by parents as an analogous issue. The National Committee for the Prevention of Child Abuse (NCPCA) has been actively seeking the primary prevention of child abuse through pamphlets, surveys, and press releases about physical punishment and spanking since the mid-1980s.

We cannot make a flat statement that the newer meanings of "spanking" are now dominant. The themes in the newer debate suggest only a partial transformation of the traditional childrearing issue into a contemporary child-protection controversy. There is certainly the potential for definitions related to abuse to become dominant. Whether the transformation proceeds further depends in part on the discourse, resources, and activities of advocates and critics in organizational, political, media, and movement contexts.

Activities in medical settings will have an impact. The Centers for the Study of Disease Control instituted a division for the study of domestic violence in 1992. The June 1992 issue of the *Journal of the American Medical Association* was devoted to family violence and included an article on spanking as a form of corporal punishment. Some physicians now claim that corporal punishment is child abuse. These medical developments, if they are recognized by the press, policymakers, and agency officials, should encourage spanking's association with child abuse.

Other activities, however, are likely to inhibit the ascendance of abuse meanings. Religious action groups are sensitive and alert to any move to broaden definitions of abuse to include spanking or to remove existing legal protections of parents who use reasonable physical discipline. We may see other spanking-related controversies develop as groups organize to resist further involvement by the state in family matters. In addition, some critics promote the idea that spanking is really a civil rights issue, and civil rights organizations may make spanking part of their agenda. Their constructions of the problem might easily bypass the issue of abuse or make it secondary to the issue of discrimination on the basis of age. Similarly, critics campaigning for state and national legislation may successfully promote the association of spanking with the violation of human or children's rights rather than child abuse. Whether spanking ever fully becomes a child-protection issue, these emergent meanings challenge the assumptions that spanking is natural, normal, and necessary on a fundamental level.

REFERENCES

Neff, D. 1993. "Dobson's New Dare" [interview with J. Dobson]. *Christianity Today* 37 (February 8):69–70.
Oliver, S. 1987. "How to Stop Spanking." *Essence* 18 (April):98.

2

Bullying as a Social Problem in Great Britain

FRANK FUREDI

Let's face it. America has been in denial about bullying. International practitioners, unions, researchers and advocates are the pioneers in the antibullying movement.

Campaign Against Workplace Bullying (1999)

Workplace bullying covers a multitude of sins. Virtually any negative, uncivil encounter can be and is defined as bullying. Bullying encompasses vandalism, gestures, withholding of important information, and making faces—even "smiling the wrong way." Bullying can include ignoring a person's contributions, flaunting status, pulling rank, making unwanted eye contact, and openly belittling individuals. Widely accepted definitions of bullying insist that these acts are determined by the victims' feelings rather than by the intention of the person who caused the offense. As the notion of "unacceptable behavior" is typically left rather vague, the range of individual acts that it can encompass becomes infinite. It is the individual's emotion, rather than any objectively defined criteria, that ultimately defines an act or an experience as harmful.

American moral crusaders rarely are as dependent on international support as the promoters of the Campaign Against Workplace Bullying (CAWB). On the contrary, they are often in the privileged position of

This chapter is excerpted from Furedi, Frank (2001). "Bullying: The British Contribution to the Construction of a Social Problem." Pp. 89–106 in *How Claims Spread: Cross-National Diffusion of Social Problems*, edited by Joel Best. Hawthorne, NY: Aldine de Gruyter.

exporting their successful causes to other parts of the world. But in the case of workplace bullying, the diffusion of the problem is in the opposite direction. In contrast to most forms of victim advocacy, American crusaders against workplace bullying systematically rely upon their international contacts for affirmation and support. They continually point to the success of their cause abroad in order to validate their own efforts. Advocates regard Sweden, which has enacted a "dignity at work" law, as a model for the United States to emulate.

While Sweden offers a model of enlightened workplace practice, the unique success of the British campaign against bullying is regarded as the exemplar: American advocates continually rely on the authority of their British counterparts to gain recognition for their causes. It is in Britain that the problem of workplace bullying has had the greatest impact on the perceptions of society. Advocates claim that workplace bullying is more prevalent there than elsewhere. According to a 1996 study carried out by the European Foundation for the Improvement of Living and Working Conditions, bullying in the European Union affected 8 percent of workers. However, this figure pales in comparison to the far more dramatic incidence of bullying that researchers claim prevails in the United Kingdom. One study claims that in the United Kingdom, 53 percent of employees have been bullied at work, and that 78 percent have witnessed bullying at work.

Now there is widespread support for the contention that Britain suffers from an epidemic of bullying. Whereas in the United States, there has been little public recognition accorded to this issue, in Britain it has become headline news. In this essay I explore the emergence of this issue and why and how workplace bullying has been transformed into a major social problem in the United Kingdom. I also reflect on the prospects for this moral crusade in the United States.

THE BRITISH EXPERIENCE

The British public first heard of bullying in 1991. Andrea Adams, who is generally recognized as the pioneering crusader of this issue, succeeded in producing two BBC radio programs on workplace bullying and in placing a few articles in the British press. Her main concern was to gain recognition of the problem. As a skilled journalist, she was able to link the problem to the existing widespread public concern with the bullying of children in school. One of the key themes of her campaign was that bullying does not stop in childhood and that millions of adults suffer in silence from this affliction. A small group of academic experts gravitated toward the promotion of this issue and were ready to affirm Adams's claim.

The public recognition accorded to childhood bullying provided an important platform from which to launch claims about adult bullying. Bullying experts projected adult bullying as the outcome of negative childhood experiences. Consequently, the antibullying campaign could tap into the existing public concern about the abusive behavior children suffered from both their peers and adults. Time and again, activists warned that bullying was not confined to children.

Another important theme pursued by Adams was the association of workplace problems with bullying—particularly bullying management styles. Adams appealed to both trade unions (on the grounds of health and safety) and to employers (on the grounds of cost to industry). Her book highlighted the claim that bullying cost millions of pounds to industry through absenteeism and reduced productivity. Newspaper reports widely publicized this burden on British industry.

By 1996, workplace bullying had entered the media vocabulary. Although reports and newspaper articles still referred to (and continue to refer to) this phenomenon as a hidden and unacknowledged problem, it acquired the status of one of the new abuse issues of the nineties. A study suggesting that more than half of employees had been bullied was presented by the media as straightforward fact. In September, the bullying of teachers by their senior colleagues emerged as a major issue. The Nottinghamshire education authority responded by introducing formal measures to combat the problem. This problem was publicized through a survey conducted by a teaching union, which stated that up to 4,000 teachers face abuse and bullying by fellow teachers every day. Individual victims also began to frame their demands for compensation in the language of bullying. Individuals' claims of bullying were regularly validated by numerous surveys and reports that suggested that this was a very serious workplace problem.

Active lobbying by antibullying campaigners has been unusually effective and has met with virtually no resistance. Although the campaign was based on a small network of advocates and professionals, its impact on British opinion makers and the media was formidable. In less than a decade, a hitherto unknown issue succeeded in winning widespread recognition as a major social problem. One reason why this campaign was so successful was that the issue of bullying was framed in a way that was unlikely to raise controversy. Campaigners carefully avoided targeting any vested interests and attempted to appeal to all the relevant interest groups. Bullying was defined as a disease that afflicted the whole of society and from which no one gained. The victims of workplace bullies were presented as normal, everyday people entitled to society's sympathy. A form of antisocial behavior, bullying fed into a more general concern with incivility in British society.

Workplace bullying became an issue that posed no threat to any interests. The issue was framed in general, diffuse terms. Virtually any form of negative behavior that offends contemporary social etiquette can be encompassed by the definition of bullying. Its only distinguishing feature is that it is not a singular event but a form of long-term, negative behavior. There is little consensus on how to define this negative behavior. One international study contends that bullying can occur in a number of different ways and that some are obvious while others are subtle and difficult to explain. Bullying serves to affirm the ideals of civil life, often expressed by the equally diffuse term of "appropriate behavior."

Unlike many other workplace problems, bullying did not raise the question of conflicting interests. Whereas the problem of sexual harassment could raise tensions between men and women and racial discrimination could provoke controversy between blacks and whites, the question of bullying was presented as a problem for everyone. Although it was often used as part of a critique of "macho" management style, business had no problem with accommodating to the issue because it blamed the individual manager rather than the company itself. This individualized focus, along with the focus on worker-to-worker relations, was clearly not perceived as a threat by employers. Indeed, many employers welcomed the discovery of the workplace bully since it provided a widely accepted explanation for personnel problems. From an early stage, antibullying crusaders were able to gain the cooperation of many employers and their organizations.

The rise of the issue of bullying coincided with the increased recognition accorded to stress as a symptom of a more widespread malaise afflicting the workplace. In the aftermath of the shakeout of British industry, human resources experts emphasized stress and problems of the emotions as negative outcomes of this process. A 1993 report published by one employer organization, the Industrial Society, claimed that bosses listed stress, emotional, and personal problems as the most important reasons for sick leave after colds and the flu. Numerous reports covering education, banking, the health sector, public-sector manual workers, and telephone companies offered alarming figures suggesting that 50 to 60 percent of employees suffered from stress. Antibullying activists were quick to link their cause to the issue of stress.

Politicians and government officials readily accepted the argument that something had to be done about workplace bullying. Guidelines on stress at work issued by the Health and Safety Executive Unions provided official recognition of this new social problem. In October 1998, the Public Health Minister officially backed the antibullying campaign. Antibullying policies were swiftly adopted in the public sector and informal pressure was placed on private enterprise to follow suit. Because the main promoters of this issue were the trade union movement and individuals closely allied to it, antibullying policy tended to be more widespread in work-places that were unionized.

At a time when Britain was in the middle of assimilating and politiciz-ing problems of emotion such as abuse and harassment, the media were quite hospitable to new claims of psychological hurt. Virtually any claim of workplace bullying was assured of national media publicity. The media did not interrogate any of the research upon which highly alarmist claims were based. The claims made about the dimensions of the problem were faithfully reported as uncontroversial facts.

The recognition that British society accorded to the adult bully encour-aged new groups of victims to frame their problems in the language of bul-lying. Victims of bullying and their lawyers were quick to convert the sympathy accorded to their plight into a demand for compensation. For their part, the British courts were distinctly responsive to the demands of those suffering from this newly discovered form of psychological injury. A number of landmark court cases lent weight to the claim that the victims of bullying suffered grave psychological harm.

THE UNION LINK

Social problems do not simply appear out of nowhere. From the stand-point of a constructionist sociology of social problems the emergence of a social problem like that of workplace bullying is most usefully understood as the outcome of "the activities of individuals or groups making asser-tions of grievances and claims with respect to some putative conditions" (Spector and Kitsuse 1977: 75). In Britain, the activities of an energetic group of skilled claims-makers played a crucial role in the construction of bullying as a social problem. Like the leading proponents of workplace bullying in the United States, many British activists claimed to have gained their expertise from their own experience of victimization; many of them insisted that personal experience encouraged them to embark on the road to discovery of this particular problem.

From the outset, antibullying experts were able to draw on therapeutic professionals to give credibility to their diagnosis of the problem. Through their informal network, the experts succeeded in gaining recognition for their campaign. Therapeutic culture today assigns an important role to victim authority. Victim-experts are expected to speak out and are treated as recognized authorities on many of the problems facing society. How-ever, professional antibullying experts on their own could not have suc-ceeded in gaining such formidable national recognition for their cause. It was the adoption of this problem as their own by the trade union move-ment that underwrote the success of the antibullying campaign.

The small group of antibullying claims-makers found influential allies in the British trade union movement. Unions associated with the International Labor Organization (ILO) became interested in the issue of workplace stress caused by "psychological violence" in the late eighties. Workplace bullying provided a new focus for raising the problem of stress. By 1994, British unions had begun to campaign around this newly discovered problem. A conference by the Manufacturing Science and Finance Union (MSF) titled "Bullying at Work," gained this union positive media recognition. This conference, which brought together union activists and expert claims-makers such as Andrea Adams, provided an important opportunity for gaining media publicity. Its success encouraged other unions to take up the issue.

The adoption of workplace bullying as a cause by a section of the British trade union movement led to its transformation into a widely recognized social problem. Union officials actively relied on their expertise to provide authority for their antibullying drive. Unions sponsored many of the surveys carried out by bullying experts. The MSF, the first labor organization to carnpaign actively on this subject, had close links with Andrea Adams. In 1994, the Public and Commercial Services Union of civil servants approached the Contributions and Benefits Agencies and demanded that bullying be made a disciplinary offence. This request was quickly accepted. Other unions published reports and launched campaigns. The issue gained greater prominence when a motion condemning the spread of bullying and hectoring management styles was passed by the 1995 national Trade Union Conference (TUC).

A closer inspection of the claim that the workplace has become traumatized by an epidemic of bullying indicates that what is under discussion is what used to be called office politics, assertive management, or the compulsion to get the job done. Trade union reports link the pressure to meet targets to the creation of an environment in which intimidation and victimization are almost unavoidable. The key focus of trade union activists is the pathologizing of workplace stress. Their reports claim a phenomenal rise of workplace stress. An increase in workload, combined with a more bullying style of management, is held accountable for the prevalence of this disease.

Trade union activists have been able to draw on a wide consensus that defines stress as harmful by definition. This medicalization of stress by health activists and the therapy lobby has helped union activists gain widespread sympathy for their claim. Consequently, claims for compensation because of stress at work are on the increase. According to a TUC report published in September 1998, stress tops the list of cases that unions are taking to the courts. By linking stress to bullying, unions have sought to portray this disease as the outcome of psychological violence.

The adoption of bullying as a major focus for its activities by the union movement was also part of its reorientation toward a new-look, consumer-oriented approach. This development was integral to the trade union response to the crisis it faced in the early eighties. During that decade, union leaders found it increasingly difficult to forge an effective role for themselves. The decline of collective solidarity and the weakening appeal of union activism diminished the movement's influence. Union leaders responded by adopting the role of workplace advocates for the individual problems facing employees. The issue of health and safety emerged as a central theme in union politics. In order to play an effective role as the advocate for the workplace victim, trade unionism has become a high-profile advocate of therapeutic services. Whereas union were once noted for their shop-floor activism and organizing, today they are far more likely to be known for their campaigns against workplace stress and bullying and for the help lines they run for those facing management bullying. British unions now offer their members stress counseling and run workshops on how to cope with the demands of a busy workplace. Buying into the culture of emotionalism has given unions a new rationale for their existence.

THE AMERICAN EXPERIENCE

It is evident that the trade union movement, a nationally influential institution, played a crucial role in placing workplace bullying on the national agenda in Britain. American campaigners have failed to attract the support of an organization whose influence is comparable to the British TUC. It is the absence of a comparable constituency of support that explains the restricted diffusion of the problem of workplace bullying in the United States. American claims-makers also face a further obstacle. The role of trade unions in the national life of the United States is far less significant than in Britain. Consequently, this potential body of support is unlikely to be as effective as the British TUC in influencing the American media and a wider body of opinion. American proponents of workplace bullying are also confronted with a reality in which there are already well-established workplace problems that touch on issues raised by their cause—sexual harassment, racial discrimination, and discrimination on grounds of disability have gained widespread recognition. It is far from clear whether the social problems market has a place for a more general form of psychological injury.

Experience suggests that workplace bullying is far more likely to become a social problem in societies where trade unions enjoy widespread legitimacy. Yet one question raised by the experience of the past decade is why workplace bullying managed to gain greater prominence in Britain than in other Western European societies that also have powerful unions. The skill and effectiveness of British moral crusaders no doubt played a part in the popularization of this issue. But probably the most significant variable has been the unique receptivity of British society to claims of abuse. Britain stands out as the European society that has most thoroughly assimilated American social problems such as child abuse, elder abuse, stalking, hate crimes, violence against women, and various forms of harassment.

Bullying, an all-purpose form of harassment, makes sense in a society that systematically anticipates psychological injury in human relations. During the nineties the meaning of bullying expanded to cover a bewildering variety of troublesome relations. Hence, the campaign against bullying has found a rich reservoir of support in a culture intensely preoccupied with the problem of abuse. That is why, in contrast to other parts of Europe, workplace bullying in Great Britain has become one of the defining social problems of the turn of the millennium. The United States shares many of the cultural preoccupations of Britain, but the absence of a credible and infuential movement ready to take up this crusade continues to consign workplace bullying to the margins of American society.

REFERENCES

Campaign Against Workplace Bullying (1999). www.bullybusters.org/home/ bullybust.html

Spector, Malcolm, and John I. Kitsuse (1977). *Constructing Social Problems.* Menlo Park, CA: Cummings.

3

The Problem with the Earthquake Problem

ROBERT A. STALLINGS

There is an old joke about the ultimate California earthquake. Several versions exist, but most go something like this:

> *Speaker:* "I just bought ocean front property in Nevada."
> *Friend:* "What are you talking about? Nevada isn't on the ocean."
> *Speaker:* "After the Big One, it will be!"

"The Big One" is most people's idea of a catastrophic earthquake. Like the joke about ocean front property, the popular image of the Big One is one of widespread destruction. Some people actually believe that parts of California will disappear into the Pacific Ocean. Indeed, earthquakes and California are synonymous. They are part of the image of California, along with Hollywood stars, violent crime, theme parks, and freeways.

Experts who study earthquakes and earthquake safety advocates have a different image of catastrophic earthquakes. Rather than what nature may do in the future, they worry about what people are doing in the present. Instead of total destruction, they see scattered pockets of vulnerability associated with structures built on certain types of soil or with design standards that did not take into account the risk of earthquakes. More than just physical destruction, they worry about economic consequences for the nation as a whole. And rather than seeing earthquakes as simply a threat in California or the West Coast, they see the risk of earthquakes existing in a majority of states in the United States.

The greatest difference between most people's view of the earthquake threat and the view of experts and safety advocates is how little concern

---

This chapter is excerpted from Stallings, Robert A. (1995). *Promoting Risk: Constructing the Earthquake Threat* (Chapter 1). Hawthorne, NY: Aldine de Gruyter.

there is in the public at large for doing something about it. The risk of future earthquakes is a low-priority issue for nearly everyone, even in California. Other issues provoke more passionate debate and louder calls for action. In fact, the existence of jokes about the Big One suggests how different the earthquake threat is from other public issues and social problems. Jokes about serial killers, child molesters, wife beaters, the homeless, AIDS sufferers, victims of gang violence, and the unemployed are more likely to be thought of as in bad taste.

To understand why there is such a difference between experts' views about the risk of earthquakes and nearly everyone else's, I will concentrate on the people who create "information" about the earthquake threat rather than on people (like me) who receive such information. I will assume that the risk of earthquakes is not self-evident. In other words, I will take the point of view that whether the risk is primarily a threat to life or a potential economic disaster, whether it is widespread or confined to one area, whether it is more important or less important than other public issues, and so forth, depends on what risk promoters are able to accomplish, rather than on self-evident "facts" about the earth.

First I will describe some of the ways that people identify what they consider to be our current social problems. Then I will describe what experts expect to happen when the catastrophic earthquake—the Big One—strikes. The difference between people's concern (or lack of concern) and what experts believe to be our future raises the question of whether the earthquake threat is unique and altogether different from other public issues and problems of the day.

EARTHQUAKE RISKS ARE NO BIG DEAL

For their victims, earthquakes are serious trouble indeed. They damage homes and ruin businesses. They injure and kill, often in grotesque ways as we saw in 1989 on the collapsed freeway in Oakland, California, and again in 1994 at the Northridge Meadows Apartment complex in Los Angeles. For most people, however, earthquakes are merely another story in the news. They lose interest long before the injured recover and the damaged buildings are repaired.

Despite the potential for death, destruction, and deprivation, the threat of future earthquakes seems to be "no big deal." At least that is the impression one gets from looking at the ways we keep track of our most pressing concerns. Public opinion polls, for instance, regularly indicate relatively little concern for the earthquake threat. Issues such as the state of the economy, poverty and homelessness, drugs and drug abuse, the federal budget deficit, "ethics and morals," unemployment, and education regularly made the list of current problems in 1991. The threat of earthquakes did not. Pollsters themselves show no more interest in the topic than the people they survey. Earthquake questions generally appear in nationwide surveys only after a major disaster actually occurs.

Politicians running for national office do not campaign on the issue of what they would do about the risk of earthquakes. The risk of earthquakes is not the sort of issue to build presidential campaigns around, and neither apparently is it the kind of cause that excites those who would change the "system." Getting government to do something about the earthquake threat does not prompt pickets to march in front of the White House nor protesters to hold rallies on the Capitol steps. Neither environmentalists, consumer groups, nor civil rights organizations have adopted earthquake risk reduction as part of their programs.

Television news both mirrors and reinforces the impression that most people do not consider earthquake safety to be a grave concern. Earthquakes themselves are often major news stories, of course, but the threat of future earthquakes becomes news only when hooked on other news pegs. For example, what households can do to prepare for future earthquakes may become a followup story in the aftermath of a small earthquake. A prediction that an earthquake will take place at a specific time and place can trigger considerable coverage of the likely consequences of a future earthquake. In contrast, public policy issues related to the risk of earthquakes rarely receive coverage in television news.

Most sociologists apparently concur with the judgments of pollsters, survey respondents, campaign managers, social change advocates, and television news directors. Textbooks written for social problems courses rarely have a chapter on the topic "Earthquakes as Social Problems" or even "Natural Disasters as Social Problems."

In short, a variety of indicators that usually give a sense of what the public at large considers to be the most pressing problems of the day all show that the earthquake threat is not of great public concern. But what do earthquake safety advocates say about this threat?

THE EARTHQUAKE THREAT RECONSIDERED

The risk of earthquakes certainly seems to have what it takes to be a social problem. Some public officials worry that even rumors of an imminent earthquake will cause panic. Mental health professionals remind parents to avoid frightening children by what they say about earthquakes and by their own reactions to small earthquakes. Many residents of the East and Midwest will not vacation in California for fear that the Big One will strike while they are there.

Earthquake safety advocates cite a potential for loss of life and personal injury that is equal to if not greater than other conditions about which there is more public concern. News accounts of earthquake disasters outside the United States graphically illustrate this potential. Due to different building practices in other countries, death tolls in foreign earthquakes can be staggering. An earthquake in Mexico City in 1985, for example, killed more than 5,000 people and injured another 30,000. In 1976, an estimated 650,000 people died and another 780,000 were injured in Tangshan, China. That same year 22,000 people died in an earthquake in Guatemala, and nearly 1,000 more died in another in Italy. In 1988 at least 25,000 people were killed in an earthquake in then-Soviet Armenia, and 40,000 or more were killed in 1990 in northern Iran.

Earthquakes kill far fewer people in the United States, but casualties can be numerous here as well. The 1994 Northridge earthquake in the San Fernando Valley region of Los Angeles killed 57 people, 16 in the collapse of one apartment building; 63 people died and another 1,400 were injured in the 1989 Loma Prieta earthquake; 131people died in the Alaska earthquake in 1964. The 1971 San Fernando earthquake killed 64 people, and the San Francisco earthquake and fire claimed 700 lives in 1906.

Experts estimate that casualty figures in a future earthquake in the United States will be much higher. They expect that as many as 23,000 people could be killed in a single worst-case earthquake in Los Angeles (a Richter magnitude 7.5 earthquake at 4:30 p.m. on a weekday afternoon on a fault running under the city along the Pacific coast). If the number of people who are likely to be killed were the only things that mattered, then the threat of future earthquakes should be a social problem.

How about economic loss? Figures produced by earthquake safety advocates match many of those offered by other social problems in their potential for financial devastation. The estimated cost of the Los Angeles riots of 1992 is $775 million in insurable damage alone. The Department of Justice lists direct expenditures for all criminal justice activities in 1988 at $61 billion. By comparison, the estimated cost of the worst-case Los Angeles earthquake is $70 billion. Such an earthquake is expected to bankrupt many businesses, disrupt the stock market, and reduce revenue to cities and towns through a decline in municipal bond markets. The federal budget also would take a big hit as a result of the cost of providing disaster relief.

IS THE EARTHQUAKE THREAT UNIQUE?

One reason the risk of earthquakes may differ from other public concerns is that the earthquake threat is somehow unique. It may be that earthquakes threaten only one part of the country (such as California) and only a fraction of the nation's total population. Conditions typically associated with a social problem, in contrast, are found anywhere. Perhaps the earth-quake threat is not sufficiently widespread?

This argument does not hold up. First, it is a mistake to think that conditions by themselves create social problems. Nor are problems and conditions one and the same. Problems are what people say and do about conditions. Second, what people say about earthquakes—at least, what scientists who study the earth say—is that earthquakes are a threat *not* limited to California. Physical conditions that can cause earthquakes are present in all fifty states. Residents of the Pacific Northwest have been told for a long time that they too are at risk, as have those in the Salt Lake City area. South Carolina's history includes a major earthquake in 1886 that killed 60 people, damaged 90 percent of the structures in Charleston, and shook such faraway cities as Boston, Chicago, and St. Louis. The Midwest has its own history of record-shattering earthquakes including three in the winter of 1811–12 centered in Missouri that destroyed an entire town, changed the course of the Mississippi River, and toppled chimneys in Cincinnati and Richmond.

The earthquake threat may be unique in another respect. It may be that earthquakes are acts of nature beyond human control. They are not like unemployment which is created by people deciding to lay off workers. Earthquakes are not like violent crimes caused by people who choose to use force. The conditions associated with social problems involve some degree of human choice. Earthquakes seem to be different. People do not cause the forces of nature that threaten them. We cannot pass laws to stop earthquakes.

This argument also does not hold up. Scientists may work in a world where earthquakes are viewed as nothing more than the release of energy, but for others earthquakes are the shaking of a house, the sound of breaking glass, cracked fireplaces, toppled utility poles, and collapsed bridges. It may be impossible to legislate the laws of nature, but it is possible to pass laws against locating buildings on top of active earthquake faults or for requiring specific construction designs and materials. People may think of earthquakes as acts of nature, but they are also capable of linking the consequences of earthquakes to prior human decisions and actions. There is no reason why these decisions and actions cannot become targets for groups mobilized to "do something."

EXPLAINING SOCIAL PROBLEMS AND NONPROBLEMS

The uniqueness of the earthquake threat, it seems to me, does not lie in the conditions that produce earthquakes. No matter how long we study the earth and its physical properties, we will never be able to explain why the earthquake threat is different from others that we often classify as social problems. Earth movements do not tell us whether the risk of earthquakes should have high or low priority, whether the hazard is more of a threat to our well-being than the risk of AIDS, whether relying on market forces or on government intervention is the better way to handle old buildings that collapse more frequently than newer ones when the ground shakes, or even whether there is so little we can do to make ourselves safe that doing nothing is a good idea. How people treat the earthquake threat is not the inevitable result of the objective reality of the earth and its dynamics.

My conclusion that the question cannot be answered by studying the earth is at odds with conventional wisdom about both earthquakes and social problems. Oversimplified, conventional wisdom holds that social problems arise when people recognize intrinsically undesirable conditions. This undesirable quality is part of the conditions themselves. In conventional wisdom, problems are "out there" in the world around us even if we are not aware of them. Sooner or later, problems get "discovered," and experts propose solutions for them. According to conventional wisdom, people who are unaware of a problem after it has been discovered are ignorant or at least uninformed. Those who dispute the seriousness of a problem are irrational.

Conventional wisdom, in other words, posits a rational view of the world in which the existence of the earthquake problem as objective reality—as fact—is taken for granted. Rational solutions to the problem are undermined by various "villains" and "fools" who, intentionally or unintentionally, let self interest get in the way of "doing the right thing." An apathetic public at large, for example, is unwilling to bear the costs of earthquake hazard reduction. Developers and business property owners are more concerned with profits than safety. Local politicians are too dependent upon business interests to take the necessary steps to minimize risk. National politicians are more concerned with other issues that have larger constituencies—and greater numbers of votes.

One hint that there are serious flaws in such conventional wisdom is that it turns out to be a thinly disguised form of name-calling. It contains "good guys" and "bad guys," right and wrong, enlightened thinking and ignorance. The trouble is that in the everyday world it is hard to tell the good guys from the bad guys. Historically, what looks like enlightened thinking at one time looks like ignorance and superstition at another. In our time, homeowners have many concerns besides the possibility of earthquakes. Given costly premiums and large deductibles that exceed the average amount of damage, it may be rational for a home owner to decide to not purchase earthquake insurance. Or, developers who ignore public safety for the sake of profits may wear the villain's hat for some, but for others they are heroes who create jobs, generate tax revenues, and provide places for people to live. Politicians who seem more concerned with things other than earthquakes may be representing their constituents very effectively on matters of more immediate interest to them.

The reason it is hard to tell the good guys from the bad guys, the ignorant from the well-informed, is that conventional wisdom about the risk of earthquakes contains a fundamental flaw. By taking for granted that risk is part of nature, it assumes that there is only one way to view risk, that there is one accurate view that correctly describes "the way things really are," that all other views are incorrect descriptions of the "true" risk that is "out there." In other words, since the risk of earthquakes is objectively real, it is a "thing" that can be perceived only correctly or incorrectly.

The problem with thinking of "risk" as objective is that it is hard to explain how the "correct" view can change without nature itself changing. The early tribes of central Europe believed that earthquakes occurred when a water buffalo carrying the earth on its back paused to shift its enormous load from one foot to another. The Algonquins of North America also must have believed that theirs was the correct view. They thought that a gigantic tortoise supported the weight of the world. The ancient Greeks were certain enough in their belief that Poseidon, god of the sea, produced earthquakes whenever he was seriously displeased that they erected sanctuaries in his honor all around the Mediterranean Sea in an attempt to prevent disaster. Today we are equally certain that our scientific description of the objective reality of earthquakes is the only accurate one.

What if scientists themselves disagree on the correct description of the objective reality of the earth? What if proponents of each competing description think that theirs is the only correct view? If reality is only one thing, you and I might not have an accurate picture of it, but how can the experts—those who really know about these things—disagree? In fact, scientists have disagreed about the structure of the earth and the causes of earthquakes. Proposed by a German scientist early in this century, the idea of continental drift was ridiculed by most earth scientists before the Second World War. Even as late as 1960, this theory of the structure and dynamics of the earth had few proponents. By 1970, however, the theory of plate tectonics that is a direct descendent of continental drift theory was the dominant paradigm in the earth sciences.

Earthquake faults, stresses and strains in rocks, p-waves and s-waves, plate tectonics, and continental drift do not tell us how important the risk of earthquakes is. They do not tell us how much money to spend on this threat compared to other issues such as health care, crime, infrastructure development, pollution control, job stimulation, or education. It is the ability of advocates to convince others that determines whether an issue such as earthquake safety is more important than some other issue. Not science but the use of science is key to understanding why one issue has higher priority than another.

In short, it is some people's ability to promote risk that determines why one threat is treated as a social problem and another is not. In order to explain what is seen as threatening and how the threat is responded to, we need to examine what people say and do. It is not nature itself we need to study but people's views of nature. We need to ask questions about the social universe, not the physical universe. We need to adopt a point of view that does not require us to figure out who the good guys are or to correctly distinguish between the informed and the uninformed. We can accomplish this by assuming that, whatever the "true" nature of objective reality, people's *ideas* about that reality is the only reality that counts. The reality of the risk of earthquakes is what people think, say, and do about that risk.

Putting people at the center of the process of promoting risk allows us to see that "doing something about the risk of earthquakes" means advancing claims in public arenas or settings such as government hearings, news reports, and meetings of civic groups. Whatever is or is not done about the earthquake threat must be due to the success or failure of the people making these claims. Who the claims-makers are, what kind of message they carry, how persuasively they argue their case, and what resources they have to carry on their fight all should make a difference in how successful or unsuccessful they are in promoting risk. If the earthquake threat is not accorded the status of a social problem, the reason must have something to do with the people who are promoting it, the way they go about it, and so forth.

What is gained by trying to answer these questions about the risk of earthquakes? Consider first what these questions are really all about. When I ask why the earthquake threat differs from other conditions that are treated as social problems, I am asking how a society decides that there is more harm in one thing than in another. When I ask how something becomes a problem, I am curious about the circumstances under which anything could attain a certain level of attention, concern, and action. If I am able to answer such questions, it will be because I have begun to understand the barriers and the opportunities that determine the fate of public issues.

4

Reality Television
Constructs Crime

GRAY CAVENDER

Reality television programming broadcasts crime dramatizations or film footage of police and other emergency personnel at work. Two of the earliest and most successful reality programs, *America's Most Wanted* (AMW) and *Unsolved Mysteries* (UM), present vignettes in which the participants or actors reenact actual crimes. The vignettes feature interviews with victims, their family and friends, and the police, as well as photographs and film of suspects. Viewers are urged to telephone the police or the program with relevant information about the crimes or the suspects. The programs update previous broadcasts, such as with film of a captured fugitive or information about sentencing.

AMW and UM employ an interesting hybrid television format. Like the news, these programs claim to present reality as a public service. However, they also are prime-time entertainment in the crime genre tradition of programs such as *Dragnet, Ironside,* and *Magnum PI.* Their emotional, fast-paced stories enjoy large audiences, and, as a result, programs like AMW and UM have proliferated on television.

Gitlin observes that the key to understanding television crime programs is to ask what they mean "as cultural objects and as signs of cultural interactions between producers and audiences" (1979:259). To understand their meaning, I examined nine half-hour-long AMW episodes and seven hour-long UM episodes broadcast during the 1989–90 television season. The crime genre is characterized by particular symbolic themes, an ideological preference for the conventional social order, and a realistic style.

This chapter is excerpted from Cavender, Gray (1998). "In 'The Shadow of Shadows': Television Reality Crime Programming." Pp. 79–94 in *Entertaining Crime: Television Reality Programs,* edited by Mark Fishman and Gray Cavender. Hawthorne, NY: Aldine de Gruyter.

THE CRIME GENRE

Genres are types or kinds of literature, film, or television programs. Genres are defined by repetitious, often formulaic plots and characterizations that yield predictability and stability in cultural production. They are not mutually exclusive, however. Reality crime programs combine news, crime drama, and even elements of the horror genre.

The crime genre covers a large territory, from Sherlock Holmes short stories to films like *Beverly Hills Cop*. Typically, it consists of simple plots in which villains commit a mysterious crime (usually murder), and the hero—a police officer, private detective, or private citizen—solves the mystery by identifying, apprehending, or killing the villains. These repetitive plots, which take on a ritualistic, almost mythic quality, feature symbolic themes: evil threatens but good intervenes and vanquishes evil. The crime genre affirms dominant interests and attitudes even as it offers the vicarious pleasure of suspense and freedom from restrictive bureaucratic rules. Indeed, the stability inherent in the crime genre rests not only in the formula's conventions, but in the degree to which these conventions reflect and reproduce a preference for social order. This traditional ideology often goes unnoticed. The crime genre obscures its penchant for order and control behind a style so realistic that its ideology seems natural and appropriate.

SYMBOLS

We represent and perceive the world through symbols. Widely used symbols affirm dominant social values and condemn threats to the social order (Durkheim 1964). In contemporary society, symbolic representations circulate widely through the media, and the media's symbolic predominance is apparent in the crime genre. The crime genre renders moralistic plots in which criminals, whose villainy symbolizes social malaise and disorder, threaten the established order. Their defeat resolves the plot's tension, reaffirming moral boundaries.

Crime on AMW and UM symbolizes the social malaise that threatens society. Crime is a vile social blight on AMW's and UM's landscape, representing the frustrations, uncertainties, and dangers of modern life: drugs figure prominently among victims and criminals; the family is victimized as children and spouses are kidnapped; and decent, hard-working people are devastated by despicable acts. The programs offer a seemingly inexhaustible array of brutal, violent crimes. These crimes are characterized sensationally as "gruesome" or "bizarre," yet they appear commonplace, a disturbing, almost defining fact of modern life. Production techniques complement the symbolic message of chaos and threat. Slow-motion cinematography captures crime's lurid, visual nature, and a soundtrack cues emotions like sorrow or fear.

AMW's and UM's criminals are recurring stereotypes, stand-ins for contemporary social concerns. The night teems with drug dealers and satanists, and crazy, cold-blooded killers prowl the mean streets of cities and small towns. The public fears what these criminals symbolize, and AMW and UM breathe life into this symbolism, giving their criminals a name and a face, and, in the process, evoking powerful symbols of disorder and social decay. Criminals are described in terms that connote physical ugliness. They are depicted as dangerous, depraved, unremorseful people.

In contrast to their loathsome criminals, AMW's and UM's victims are depicted as respectable, often physically attractive people, such as "a good-looking college kid" or "a pretty, young wife." The victims, who symbolize innocence and beauty, shape our sense of the crime problem as dirty and threatening. The programs foster audience identification with these attractive victims. Family and friends personalize them, hosts speak as if they know them, and the camera dramatizes crimes from the victim's point of view. Victims recount their emotions during the crime, prompting the audience to share the victimization experience. Sometimes the host speculates on the victim's fear, or encourages the audience to do so. AMW's and UM's victims are like sacrificial lambs; they are innocent and vulnerable, but, as in the horror genre, the narrative moves inexorably toward their destruction. The symbolism is straightforward: the victim's plight should be felt by the audience, who are the "not yet victimized."

The fear of victimization is at the heart of the social malaise that crime symbolizes. This fear reflects and reproduces a loss of trust in contemporary society. Misplaced trust is a frequent subplot in AMW's and UM's narratives. Seemingly normal situations and people turn out to be not so normal, again, in ways that reflect common contemporary concerns, such as a policeman, trusted by other officers and by citizens, who molests children, or a respected community leader who is an escaped murderer. The resulting sense of malaise creates a tension that the programs must resolve.

The crime genre's mythic narrative constructs and then resolves the tension: the villain is ritually defeated by the hero, restoring order. In AMW's and UM's version, crime disrupts the social order, but resolution comes with the criminal's condemnation, capture, or punishment. Shocking, tragic crimes not only offend common sensibilities, they disrupt life's normal routines. Families lament that they cannot get on with their lives until a victim's fate is known, an assailant's identity is revealed, or until a fugitive is captured. Crime undoes the rightful order of things, generating the vignette's tension.

Once generated, tension is converted into outrage focused on the criminal. Outrage, which follows "naturally" in the crime genre, is not left to chance on AMW and UM. Victims or their survivors explicitly express anger at the criminal, or the host conveys to the victim's family his outrage at their loss. Visuals and soundtracks heighten these emotions.

Like the crime genre, AMW and UM resolve tension in a ritualistic catharsis. Of course, since most of the fugitives are "at large," the catharsis differs from the killings or captures that characterize most television crime drama. Instead, vignettes culminate in denunciation or condemnation. In one vignette, a police officer denounces the criminal as someone who "doesn't belong in society." The ultimate resolution comes in updates that combine film or photographs of a captured fugitive, often in handcuffs, or that announce a prison sentence.

IDEOLOGY

The symbols that circulate in media crime presentations carry ideological meanings. The crime genre privileges authority and order. Authority is located in the hero/detective who triumphs over evil, defining the "good" in terms of a preference for the social order. The audience experiences ideological pleasure when it identifies with the detective, whose sense of justice reflects the dominant ideology.

Genres are sensitive, at least indirectly, to ideological shifts in society. The crime control model has emerged as the ideological foundation of U.S. crime policy. This model posits crime as a serious threat to the social order, and is accompanied by *controltalk*, the language that discusses the crime problem and its solution (Cohen 1985:272-74). Controltalk is a form of political language; like all political language, it defines what constitutes the (crime) problem and what might be done about it. Because television crime programming constantly relays and reproduces ideology, crime control ideology on reality programming seems so natural that it goes unnoticed.

AMW's and UM's vignettes typically open in a state of equilibrium. The soundtrack, the visuals, and the narrative convey a pastoral or small-town sense of equilibrium. Crime shatters this tranquillity. Discordant music, jump-cut editing, and lurid close-ups frame the criminal act, and interviews with devastated victims and families detail the resulting disruption. Vignettes depict crime as out of control. Small towns that were safe havens no longer are safe, and caution is no guarantee against horrible victimization. Crime appears to be random and pervasive, confirming the crime control model's view that crime has disrupted the rightful order of things.

The police are authority figures on AMW and UM. The police may be clueless, but they are portrayed as "on the case." The program host is an authority figure, too. Like the genre detective, he narrates the story and exudes knowledge about the case and about crime in general. The host is seen examining evidence with the police or receiving praise from them, an apparent partnership that enhances authority for both.

The crime control model detaches crime from its social context. Moreover, the fugitive is depicted as guilty though not yet convicted of a crime. This portrayal of guilt squares with the crime control model's working presumption of guilt. Although the narratives often use cautious language, such as "alleged" or "only a suspect," the visuals tell a different story. In one vignette, a victim notes that his injury left him with no memory of the crime, yet the dramatization depicts the suspect clubbing the victim. In another, the host reminds the audience that the person sought is only a suspect, but adds, "The police would like to talk to him so that if he is innocent, he can clear his name."

AMW and UM foster a notion of community to which the audience can belong by watching the programs and by participating in the common effort to capture fugitives. The community exhibits a set of idealized shared values, including group commitment and even a kind of televised intimacy—the audience sees families struggle to maintain composure during an emotional interview. In other vignettes, the hosts reference the audience as a community, "Thanks for caring, thanks for helping," or, they appeal to both community and patriotism, "Thanks, America."

Justice on AMW and UM connotes the punitive outcomes of crime control ideology, "Help bring [the fugitive] to justice," or "Put him back behind bars." This sense of justice is rationalized by the language of controltalk, which casts crime as a kind of war. War imagery depicts criminals as the enemy who must be defeated if the social order is to be preserved.

REALISM

AMW and UM stake their reality claim on television formats that suggest realism: they appropriate the realistic style of the crime genre, and the televisual empiricism of the news. Interestingly, AMW's and UM's adherence to the crime genre format bolsters their reality claim. The crime genre adopts a seemingly realistic naturalism, which AMW and UM mimic in production style, in story construction, even in their hosts.

AMW and UM feature the sort of violent, sensational crimes that are a staple of television crime drama. These crimes attract an audience—viewers have learned to enjoy the vicarious experience of suspense—and also maximize television's visual capabilities. Narratives about "real" crimes combine with the visuals to lend a sense of objective, empirical reality to their vignettes.

AMW's and UM's story construction mirrors a standard crime genre plotting device: the story opens as the detective addresses the audience, narrates the tale in flashback, and addresses the audience at the story's end. A UM vignette about a murder on an isolated highway opens as host Robert Stack emerges from the shadows. Stack epitomizes the detective/storyteller as he recounts the victim's past, the dramatized murder, and addresses the audience at vignette's end. AMW's vignettes open and close with host John Walsh, in the studio, addressing the audience, using argot that could be drawn from the pages of a hard-boiled detective novel, "hit the safe," "the take," and "face the music." This narration gives the teller and the tale the ring of authenticity.

AMW's and UM's hosts enjoy credibility based on audience familiarity with their television characters. UM's host, actor Robert Stack, played a tough federal cop on the television drama *The Untouchables*. John Walsh, AMW's host, was portrayed in *Adam*, a television docudrama about the tragic kidnapping of his young son. Their television credentials allow Stack and Walsh to play the role of host/crimefighter. Story construction reinforces this role: as the credits roll in one AMW episode, Walsh and the police study a map, apparently closing in on a fugitive. His and Stack's knowledge of exact dates, locations, and other details privileges their authority, and gives the vignettes a police-blotter effect that imitates the crime genre. Realism in the crime genre is an effect produced by such attention to detail.

AMW and UM imitate a subgenre of crime film, the "police procedural," which was popular during the 1940s and 1950s. This subgenre was characterized by documentary production techniques and plots that were drawn from actual police cases. Like those films, AMW and UM employ production techniques that produce a gritty realism. Lighting and camera work, such as freeze frame and slow-motion shots, yield a sense of intense emotional reality. They also achieve a careful compromise between documentary and drama. Television and film establish a documentary-like realism when characters directly address the camera and the audience; dramatic characters do not address the camera. When AMW's Walsh directly addresses the audience as host, he establishes the program's realism; direct address also invites the audience to share his view of reality. At other times, the camera might catch Walsh, in his crimefighter role, seemingly unaware that a commercial break has ended, sans jacket with shirt sleeves rolled back, examining stolen gems through a jeweler's eyepiece.

A Television Reality

Our reality, even our criteria for what counts as real, are mediated through television, which claims to present an unmediated picture of reality. Although AMW and UM note that they are not news broadcasts, they establish the "reality" of their presentations with techniques that suggest the news. The hosts often introduce vignettes with crime statistics or other public service-type material that resembles news and information programming. In their closing credits, staffers are identified as reporters or correspondents.

AMW's and UM's most significant reality claim is that they dramatize actual crimes. Frequent invocations such as "police say" or "according to the police" construct a credibility premised on official sources. Not only are the police an authoritative source, narrative statements such as "the police suspect" are accompanied by visuals that conform their suspicions. AMW deliberately establishes its credibility. Broadcast from Washington, D.C., the home of federal law enforcement agencies, AMW displays its own law enforcement-type seal, and wanted posters and seals from official enforcement agencies dot its studio set, which was designed to resemble a police squad room to enhance credibility.

AMW's and UM's staccato pace resembles the crime genre, but also reinforces their reality claims. Vignettes appear as fast-breaking stories, generating the immediacy that makes television news credible. Hosts speculate that viewer tips might locate a fugitive "tonight," or urge viewers to call "right now." The programs seem to be "live" broadcasts (AMW announces "live from Washington, D.C." although it is taped), when, for example, the host communicates directly with the police or a victim. Comments such as "We'll continue to update you as developments occur" combine with frequent updates to produce a sense of immediacy.

The claim that real cops are investigating real crimes validates the hosts' crimefighter image, enhances AMW's and UM's realism, and pulls the viewer into that reality: if a television character can work with the police, so can the viewer. The programs' format reproduces television's characteristic sense of "being there." The viewer knows what the police know, and, because of the camera's omnipotence, seemingly sees events—the criminal committing the crime—that the police only suspect. Indeed, the premise of these programs is that the viewer knows more than the police, "Detectives are eager to know what you know." AMW and UM urge viewers to envision a reality that consists of themselves, the police, and television, working in a common effort to fight crime.

CONCLUSION

Reality programs are designed to draw the audience into this reality. The line between television fact and fiction, already indistinct, becomes even more hazy on these programs. Often it is difficult to discern if a vignette is depicting a dramatization or actual footage, a suspect or an actor playing suspect. In several instances, viewers have turned in the actor who played the fugitive in a dramatization. The audience's confusion is no surprise.

AMW, UM, and their progeny abound on television, and their meaning is clear. These programs reinforce the public's fear of crime and sentiment toward the more punitive crime control model. Reality programming points up television's potential either to serve the common good—capturing criminals—or to create illusions that are dangerous, not only because they confuse television and reality, but because they are a powerful tool for a repressive ideology. These programs blame crime for society's ills, ranging from loss of community to the alienation and frustration that characterize contemporary life, and pin their hopes for a better future on catching and punishing criminals. Were it that simple. . . .

REFERENCES

Cohen, Stan. 1985. *Visions of Social Control*. Cambridge: Polity.
Durkheim, Emile. 1964. *The Division of Labor in Society*. New York: Free Press.
Giltlin, Todd. 1979. "Prime Time Ideology: The Hegemonic Process in Television Entertainment." *Social Problems* 26:251–66.

II
Claims-Makers and Audiences

Introduction to Section II

Social constructionists argue that people create the meanings we assign to the objective world around us. This means that any particular condition—drug use, earthquakes, crime, and so on—is not a social problem until people evaluate the condition as frequent, very troublesome, and in need of change. Understanding why we respond to some conditions—and not others—as social problems requires that we look at this process of meaning-making. Within a constructionist perspective, a *claim* is any verbal, visual, or behavioral statement that tries to persuade audience members to take a condition seriously and respond to it as a social problem, *claims-makers* are the people who make claims, and *audiences* are the people who evaluate the believability and importance of claims.

We begin with the importance of *audiences* for social problems claims. In daily life we each are members of audiences for social problems claims—we see them on the news and on flyers taped to the stairs leading to classrooms, we hear them in those classrooms. Audiences are the people who claims-makers must persuade, and this persuasion can be difficult. Every day, for example, we are bombarded with claims about conditions we are told we should worry about. While the potential supply of social problems seems limitless, public worry is limited: It is not possible to worry simultaneously about the problems of crime, and poverty and abuse and terrorism and the economy and the environment. Claims-makers therefore compete for audience members' attention. Also, claims that might persuade some people that a social problem is at hand and that something must be done might not persuade others. The most general audience, the United States population (what often is called the "public"), typically unites in its worry only around the most extreme events such as the terrorist attacks or the Colombine High School massacre. Most claims about social problems do not find such united audiences: Some audience members vehemently defend the rights to own guns or burn flags or physically discipline children, while others want gun control or a ban on flag-burning or laws prohibiting parents from spanking their children.

It's important for audience members to be thoughtful in evaluations of the believability and importance of claims we see or hear because, in the final analysis, claims-making is successful only if audience members support claims-makers. Yet, in "Audiences Evaluate Statistics," Joel Best raises a perplexing point: While claims-makers often use statistics to describe the prevalence and nature of social problem conditions, people in American audiences for these claims tend to be innumerate. We do not know much about statistics so we tend to not think much about them. We either accept what we hear without challenge, or dismiss statistics as probably misleading, again without thinking about it. Best outlines a critical approach to thinking about social statistics: Rather than being naïve and simply accepting what claims-makers say or being cynical and refusing to accept what they say, we can be critical and ask questions. Because statistics are the result of organizational practices in places such as police stations (crime), coroner's offices (suicide), or pollster's offices (public opinion) we can ask where statistics came from and how they were gathered. Because numbers are meaningless without interpretation we can ask how statistics were interpreted, what they mean. Claims about social problems are all around us, so it is important that we train ourselves how to be good consumers of statistics.

Audiences are the judges and juries for social problems claims and these claims are made by *claims-makers*. We each can be claims-makers in daily life when we tell friends our opinions on social problems or when we write letters to local editors, sign petitions, or drive cars with bumper stickers advertising social problems themes. More obvious claims-makers include politicians; political lobbyists; social movement activists; academics and scientists; television talk show hosts; people who produce television shows such as "60 Minutes" or "Dateline"; people who write articles, books, magazines and film scripts; teachers; and so on. Clearly, claims-makers don't speak with one voice—the social problems constructed by rap musicians are not those constructed through college textbooks; The *New York Times* constructs different visions of social problems than the *National Enquirer*; there are "pro-life" and "pro-choice," "pro-gay" and "anti-gay" claims-makers; some claims-makers feel passionately about the problem they are constructing, others might care primarily about how much they might gain financially if they persuade others to take a condition seriously. As with audiences, there are many differences among claims-makers. Within this incredible diversity among claims-makers, we look at the three most important types.

First, there are *social movement activists*, the people who work precisely to convince audience members that a social problem exists. Activists band together in organizations such as NOW (National Organization for Women), PETA (People for the Ethical Treatment of Animals), AARP

(American Association of Retired Persons), and so on. Valerie Jenness and Kendal Broad consider how several of these social change groups banded together to transform the meanings of violence against powerless people. This condition was not new, but the activists gave it a new name: "hate crime" or "bias motivated crime," terms used to categorize behaviors whose victims suffer due to their status as racial, ethnic, gender, religious, and/or sexual orientation minorities. In "Promoters of Hate Crime Legislation" we see how particular social problems reflect the larger culture: It was social movements on behalf of African Americans, women, gay/lesbians, and crime victims that set the stage for hate crimes to be constructed as a specific type of social problem. Through a variety of claims-making activities—publishing books and pamphlets, tracking statistics, public education, research, sponsoring legislation, legal advocacy, organizing shelters for battered women—social activists transformed what always had existed into a new type of crime.

A second important type of claims-maker is *scientists*. Scientists are critical players because they are at the top of the hierarchy of credibility, which means that many audience members in the United States simply accept the claims of scientists as true. Yet the backstage of science—how science is actually done—sometimes is far different from the front stage of science—how science presents itself to the public. In "Psychiatrists Construct Homosexuality," Stuart Kirk and Herb Kutchins examine the claims-makers and the claims-making process behind the *Diagnostic and Statistical Manual of Mental Disorders, Third Edition (DSM III)*. The *DSM* is the most powerful reference book in psychiatry: As the official system of psychiatric diagnosis, the *DSM* defines what is—and what is not—mental pathology. Their particular topic is explaining why homosexuality, which had been included as a "pathology" in the previous *DSM*, was dropped from the new edition. Although college students taking psychology courses are taught that the *DSM* is a scientific document based on scientific principles and data, Kirk and Kutchins argue that the revised listing was *not* the result of new knowledge. Rather, revisions in the construction of homosexuality were the result of the claims-making activities of gays/lesbians as well as internal problems in the American Psychiatric Association.

The third type of claims-maker is the *mass media* for the simple reason that most Americans now get most of their information about the world from watching television, surfing the Web, reading magazines, and so on. As an example, we turn to a most unlikely place of social problem construction: television talk shows such as those hosted by Montel Williams and Jerry Springer. Kathleen S. Lowney examines how "Television Talk Shows Construct Morality." Her close examination of the *form* and *content* of these shows leads her to argue that, rather than promoting immorality (as some critics charge), these shows promote a very distinct morality.

They are a modern-day version of the religious revivals and traveling circuses of the 1800s where hosts, audience members, and guests construct deviance and then construct the route to salvation. When viewed in this light, talk shows appear as social problems claims-makers, preaching a distinct morality within a circus-like form.

The articles in this section each speak to general issues about the process of claims-making. They demonstrate how different types of people (social activists, psychiatristics, talk show hosts) make social problems claims to many types of audiences (government officials, psychiatrists, the general public); they demonstrate how images of particular conditions as "social problems" depend on the activities of people who say things and do things, as well as on how audience members evaluate the believability and importance of claims they see or hear.

5

Audiences Evaluate Statistics

Joel Best

Most claims drawing attention to new social problems aim to persuade all of us—that is, the members of the general public. We are the audience, or at least one important audience, for statistics and other claims about social problems. If the public becomes convinced that prostitution or homelessness is a serious problem, then something is more likely to be done: officials will take action, new policies will begin, and so on. Therefore, campaigns to create social problems use statistics to help arouse the public's concern.

This is not difficult. The general public tends to be receptive to claims about new social problems, and we rarely think critically about social problems statistics. The media like to report statistics because numbers seem to be factual, little nuggets of truth. The public tends to agree; we usually treat statistics as facts.

In part, this is because we are *innumerate*. Innumeracy is the mathematical equivalent of illiteracy; it is an inability to deal comfortably with the fundamental notions of number and chance. Just as some people cannot read or read poorly, many people have trouble thinking clearly about numbers.

One common innumerate error involves not distinguishing among large numbers. A very small child may be pleased by the gift of a penny; a slightly older child understands that a penny or even a dime can't buy much, but a dollar can buy some things, ten dollars considerably more, and a hundred dollars a great deal (at least from a child's point of view). Most adults clearly grasp what one can do with a hundred, a thousand, ten thousand, even one hundred thousand dollars, but then our imaginations

This chapter is excerpted from Best, Joel (2001). *Damned Lies and Statistics: Untangling Numbers from the Media, Politicians, and Activists* (pp. 19–29, 160–71). Berkeley: University of California Press. 2001.

begin to fail us. Big numbers blend together: million, a billion, a trillion—what's the difference? They're all big numbers. (Actually, of course, there are tremendous differences. The difference between a million and a billion is the difference between one dollar and one thousand dollars; the difference between a million and a trillion is the difference between one dollar and a million dollars).

Because many people have trouble appreciating the differences among big numbers, they tend to uncritically accept social statistics (which often, of course, feature big numbers). What does it matter, they may say, whether there are 300,000 homeless or 3,000,000—either way, it's a big number. They'd never make this mistake dealing with smaller numbers; everyone understands that it makes a real difference whether there'll be three people or thirty coming by tomorrow night for dinner. A difference (thirty is ten times greater than three) that seems obvious with smaller, more familiar numbers gets blurred when we deal with bigger numbers (3,000,000 is ten times greater than 300,000), If society is going to feed the homeless, having an accurate count is just as important as it is for an individual planning to host three—or thirty—dinner guests.

Innumeracy—widespread confusion about basic mathematical ideas—means that many statistical claims about social problems don't get the critical attention they deserve. This is not simply because an innumerate public is being manipulated by advocates who cynically promote inaccurate statistics. Often, statistics about social problems originate with sincere, well-meaning people who are themselves innumerate; they may not grasp the full implications of what they are saying. Similarly, the media are not immune to innumeracy; reporters commonly repeat the figures their sources give them without bothering to think critically about them.

The result can be a social comedy. Activists want to draw attention to a problem—prostitution, homelessness, or whatever. The press asks the activists for statistics—How many prostitutes? How many homeless? Knowing that big numbers indicate big problems and knowing that it will be hard to get action unless people can be convinced a big problem exists (and sincerely believing that there is a big problem), the activists produce a big estimate, and the press, having no way to check the number, simply publicizes it. The general public—most of us suffering from at least a mild case of innumeracy—tends to accept the figure without question. After all, it's a big number, and there's no real difference among big numbers.

ORGANIZATIONAL PRACTICES AND OFFICIAL STATISTICS

One reason we tend to accept statistics uncritically is that we assume that numbers come from experts who know what they're doing. Often these experts work for government agencies, such as the U.S. Bureau of

Census, and producing statistics is part of their job. Data that come from the government—crime rates, unemployment rates, poverty rates—are *official statistics*. There is a natural tendency to treat these figures as straightforward facts that cannot be questioned.

This ignores the way statistics are produced. All statistics, even the most authoritative, are created by people. This does not mean that they are inevitably flawed or wrong, but it does mean that we ought to ask ourselves just how the statistics we encounter were created.

Consider, for example, statistics on suicide. Typically, a coroner decides which deaths are suicides. This can be relatively straightforward: perhaps the dead individual left behind a note clearly stating an intent to commit suicide. But often there is no note, and the coroner must gather evidence that points to suicide—perhaps the deceased is known to have been depressed, the death occurred in a locked house, the cause of death was an apparently self-inflicted gunshot to the head, and so on. There are two potential mistakes here. The first is that the coroner may label a death a "suicide" when, in fact there was another cause (in mystery novels, at least, murder often is disguised as suicide). The second possibility for error is that the coroner may assign another cause to death to what was, in fact, suicide. This is probably a greater risk, because some people who kill themselves want to conceal that fact (for example, some single-car automobile fatalities are suicides designed to look like accidents so that the individual's family can avoid embarrassment or collect life insurance benefits). In addition, surviving family members may be ashamed by a relative's suicide, and they may press the coroner to assign another cause of death such as accident.

In other words, official records of suicide reflect coroners' judgments about the causes of death in what can be ambiguous circumstances. The act of suicide tends to be secretive—it usually occurs in private—and the motives of the dead cannot always be known. Labeling some deaths as "suicides" and others as "homicides," "accidents," or whatever will sometimes be wrong, although we cannot know exactly how often. Note, too, that individual coroners may assess cases differently; we might imagine one coroner who is relatively willing to label deaths suicides, and another who is very reluctant to do so. Presented with the same set of cases the first coroner might find many more suicides than the second.

It is important to appreciate that coroners view their task as classifying individual deaths, as giving each one an appropriate label, rather than as compiling statistics for suicide rates. Whatever statistical reports come out of coroners' offices (say, total number of suicides in the jurisdiction during the past year) are byproducts of their real work (classifying individual deaths). That is, coroners are probably more concerned with being able to justify their decisions in individual cases than they are with whatever overall statistics emerge from those decisions.

The example of suicide records reveals that all official statistics are products-and often byproducts—of decisions by various officials; not just coroners, but also the humble clerks who fill out and file forms, the supervisors who prepare summary reports, and so on. These people make choices (and sometimes errors) that shape whatever statistics finally emerge from their organization or agency, and the organization provides a context for those choices. For example, the law requires coroners to choose among a specified set of causes for death: homicide, suicide, accident, natural causes, and so on. That list of causes reflects our culture. Thus, our laws do not allow coroners to list "witchcraft" as a cause of death, although that might be considered a reasonable choice in other societies. We can imagine different laws that would give coroners different arrays of choices: perhaps there might be no category for suicide; perhaps people who kill themselves might be considered ill and their deaths listed as occurring from natural causes; or perhaps suicides might be grouped with homicides in a single category of deaths caused by humans. In other words, official statistics reflect what sociologists call *organizational practices*—the organization's culture and structure shape officials' actions, and those actions determine whatever statistics finally emerge.

Now consider an even more complicated example. Police officers have a complex job; they must maintain order, enforce the law, and assist citizens in a variety of ways. Unlike the coroner who faces a relatively short list of choices in assigning cause of death, the police have to make all sorts of decisions. For example, police responding to a call about a domestic dispute (say, a fight between husband and wife) have several, relatively ill-defined options. Perhaps they should arrest someone; perhaps the wife wants her husband arrested—or perhaps she says she does not want that to happen; perhaps the officers ought to encourage the couple to separate for the night; perhaps they ought to offer to take the wife to a women's shelter; perhaps they ought to try talking to the couple to calm them down; perhaps they find that talking doesn't work, and then pick arrest or a shelter as a second choice; perhaps they decide that the dispute has already been settled, or that there is really nothing wrong. Police must make decisions about how to respond to such cases, and some—but probably not all—of those choices will be reflected in official statistics. If officers make an arrest, the incident will be recorded in arrest statistics, but if the officers decide to deal with the incident informally (by talking with the couple until they calm down), there may be no statistical record of what happens. The choices officers make depend on many factors. If the domestic dispute call comes near the end of the officers' shift, they may favor quick solutions. If their department has a new policy to crack down on domestic disputes, officers will be more likely to make arrests. All these decisions, each shaped by various considerations, will affect whatever statistics eventually summarize the officers' actions.

Like our earlier example of coroners labeling suicides, the example of police officers dealing with domestic disputes reveals that officials make decisions (these are complicated for coroners, and even more complicated in the case of the police), that official statistics are byproducts of those decisions (police officers probably give even less thought than coroners to the statistical outcomes of their decisions), and that organizational practices form the context for those decisions (organizational practices likely differ among coroners' offices, and there is great variation in how police deal with their complex decisions, with differences among departments, precincts, officers, and so on). In short, even official statistics are social products, shaped by the people and organizations that create them.

THINKING ABOUT STATISTICS AS SOCIAL PRODUCTS

The lesson should be clear: statistics—even official statistics such as crime rates, unemployment rates, and census counts—are products of social activity. We sometimes talk about statistics as though they are facts that simply exist, like rocks, completely independent of people, and that people gather statistics much as rock collectors pick up stones. This is wrong. All statistics are created through people's actions: people have to decide what to count and how to count it, people have to do the counting and the other calculations, and people have to interpret the resulting statistics, to decide what the numbers mean. All statistics are social products, the results of people's efforts.

Once we understand this, it becomes clear that we should not simply accept statistics by uncritically treating numbers as true or factual. If people create statistics, then those numbers need to be assessed, evaluated. Some statistics are pretty good; they reflect people's best efforts to measure social problems carefully, accurately, and objectively. But other numbers are bad statistics—figures that may be wrong, even wildly wrong. We need to be able to sort the good statistics from the bad.

THE CRITICAL APPROACH TO THINKING
ABOUT SOCIAL STATISTICS

There are cultures in which people believe that some objects have magical powers; anthropologists call these objects fetishes. In our society, statistics are a sort of fetish. We tend to regard statistics as though they are magical, as though they are more than mere numbers. We treat them as powerful representations of the truth; we act as though they distill the complexity and confusion of reality into simple facts. We use statistics to convert complicated social problems into more easily understood estimates, percentages, and rates. Statistics direct our concern; they show us what we ought to worry about and how much we ought to worry. In a sense the social problem becomes the statistic and, because we treat statistics as true and incontrovertible, they achieve a kind of fetish-like, magical control over how we view social problems. We think of statistics as facts that we discover, not as numbers we create.

But of course, statistics do not exist independently; people have to create them. Reality is complicated, and every statistic is someone's summary, a simplification of that complexity. Every statistic must be created, and the process of creation always involves choices that affect the resulting number. People who create statistics must choose definitions—the must define what it is they want to count—and they must choose their methods—the ways they will go about their counting. Those choices shape every good statistic, and every bad one. Bad statistics simplify reality in ways that distort our understanding, while good statistics minimize that distortion. No statistic is perfect, but some are less perfect than others.

In order to interpret statistics we need a general approach, an orientation, a mind-set that we can use to think about new statistics that we encounter. We ought to approach statistics thoughtfully. This can be hard to do, precisely because so many people in our society treat statistics as fetishes. We might call this the mind-set of the *Awestruck*—the people who don't think critically, who act as though statistics have magical powers. The Awestruck know they don't always understand the statistics they hear, but this doesn't bother them. After all, who can expect to understand magical numbers? The reverential fatalism of the Awestruck is not thoughtful—it is a way of avoiding thought.

The *Naive* are slightly more sophisticated than the Awestruck. Many people believe they understand a bit about statistics but their approach is basically accepting. They presume that statistics are generally accurate, that they mean what they seem to mean. The Naive are often at least somewhat innumerate and they tend to be innocent and trusting. The Naive are unlikely to question numbers—not even the most implausible exaggerations; after all, the Naive usually don't suspect statistics might be bad, and even if they do, they have no good ways of detecting bad statistics. They are unlikely to wonder about definitions or measurements, or to spot inappropriate comparisons, and they find debates over statistics completely bewildering. The Naive also can create and disseminate statistics. Once a number is in circulation, Naive reporters may be willing to repeat it and pass it along. When they are innumerate, the Naive often generate mutant statistics; when they try to repeat figures they don't completely understand, it is easy for them to produce new, mangled numbers.

Fewer people can be described as *Cynical* but they are extremely important. The Cynical have a mind-set of suspicion about statistics; they are convinced that numbers are probably flawed, and that those flaws are probably intentional. The Cynical are the most important as originators of statistics. The Cynical design research that will produce the results they want: they word questions so as to encourage particular responses; they choose samples likely to respond the way they want; they massage the data until the results take the form they desire; in extreme instances, they simply lie and make up whatever numbers suit their purposes. The Cynical count on their audience being mostly Naive; the Naive will accept whatever numbers they're given. When the Cynical are audiences for statistics they suspect there must be something wrong with whatever numbers they hear. They can justify ignoring all numbers—particularly those challenging their beliefs.

The final stance to approaching statistics is *Critical*. Being critical does not mean being negative or hostile—it is not cynicism. The Critical approach statistics thoughtfully; they avoid the extremes of both naive acceptance and cynical rejection of the numbers they encounter. Instead, the Critical attempt to evaluate numbers, to distinguish between good statistics and bad statistics.

The Critical understand that, while some social statistics may be pretty good, they are never perfect. Every statistic is a way of summarizing complex information into relatively simple numbers. Inevitably, some information, some of the complexity, is lost whenever we use statistics. The Critical recognize that this is an inevitable limitation of statistics. Moreover, they realize that every statistic is the product of choices—the choice between defining a category broadly or narrowly, the choice of one measurement over another, the choice of a sample.

Being Critical means more than simply pointing to the flaws in a statistic. Again, every statistic has flaws. The issue is whether a particular statistic's flaws are severe enough to damage its usefulness. Is the definition so broad that it encompasses too much, or so narrow that it excludes too much? How would changing the definition alter the statistic? What would happen if different measures or samples were chosen? And how is the statistic used? Is it being interpreted appropriately? Are the comparisons that are being made appropriate, or are apples being confused with oranges? These are the sorts of questions the Critical ask.

At first, these questions might seem overwhelming. How can an ordinary person—someone who reads a statistic in a magazine article or hears it on a news broadcast—determine the answers to such questions? Being Critical, it seems, involves an impossible amount of work. In practice, however, the Critical need not investigate the origin of every statistic. Rather, being Critical means appreciating the inevitable limitations that affect all statistics, rather than being Awestruck in the presence of numbers. It means not being too credulous, not accepting every statistic at face value (as the Naive do). But it also means appreciating that statistics, while always imperfect, can be useful. Instead of automatically discounting every statistic (in the fashion of the Cynical), the Critical reserve judgment. When confronted with an interesting number, they may try to learn more, to evaluate, to weigh the figure's strengths and weaknesses.

Of course, this Critical approach need not—and should not—be limited to statistics. It ought to apply to all the evidence we encounter when we scan a news report, or listen to a speech, whenever we learn about social problems. Claims about social problems often feature dramatic, compelling examples; the Critical might ask whether an example is likely to be a typical case or an extreme, exceptional instance. Claims about social problems often include quotations from different sources, and the Critical might wonder why those sources have spoken and why they have been quoted. Claims about social problems usually involve arguments about the problem's causes and potential solutions. The Critical might ask whether these arguments are convincing. Are they logical? Does the proposed solution seem feasible and appropriate? And so on. Being Critical—adopting a skeptical, analytical stance when confronted with claims—is an approach that goes far beyond simply dealing with statistics. Being Critical requires more thought, but failing to adopt a Critical mind-set makes us powerless to evaluate what others tell us.

6

Promoters of Hate Crime Legislation

VALERIE JENNESS AND KENDAL BROAD

History reveals that what is now commonly referred to as bias- or hate-motivated violence is not a new phenomenon. Rather, it is an identifiable feature of human societies across the globe, both historically and at present. Hate- or bias-motivated violence has taken and continues to take a variety of forms, from symbolic to fatal assaults. It also has implicated and continues to implicate a range of perpetrators, from intimates to strangers to institutions such as the state, religion, and medicine.

From the discovery of North America to modern times, there have been acts of atrocity, mayhem, murder, and intimidation perpetuated on the grounds of racial or religious prejudice. Violence against homosexuals and people presumed to be homosexual has been recorded for as long as the lives of gay men and lesbians have been documented. In the last few decades, feminist historians, activists, and scholars have documented literally thousands of cases of violence against women. The historical record is clear that violence directed at individuals because of their real or imagined social characteristics and group membership is as old as humankind. What is new, at least from a historical point of view, is the emergence and institutionalization of so-called new social movements that have inspired and sponsored organizations whose reason for existence is to monitor and publicize the evolving characteristics and consequences of violence born of racism, nationalism, anti-Semitism, sexism, and heterosexism. In particular, the civil rights movement, the contemporary women's movement, the gay and lesbian movement, and the victims' rights movement have fundamentally (re)shaped the politics of violence in the United States and abroad. The discursive themes emanating from the "rights" movements of

This chapter is excerpted from Jenness, Valerie and Kendal Broad (1997). *Hate Crimes: New Social Movements and the Politics of Violence* (Chapter 2). Hawthorne, NY: Aldine De Gruyter.

the 1960s and 1970s formed the sociopolitical terrain that inspired and continues to fuel the contemporary movement to recognize, respond to, and criminalize violence motivated by bigotry in the United States. Accordingly, a brief overview of each of these movements is in order.

THE MODERN CIVIL RIGHTS MOVEMENT

The emergence, organization, evolution, and success of the modern civil rights movement has been well documented and analyzed. Emerging in the mid-1950s, the modern civil rights movement has remained committed to enhancing the legal, social, and economic status and welfare of blacks in particular and racial/ethnic minorities in general in the United States. Early on, the modern civil rights movement focused on contesting legal prohibitions based on skin color in public accommodations and voting, and injustices rooted in economic disparities.

Contemporary civil rights organizations, associations, and task forces continue to grow in number and comprise the modern civil rights movement. Individually and collectively, they continue to contest legal, social, and economic discrimination on a variety of fronts. From the mid-1970s on, one issue in particular—physical and symbolic violence directed toward blacks, as well as other racial minorities and religious and ethnic minorities—has received increasing attention from civil rights organizations. This component of what is often referred to as the "the racial justice movement" focuses on such things as police brutality and other forms of violence against people of color and other minorities.

History already has revealed that early advances by the modern civil rights movement spurred more than awareness of racial inequality. They also defined for other groups the potential of mobilization. As a model and groundbreaker, the black struggle facilitated the mobilization of future movements in the United States. The modern civil rights movement did so by sensitizing opinion makers, polity members, authorities, and the wider public to the challenges, promises, and consequences of protest. The modern civil rights movement has had a precedent-setting effect on subsequent civil rights-minded movements and social movement organizations, especially the contemporary women's movement and the gay and lesbian movement.

THE CONTEMPORARY WOMEN'S MOVEMENT

Like other causes of the 1960s, women's activism in the middle part of the twentieth century evolved in an environment conditioned by the civil rights movement and culminated in the coalition of groups collectively labeled the women's movement. Although the contemporary women's movement addresses a broad set of concerns, sexuality and the social control of sex and sexuality have dominated its agenda. For example, feminists' fight for reproductive rights, especially access to legal abortions, historically has been packaged as a struggle for women's absolute right to control their own bodies.

Identifying various forms of violence against women as a manifestation and consequence of patriarchal oppression has been one of the lasting contributions of the contemporary women's movement. It has done this by documenting instances of violence against girls and women, bringing attention to the types of violence against women and girls, developing crisis intervention and assistance programs, founding and sustaining shelters and networks of "safe homes," establishing and maintaining telephone hotlines, sponsoring public education campaigns and public protests, challenging law enforcement practices that fail to intervene effectively to assist injured women, and drafting new legislation to protect women from violence. Combined, this activity has ensured that battery, rape, sexual harassment, forced prostitution, and other forms of violence directed at girls and women are no longer seen as a personal problem to be resolved within the private sphere of the family and home. Instead, such conduct is now accorded the status of a social problem—violence against women.

THE GAY/LESBIAN MOVEMENT

Like the contemporary women's movement, the gay and lesbian movement addresses a broad set of concerns. Although the founding of the Mattachine Society in 1950 and that of the Daughters of Bilitis in 1955 are often cited as the first signs of a gay and lesbian movement in the United States, it was not until the late 1960s that gay men and lesbians became politically mobilized to fight discrimination. The struggle against homophobic discrimination has been fought on many levels. The initial intent of the early gay and lesbian movement was to disrupt stereotypical perceptions of homosexuality as a peculiar condition. Since then, it has continually sought to establish homosexuality as a nonstigmatized public alternative to heterosexual standards, one worthy of public respect and legal protection.

The presence of the gay/lesbian movement has served to fundamentally shape the discourse of contemporary sexual politics in general and the politics of violence more particularly. One of the ways in which the gay and lesbian movement has played a key role in shaping contemporary "politics of violence" in the United States is by establishing and institutionalizing gay- and lesbian-sponsored antiviolence projects throughout the United States, just as the contemporary women's movement did earlier.

THE CRIME VICTIM MOVEMENT

Consistent with and drawing from the antiviolence movements established and sustained by the civil rights movement, the women's movement, and the gay and lesbian movement, three kinds of antiviolence movements currently operate in the United States: (1) the citizen-action model of communities mobilizing to mount patrols, run neighborhood watch programs, and try to make the streets and neighborhoods safer; (2) the victim services movement, which staffs hotlines, centers, and support groups; and (3) the racial justice movement organized against police brutality, state-sanctioned violence, and violence against people of color and other minority groups. Each of these antiviolence movements organizes around the framework of civil rights and each pursues legal reforms through legislative activity and education promoting understanding, awareness, prevention, and support for victims of violence.

A central component of these antiviolence efforts—the support for victims of violence—has been recognized as a key element in a larger crime victim movement. Emerging in the face of rising fear of victimization, penal reforms perceived to benefit criminals, and diminished confidence in the legal system, the crime victim movement in the United States is a national reform movement promoting the rights of crime victims. The basic claim put forth by the crime victim movement is simple: victims of crime, especially violent crime, need and are entitled to special assistance, support, and rights. From the point of view of those involved in the crime victim movement, legal and extralegal mechanisms need to be put in place to recognize and serve those injured by crime. This is done by expanding the rights of crime victims.

SOCIAL MOVEMENT ORGANIZATIONS AND NEW
ATTENTION TO AN OLD PROBLEM

Consistent with the foci of the modern civil rights movement, the contemporary women's movement, the gay and lesbian movement, and the crime victim movement in the United States, beginning in the late 1960s and continuing to the present, many organizations emerged to bring attention to and curb violence directed at minority groups. In the latter part of the twentieth century, watchdog organizations emerged at the national, regional, state, and local levels to play a key role in documenting instances of violence that target minority members of the community, identifying and publicizing harm associated with bias-motivated violence, submitting proposals for reform, calling on the law to intervene on behalf of select injured groups, and providing social services to victims of bias-motivated violence. In the process, these organizations have collectively redefined age-old conduct and constructed new portraits of victimization.

A brief description of seven of the larger, more established, and pivotal antiviolence organizations that have accompanied the social movements described above demonstrates how these types of organizations play a decisive role in the politics of violence. Specifically, the following seven organizations have emerged to engage in activism that brings newfound attention to hate-motivated violence. At the same time, they promote the interests of select groups by demanding changes in public policy, including the law. The description that follows is not a comprehensive overview; rather, it illustrates the ways in which various organizations emerged and responded to what they perceive to be an escalation of racial, ethnic, religious, and other forms of intergroup conflict.

The Antidefamation League of B'nai B'rith

As the most established antiviolence organization in the United States, the Anti-Defamation League of B'nai B'rith (ADL) was founded in 1969; its primary focus is on anti-Semitic violence. Since 1979, the ADL has been tracking anti-Semitic violence and has published an annual *Audit of Anti-Semitic Incidents*. In 1981, the ADL's Legal Affairs Department drafted a model hate crime bill to be introduced in state legislatures. Like other lesser known organizations, including many civil rights groups, the ADL's work has underscored the victim status of those harmed by violence because of their race and/or religion.

The National Institute Against Prejudice and Violence

Like the ADL, the National Institute Against Prejudice & Violence (NIAPV) in Baltimore, Maryland, has focused on what is now termed "ethnoviolence"— acts motivated by racial, religious, or ethnic prejudice. Ethnoviolence includes physical assaults, verbal harassment, attacks on people's homes, and various forms of vandalism. Since its founding in 1984, the NIAPV has published documents inventorying the criminal and civil remedies available under federal and state law for violence motivated by racial, religious, and ethnic hatred. They are intended primarily to inform victims of these crimes and their attorneys of the various avenues of legal recourse against offenders of bias crime; the goal is to enable attorneys and their clients to arrive at the most effective combination of legal remedies to fully vindicate the victims' rights.

The Center for Democratic Renewal

Founded in 1979, the Center for Democratic Renewal (CDR), formerly known as the National Anti-Klan Network, is an Atlanta-based antiracist organization with offices in Kansas City and Seattle. According to its bimonthly newsletter, *The Monitor*, the CDR is "leading the fight against bigoted violence and hate group activity in America today. The CDR is a multiracial, multiethnic, interfaith, nonprofit organization dedicated to promoting constructive, nonviolent responses to hate violence and the white supremacist movement." Like the ADL and the NIAPV, the CDR acts as a national clearinghouse for efforts to counter hate group activity and bigoted violence through public education, community response, leadership training, and research. The CDR has been primarily concerned with monitoring and addressing antiracist violence associated with the Ku Klux Klan (KKK). Although the CDR's original focus was on racist violence, over the years it has developed a much broader agenda. Like the ADL and the NIAPV, the CDR currently includes in its purview violence motivated by bigotry and directed at homosexuals.

The Southern Poverty Law Center

As a nonprofit foundation supported by private donations, the Southern Poverty Law Center (SPLC) in Montgomery, Alabama, was founded in 1971. The SPLC's Klanwatch Project was established in 1980 to address racist violence through litigation, education, and monitoring. Since then, the SPLC's Klanwatch Project continues to operate as a private intelligence agency. It collects data on the KKK and other white supremacist groups and sustains one of the most complete lists of hate groups and hate leaders in the United States; it compiles perpetration and victimization data based on police and news sources; and pursues legal redress by bringing lawsuits against members of the Klan's Invisible Empire in Alabama, Texas, North Carolina, and Georgia. While the Klanwatch Project primarily focuses on racist violence, it nonetheless acknowledges the importance of devoting attention to antigay and lesbian violence.

The National Gay and Lesbian Task Force

The National Gay and Lesbian Task Force (NGLTF) was founded in Washington, D.C., in 1973 to promote the interests of gays and lesbians in the United States. The NGLTF has over 17,000 members and houses various projects, including the Privacy/Civil Rights Project, the Lesbian and Gay Families Project, the Campus Organizing Project, and the Anti-Violence Project. The NGLTF's AntiViolence Project was established in 1982 to contribute to the overall goals of the NGLTF, including the specific civil rights and social change goals articulated by other divisions within the NGLTF.

The National Coalition Against Domestic Violence

The National Coalition Against Domestic Violence (NCADV) was formally organized in 1978 when over 100 battered women's advocates from all parts of the nation attended the U.S. Commission on Civil Rights hearing in Washington, D.C., on battered women. The NCADV currently has members from over two thousand programs across the United States. Governed by a working board of directors comprised of women from all over the country and representatives of task forces, who are themselves active in domestic violence programs in their communities, the NCADV's mission is to offer assistance with common problems faced by programs operating in isolation at the local level.

The National Victim Center

As a nonprofit organization, the National Victim Center (NVC) engages in a number of activities designed to reduce the consequences of crime on victims. Most notably, the NVC: (1) compiles statistics and produces a national report, which is made available to libraries, governmental agencies, and political organizations across the United States; (2) publishes the academic journal *Victimology*, which is distributed to libraries, governmental agencies, and political organizations across the United States; (3) engages in legal advocacy at the state and national level in order to protect and restore the rights of crime victims; (4) raises funds to support programs and efforts across the country; and (5) sponsors educational efforts designed to make citizens, law enforcement officials, crime victims, and offenders aware of the rights of victims.

THE POLITICS OF VIOLENCE AND ATTENDANT LEGAL TRANSFORMATIONS

Historically speaking, the efforts and activities of the organizations described above, as well as many of their affiliates and other civil rights organizations across the United States, were inspired by and rode the coattails of the liberal movements of the 1960s and the 1970s. In large part because of these movements and their organizations, throughout the last thirty years there has been a virtual explosion of political work around the status of all sorts of minorities, but especially those defined by their race, religion, ethnicity, gender, or sexual orientation/preference.

One of the most obvious results of this political work is recent legal changes. Specifically, in the late 1970s, throughout the 1980s, and continuing into the 1990s, legislation that criminalizes violence and intimidation motivated by bigotry and targeting minority groups has been introduced, adopted, and invoked for both symbolic and prosecuting purposes. This has occurred at both federal and state levels. These changes in law suggest that violence against select types of people has been institutionalized as a social problem. The new social movements and organizations described here in large part have been credited with inducing and institutionalizing both large-scale legal change and cultural change. Activists capitalized on the discourse, established networks, and collective identities developed by the civil rights movement, the women's movement, the gay/lesbian movement, and the crime victim movement in the United States. They effectively framed grievances, developed collective action frames, pressed claims, marshaled support, and interacted with institutions in ways that led to social change.

7

Psychiatrists Construct
Homosexuality

STUART A. KIRK AND HERB KUTCHINS

Although changing leadership of the American Psychiatric Association (APA) did not propel the organization into the forefront of social activism in the United States, it reflected a greater responsiveness to the social problems from which psychiatrists had traditionally insulated themselves. This change was evident in the dramatic events surrounding the controversy over the diagnosis of homosexuality, which occurred just as plans for the third edition of the *Diagnostic and Statistical Manual (DSM-III)* were being formulated. This controversy illustrates both the sensitivity of the APA to public opinion and its organizational difficulties in dealing with internal dissension or external critics. These dual vulnerabilities allowed an enterprising and able nosologist (a specialist in the classification of diseases), Robert Spitzer, to step into the breach. His eagerness to do so and his tenuous success at managing the controversy placed him at the political heart of psychiatric diagnosis and foreshadowed his subsequent efforts to develop DSM-III.

The principal source of information about the *DSM* controversy over homosexuality is Spitzer. Bayer's (1981) book-length description of these events was heavily dependent on material provided by Spitzer. Bayer and Spitzer reveal a good deal of information, some of it critical of Spitzer. While the story that is presented could be incomplete, the recounting of a key episode illustrates some of the politics of psychiatric diagnosis that existed just as the campaign to transform *DSM* was about to begin.

This chapter is excerpted from Kirk, Stuart A. and Herb Kutchins (1992). *The Selling of DSM: The Rhetoric of Science in Psychiatry* (Chapter 4). Hawthorne, NY: Aldine de Gruyter.

At stake was a minor modification of *DSM*-II. At the 1970 annual convention of the APA in San Francisco and at subsequent psychiatric meetings, gay activists picketed and disrupted conference events in order to draw attention to their demand that homosexuality be dropped as a psychiatric category. In addition to disrupting the presentations by psychoanalysts who were well known for their views that homosexuality was a form of pathology, gay activists forced the APA to schedule panels at the. annual meetings where the protesters presented an alternative view of homosexuality as a normal variation of sexual activity. This pattern of protest persisted for several years and at the 1972 meeting a masked and cloaked psychiatrist, "Dr. Anonymous," joined the panel and declared that he was a homosexual as were more than two hundred of his associates, some of them members of the Gay Psychiatric Association, which met socially but secretly during the annual APA meetings.

A standoff persisted until late in 1972 between the protesters and some psychoanalysts who insisted that the "scientific evidence," principally derived from studies that they had conducted, demonstrated that homosexuality was a pathological condition, and that a positive response to gay demands would constitute an unjustified political accommodation. Enmeshed in the controversy was a challenge to psychoanalytic orthodoxy.

The man who took control was Robert Spitzer. Although he was a member of the Committee on Nomenclature and Statistics, which produced *DSM*-II, he had not been assigned to resolve the conflict. As the story has been told, he was at a meeting in October 1972, when more than a hundred gay activists protested antihomosexual bias. This was his first contact with gays protesting against psychiatric mistreatment and he stayed afterward to talk with one leader of the protest, Ron Gold. The result of this encounter was that Spitzer agreed to arrange a meeting with the Committee on Nomenclature and to schedule a panel at the next meeting of the APA in May 1973 in Honolulu.

Spitzer conveyed the request to meet with the Committee on Nomenclature and Statistics to its chairman, Henry Brill, who agreed. Spitzer's explanation for the decision: "We couldn't think of any good reason not to meet them" (Spector 1977:54). Perhaps not, but there were many good reasons for the members of the committee to proceed in a different manner than they did. When they met with gay spokesmen in February 1973, they did not invite the established psychiatrists who vehemently opposed dropping homosexuality from the manual. And they made their deliberations public. The following day there was an article in the *New York Times* about the meeting, and Brill was quoted as saying that some change was indicated.

Actually, as early as 1971 Brill had reported that there was strong sentiment within the Committee on Nomenclature and Statistics to recognize "that homosexual behavior was not necessarily a sign of psychiatric disorder; and that the diagnostic manual should reflect that understanding" (Brill to Barton in Bayer 1981:113). But the story in the *New York Times* was different because these private sentiments were now a part of the public record. Furthermore, Brill indicated that the committee hoped to have a resolution prepared within two months, in time for the APA annual meeting. This deadline was not met despite the apparent enthusiasm of the Committee on Nomenclature and Statistics and its chairman, because Spitzer balked and would not agree to incorporate a recommendation to declassify homosexuality in a position paper he was asked to coauthor for the committee.

Although the May 1973 convention was not punctuated by the dramatic disruptions that had occurred in prior years, there were several events that had a major impact on the conflict over the diagnosis of homosexuality. First of all, as he had promised, Spitzer arranged for a panel that included leading psychiatrists on both sides of the controversy as well as a gay speaker. This program was unlike the previous year's panel, which had consisted of gay activists and their psychiatrist supporters. The whole atmosphere had changed dramatically in the three years since protestors first disrupted a panel on "Issues of Homosexuality" and created so much pandemonium that some conventioneers demanded a refund of their airfares, and at least one physician asked that police shoot the protesters. By contrast, the panel at the 1973 convention was very well attended by almost a thousand people, and there was a positive response to those who criticized the view that homosexuality was a pathological condition. The media made optimistic predictions that homosexuality would be dropped soon from *DSM*.

Another event at the conference had a profound effect on Spitzer, who was still undecided about homosexuality. Spitzer, who, we are told, had never knowingly met a gay psychiatrist, was invited to attend a social meeting of the Gay Psychiatric Association. Although participants were upset by Spitzer's unannounced appearance, many were persuaded to explain how they felt. "Spitzer heard homosexual psychiatrists declaring that 'their lives had been changed by what they had heard at the panel discussion'" (Bayer 1981:126). They confirmed Spitzer's belief that many homosexuals (among them psychiatric colleagues) functioned at a high level. His encounter gave Spitzer such "an emotional jolt" that he prepared a proposal within a month for the deletion of homosexuality from *DSM*.

Actually, Spitzer's position paper, "Homosexuality as an Irregular Form of Sexual Development and Sexual Orientation Disturbance as a Psychiatric Disorder," did not recommend the entire elimination of homosexuality from the manual. Although homosexuality per se was not enough to warrant a diagnosis, those who were troubled should be given a new diagnosis of Sexual Orientation Disturbance. Spitzer did not accept the position of gay activists that homosexuality was a normal variant of sexual behavior. He proposed a middle ground between their position and the assertion that homosexuality was pathological.

Spitzer's reasoning was as follows. In order to answer the question of whether homosexuality was an illness, he felt that it was necessary first to define mental disorder as a behavior that was accompanied by subjective distress or a general impairment in social effectiveness or functioning. Since some gays, such as those he met at the APA meeting, did not suffer from subjective distress because of their sexual orientation and were obviously high functioning, they could not be considered mentally ill.

On the other hand, he did not want to give homosexuality the stamp of normalcy. He decided that homosexuality was a form of irregular sexual behavior. But, if psychiatry was to broaden its diagnostic system to include "suboptimal" behaviors as mental disorders, he reasoned, it would have to recognize celibacy, religious fanaticism, racism, vegetarianism, and male chauvinism as diagnostic categories. The choice of examples, obviously meant by Spitzer to be humorous, reveals what was likely to persuade his audience composed primarily of white males who understood the distinctions between racism, sexism, and the disorders they diagnosed and treated. Bayer (1981:129) offered an admiring evaluation of the proposal:

> The position paper as well as the proposed new diagnostic category thus attempted to provide a common ground for those who had been locked in combat for the past three years. To homosexual activists it granted the removal of homosexuality from the *Diagnostic Manual*, allowing them to claim a stunning victory. To psychoanalytically oriented psychiatrists, it stated that their own view of homosexuality as suboptimal was not being challenged but rather was not central to the restricted concept of psychiatric disorder. To those seeking an end to the pattern of disruptions that had beset psychiatric meetings, the new classification provided a formula that could remove the APA from the center of controversy. Finally for psychiatrists concerned with the extent to which the psychiatric nosology had become a tool in the hands of government officials attempting to deprive homosexuals of their rights, the proposed shift promised to put an end to such unwanted collaboration. That all this could take the form of a theoretical refinement rather than a political accommodation made the proposal more attractive to those willing to yield polar positions defined in the course of conflict.

However, few of the participants in this controversy viewed Spitzer's handiwork in this way. The Committee on Nomenclature and Statistics refused to adopt his proposal. The chairman, Brill, seemed to back away from his earlier position that the committee should do something about the diagnosis of homosexuality. Instead, he suggested a survey of APA members to determine whether Spitzer's proposals would elicit a strong reaction. Spitzer's proposal, without committee approval, was sent to the Council on Research and Development. The chair of the council rejected Brill's suggested survey as "ridiculous," saying, "You don't devise a nomenclature through a vote" (p. 130).

The Committee on Nomenclature and Statistics was not the only group that refused to accept Spitzer's compromise. Ron Gold objected to Spitzer's proposal, particularly the new diagnosis, Sexual Orientation Disturbance, which would be used only for homosexuals. Gold urged the council to limit its action to deletion of homosexuality from *DSM*. Despite reservations by many of its members, the council voted unanimously to adopt Spitzer's proposal. The reasoning of the council was that they should not override the recommendation of a committee they had appointed to evaluate a scientific issue. Their logic was questionable, since the proposal was not recommended to them by the Committee on Nomenclature and Statistics; it was solely Spitzer's work.

Next to review the proposal was the Assembly of District Branches, which overwhelmingly approved it. However the assembly called upon the Council on Research and Development to reword the proposal to eliminate pejorative phrasing such as the reference to homosexuality as an irregular form of sexual behavior.

Finally, in December 1973, the matter was considered by the board of trustees. After listening politely to the objections of opponents, the board voted unanimously to delete homosexuality and to replace it with the diagnosis of Sexual Orientation Disturbance. The final text made a distinction between homosexuality per se and Sexual Orientation Disturbance. According to a press release from the American Psychological Association (cited in Bayer 1981:137), "This diagnostic category is distinguished from homosexuality which by itself does not necessarily constitute a psychiatric disorder."

The meeting was followed by a press conference attended by the president of the APA, gay activists, and Robert Spitzer. Major newspapers across the country carried stories announcing the revision. Many reports missed the nuances of the compromise. For example, the *Washington Post* reported "Doctors Rule Homosexuals Not Abnormal" (December 12, 1973, p. 1). Their headline ignored the careful denials of the APA president and Spitzer that the board had not declared that homosexuality was normal. Spitzer's statement infuriated gays, but it made little difference in the public perception of what had happened.

Other participants had scores to settle. One member forced the board to submit its decision to a referendum of the APA membership; many people ridiculed the idea that a scientific issue should be settled by a plebiscite. The reputation of the organization was not the only thing at risk. Individual careers were deeply affected. A new group of experts, many with views more sympathetic to gays and lesbians, was called on to express their opinions about issues related to homosexuality in court proceedings, in the popular media, and in professional publications.

Spitzer was among those most directly affected. Although he expressed "severe discomfort" (Bayer 1981:143) over the idea of a referendum, he and gay activists drafted a letter that was signed by all of the candidates in an upcoming election for president and vice president of the APA. The letter was sent to the entire APA membership, paid for by funds raised by gay groups, although their participation was concealed. This was a risky strategy, but he felt that the stakes were very high. Spitzer's career was directly linked to the outcome of the vote, since he had just been appointed to oversee the publication of *DSM*-III.

The vote was not close although it was described this way in later accounts: 58 percent were in favor of deleting homosexuality from *DSM*, while only 37 percent voted against the proposal. Those familiar with voting patterns among large groups of people would characterize this as a landslide, but describing the vote as close served other purposes in subsequent conflicts over the diagnosis of homosexuality.

Four aspects of the controversy deserve to be highlighted, since they recurred repeatedly in the conflicts over the revisions of *DSM*. One is the claim of the proponents on every side that they were being scientific and their opponents were not. Even though they had done little research and had very little hard data to support their position, psychiatrists who wanted to change the diagnostic system claimed that they were making informed, scientific decisions. A fallback position was that the scientific evidence presented by their opponents was invalid and should be discounted, which was easy enough to show by looking at it in terms of basic scientific standards. Few of the psychiatrists involved in the controversy had done studies that could pass muster as credible research, but before a decision could be made each side had to couch its arguments in the terms of science. The presentations by gay activists were very important in this respect, because they were careful to mobilize whatever scientific reports were available to support the declassification of homosexuality. The earlier disruptions by gay rights groups were crucial, but a scientific rationale was also needed before the APA and its committees could act. Science was a rallying cry; politics a term of denigration.

A second factor involves the strategy of presenting issues as though they came from a position of organizational authority. For example, even when Spitzer did not have the support of the Committee on Nomenclature and Statistics, his proposal was seen as its recommendation. Perhaps the best illustration of this strategy was in the final referendum. In addition to the circulation of the letter signed by the leaders of the organization, the strategy was reflected in the way that the referendum was worded. Members were asked to vote whether they were in favor of the decision of the board of trustees or whether they opposed it. In this way the proposal was persuasive to both liberals who wanted to declassify homosexuality and to some conservatives who wanted to maintain the status quo and to reestablish traditional authority of the organization.

A third very important phenomenon that would reappear in the struggles about *DSM*-III was the sense that someone took control in a stalemated situation and resolved it; without active intervention the more conservative membership of the APA would not have acted.

The final consideration about this episode is how important it was symbolically, but how *unimportant* its consequences were. Lawrence Hartmann, who headed the initiative of the Massachusetts Psychiatric Association to declassify homosexuality, told an interviewer:

> If you're seeing a homosexual patient and had to fill out an insurance form, I would still . . . not use the word homosexual. I think it is such a damaging word. [Interviewer: What is the most convenient one?] Depression is easy, anxiety neurosis is easy, adjustment reaction of adulthood or adolescence. Usually a patient has quite a few worries. I write as brief notes as I can. I use as vague and general categories as I think are compatible with the truth. Insurance companies realize that they are getting watered down diagnostic labels in order not to harm the patient. (Spector 1977:56)

The gay activists clearly realized the symbolic significance of the decision about the diagnosis. Although they were angry with Spitzer for the way that he had formulated the diagnosis of Sexual Orientation Disorder and for his continued unwillingness to recognize that homosexuality was a normal variation of sexual activity, they pushed for the APA press conference that announced the change in the nomenclature.

REFERENCES

Bayer, R. 1981. *Homosexuality and American Psychiatry*. New York: Basic.
Spector, M. 1977. "Legitimizing Homosexuality." *Society* 14 (July): 52–56.

8

Television Talk Shows
Construct Morality

KATHLEEN S. LOWNEY

Lots of people seem to be uneasy with talk shows. A wide variety of people seem to think that talk shows have gone "too far," although not everyone agrees about what "too far" means. Some critics feel that the shows reflect a growing national moral decline. They assume that there is no moral code operating on these shows; they feel the shows simply celebrate the worst in sexual perversions, interpersonal violence, and family misfortunes. I disagree. There *is* a moral code on talk shows, and we need to explore it, asking: What is the code? And just whose morality is being espoused? These questions are critical for understanding the role of talk shows in American popular culture.

I want to explore the normative order on talk shows by examining the shows themselves. Having just written this sentence, I took a bit of a break and watched *The Jerry Springer Show*. The show focused on just one family. Amber was introduced first; she was 12 years old and had been dating, with her parents' approval, a 24-year-old guy named Glenn, who was another one of the guests. Her parents knew that she and Glenn were sexually involved. Amber's mother (Pam, the third guest) also was dating Glenn and wanted to marry him. About 20 minutes into the show, Amber's father, Frank, came out on the stage, promptly threatened Glenn with bodily harm, and had to be restrained by well-muscled guards. As the show progressed, emotions became extremely intense. Pam told her daughter that it was time that her own needs came first and her daughter would have to cope with Glenn as her new stepfather or else Amber would

---

This chapter is excerpted from Lowney, Kathleen S. (1999). *Baring Our Souls: TV Talk Shows and the Religion of Recovery* (Chapter 1). New York: Aldine de Gruyter.

just have to get lost. The mother went on to say more hurtful and embarrassing things about her daughter, such as the fact that she smelled due to poor hygiene.

On the surface, this show could be an excellent typifying example of what critics mean when they say that talk shows are destroying America's moral fabric. One whole television hour was devoted to discussing the sexual appetites of a 12-year-old girl and her mother. Viewers learn that Pam thought that Glenn was "stupid and slow"; Pam admitted to prostitution, a drug habit, and serving time in prison; Frank sort of admitted to having a violent relationship with Pam; Pam called Amber lots of names (many were bleeped out).

But there was more to the show. The host, Jerry Springer, played a significant role. He was constantly interrupting the guests, especially Pam, and most interruptions communicated one of two emotions. The first was incredulity—that a mother would say such hurtful, selfish things to her daughter. The second emotion was sarcasm. Jerry made pointed comments about Pam and Frank's parenting skills, Glenn's decision-making capabilities, and even Amber's choices (though he was careful to say repeatedly that she was a child and children make mistakes and that she shouldn't be judged too harshly). Jerry definitely was grounding his remarks in a moral code: children should not be having sex and parents should protect their children, even if it means putting the needs of the children above those of the parents. Near the end of the show, a psychologist joined the family on stage. He promptly added his critical voice by telling Glenn to leave this family alone. He told Pam to start acting like a mother to her daughter, and told both parents to start loving their daughter more if they wanted her to have any self-esteem.

Clearly there was a quite strong moral message to this show. It didn't come only at the end of the show; Springer wove it throughout the program. The morality was hard to ignore. In addition to Jerry's sarcasm and his outrage, the audience was there, booing and hissing Pam, Glenn, and Frank. They clapped wildly when Springer moralized; when he finished a three-minute harangue against Pam, the audience gave him a standing ovation. Jerry Springer, the audience, and the psychologist reiterated time and again a moral code that valued sexual restraint and honoring commitments to others (such as mother to daughter). Still, television talk show critics probably would say that this moral message should not be couched in the public humiliation of a 12-year-old girl. The viewing public now knows about her promiscuity and her troubled family life, and for what? What did that show cost Amber, her family, and perhaps our nation's very soul?

Such questions about the presence (or absence) of and the kinds of moral discourse on talk shows often occur in an intellectual vacuum. We think of television, and especially talk shows, as a relatively new, yet powerful medium of entertainment that can lead children and adults down the path to depravity. But there always has been some type of entertainment that has bothered a portion of the population. There are historical parallels to talk shows that bear investigating. I remember my parents hating some of the music that I liked; there was a national debate over Elvis' swinging hips and how much—or even if—they should have been shown on *The Ed Sullivan Show*. Both critics and apologists of talk shows need to understand the historical roots of talk shows in order to comprehend their role in American society today. Journey back in time with me for a moment.

SECULAR FUN: THE CIRCUS AS ENTERTAINMENT

It's the middle of the nineteenth century. For now, let's shun the big cities and instead go traveling in rural America. Most adult males worked on the land or were involved in a few central industries. The women were involved in agriculture as well as taking care of the home. Children worked hard to help the family economically. Book learning would be squeezed in around the patterns of planting, tending, and harvesting the crops. It's easy to think of this as a hard life by our twentieth-century standards: Appliances were rare, food took much longer to prepare, walking a few miles to a neighbor's home or into town was not seen as extraordinary.

What would these people do after a long day of working in the fields? Save for relaxing with other family members, most of their leisure time would be spent in two activities: church and secular entertainment. Carnivals and circuses provided much of the secular entertainment, in town for a few days and then gone for another year; religious revivals likewise were an important activity. These nineteenth-century carnivals and revivals are two roots—perhaps the most important roots—of modern talk shows. Each has left an important legacy that has shaped the moral discourse on talk shows.

Carnivals were significant national diversions by the 1830s. But although enjoyable, they were not without their critics. Many people felt that circuses and carnivals were morally ambiguous; people worried about their effects on impressionable children. But just what was so immoral about circuses? The laughter and the bawdiness of the activity under the big top fractured the routines of production and home life. There was a fascination with the giant, the bearded woman, the dwarf, and the daredevil humans with their animal acts. These were people quite different from one's neighbors. Townspeople joined in the revelry, not paying much attention to social status. The normative order was suspended during the performance; for example, many female circus performers wore provocative clothing (for that time period, mind you) while they entertained the crowds, and fortune-tellers and seers transgressed religious admonitions. Ministers felt the dangers of disrupting the moral order, even if it was for momentary amusement. The thought of parishioners wasting time—and hard-earned money—in such frivolous pursuits flew in the face of the work ethic preached from pulpits every Sunday.

But despite warnings from the pulpit, people flocked to this form of amusement. And the most entertaining part of carnivals were the "freaks." Some had genetic abnormalities; others simply had physical characteristics they accentuated for monetary gain. They were displayed in ways emphasizing their distinctiveness from the "good citizens" who had paid to watch them. There was little public outrage over the exploitation of such performers (especially those who we would now call mentally handicapped) until early in the twentieth century.

Circuses not only brought new people into the town, they also brought an ambiance. The scurrying to put up the huge tent, the sights and smells of exotic animals, the strangely dressed entertainers—all these were part of the circus environment. An assemblage of strangers had invaded town; their behavior was not the same as the community's. Whether deserved or not, there was a veneer of fraud that permeated the circus company. Circus performers played with moral boundaries, in reality or through illusion. Thus the unique circus moral code, vehemently condemned by ministers, only highlighted to members of the audience that there were other ways of living, other ways of being human. The circus performers allowed spectators to imagine that their own lives could be different, but without much risk to the community's moral standards. The carnivals and circuses of that century provided entertainment, but it was all in fun. The next morning another day would dawn and the community would settle back into its routines, which focused on the institutions of work and family, with their sex/gender, racial, and socioeconomic systems of stratification. The circus would leave after a few days and, fostered by the community's religious institutions, life would go back to normal.

TURNING AWAY FROM SIN: RELIGIOUS REVIVALS AS OPPORTUNITIES FOR CONVERSION

America in the early 1800s was changing: it was growing territorially and with that growth came new people who somehow were to fit into the social contract. Technology began to transform how our ancestors lived, where they worked, and for whom they toiled. With such rapid change came anxiety, even fear of the future. People began to question the moral order—would it still work in these new times? How should one live in this new time? What norms would be there to guide people's interactions with each other? For many, a turn, or return, to religion answered these questions. Religion became a comfort, a guidepost in unsettling times. No matter what faith people chose, most believers took their faiths very seriously. They examined their consciences and tried to reign in, if not extinguish, immoral behaviors. This period of religious fervor is usually referred to as the Second Great Awakening (1800–30).

A key feature of this Awakening was the religious revival. Preachers would come into a town for a few days and preach salvation to all who attended. These services were often held under a tent, perhaps on the very site occupied a few days earlier by a circus. The revivals were most often held at night during the workweek, so that all could attend and hear God's word. Frequently a large crowd would gather. The services were full of emotionality and drama. The key to a successful revival was excitement.

The revivalist's responsibility was to create this emotion-filled experience so that conversions would occur. The main way to accomplish this was preaching. Sermons had to deliver word pictures that gave graphic images of the damned eternally suffering in Hell, for then large numbers would convert or rededicate their lives to God. If it was necessary to make someone uncomfortable in the pit of the stomach, or in the depths of the soul, then these ministers were ready to make their audience very, very uncomfortable.

After the sermon, the testimonial was the most effective conversion technique in the revivalist's arsenal. Attendees would share stories of a life full of sinfulness now redeemed by a right relationship with God. The testimony about life before conversion needed to be truly horrific for others to want to convert. These revival meetings were full of sinners openly confessing to all sorts of sins—of failing to resist the temptations of alcohol, gambling, "the flesh," violence, theft, pride, self-indulgence, and so forth. The successful revivalist knew just what to do with these stories of sin. He used them to fill the mourner's bench, seeker's bench, or anxious seat, which was near the front of the tent, sometimes even on the stage. Sitting there was a public symbol that the person was undergoing an internal battle. Such visibility of self-identified deviants served a profound social function. Once a person had taken, voluntarily, a seat on the anxious bench, it was difficult not to complete the process with a confession and a promise to change one's life. Forgiveness and acceptance by one's neighbors flowed from giving testimony and from public conversion. This not only helped the individual find peace, but fostered solidarity in the community.

So it was that the carnival/circus and the revival were almost perfect opposites. The former were times when frivolity, deviance, and eternal damnation lurked under the big tent awaiting the sinner, whereas the latter beckoned the sinner to undergo public humiliation, in return for ultimate redemption.

TELEVISION TALK SHOWS AS CIRCUS AND REVIVAL

We are not like our ancestors in these rural communities. Not as many of us identify ourselves as religious, we often have less familial interaction and support. We feel that our society is more violent, more out of control than ever before. We seek protection from each other by attending self-defense classes, by making our homes armed and secure fortresses, or by choosing to carry weapons. Poverty and drugs seem rampant and they worry us, even if we are not directly affected by either. We especially worry about our children: what they are downloading off the Internet, what they are or aren't learning in school. We are scared about the kind of future our children will inherit from us. As a nation we seem more interested in being assertive than compassionate, self-indulgent than self-sacrificing. We appear to be fascinated by those who break social norms rather than by those quiet, unassuming citizens who embody them.

We, of course, watch television whereas our ancestors could not. Perhaps the "lowest" form of entertainment we could publicly admit to watching is the talk show. But as a culture, watch them we do. We watch them just as we flocked to carnivals and revivals a century ago. Our reasons have changed little; talk shows serve useful social functions, just as carnivals and revivals did in the 1800s. Talk shows provide us with public entertainment, a time to play with and then ultimately affirm moral boundaries, and the opportunity to listen to people tell their stories of despair and then redemption.

The roots of the modern-day talk shows lie in the nineteenth century's carnivals and revivals. The parallels are striking. The talk show and the carnival both tempt us to watch portrayals of otherness. We see behaviors that are neither common nor publicly discussed exhibited for all to see. Just as the circus performers were displayed one dimensionally, so are talk show guests. Indeed, this atypical or deviant position is what earns them an invitation to appear on the show. And it is the talk show host, like the circus ringmaster of old, who identifies the guests' particular deviance for us from the outset, just in case those in the audience missed it. A person's complex life becomes summarized in a simplistic, made-for-TV label just as freaks were publicized for their unique characteristics on circus handbills. These labels are reinforced throughout the program by subtitles shown just under guests' faces. Just this one aspect of the guests' lives is lifted up for moral judgment.

Carnivals, circuses, and talk shows highlight behavior that falls outside the realm of normality for mainstream society. Most of us do not traipse on high wires, work with animal acts, or read the future; neither are most of us "mothers who covered up their daughters' pregnancies," "high-powered women derailed by menopause," or a "father who abused all four of his sisters." It seems unlikely that any one of us can personally relate to more than a small percentage of show topics. So why then do we watch? In the circus act, the performance was fraught with risk; we knew that no matter how practiced a performer might be, he or she was always flirting with injury, possibly even death. Likewise, guests on talk shows take risks. They expose their lives in ways that some of us might fantasize about and others might find repellent. We know that secrets are a moment away from being spilled. Anxiously we watch both the carnival and the talk show "acts," always aware of the precariousness of the situation. Talk shows become glimpses into the pain (much less often the joy) that is life. Watching deviant people suffer can make us rejoice at the life that we have while at the same time they can remind us of the need for a morality that binds people together. These shows do, then, feature a moral discourse.

Talk shows do not just entertain us—they are also a site for American revivalism, of a novel sort. They provide an "electronic tent" under which we can gather together and watch sinners confess, sometimes receiving absolution from the people whom they have hurt, and be reinstated into the moral community. The hosts are contemporary preachers, cajoling guests, studio audiences, and those of us at home to obey the normative order. And any good preacher knows that an excellent technique to facilitate conversion is to offer oneself as an exemplar of a sinner now redeemed. Talk show hosts make good use of this rhetorical strategy; thus audiences know about Oprah Winfrey and Ricki Lake's weight loss, Sally Jessy Raphael's daughter's drug use and subsequent death, Oprah's shame over and healing from sexual abuse, and Geraldo Rivera's numerous sexual escapades. These admissions of failing are used to establish a parasocial sense of solidarity among host, guest, and audience members. This parasocial connection is exhibited when the public thinks that we "know" all about celebrities even though we haven't met them—and probably never will. And hosts manipulate this parasocial relationship.

The hosts' life stories, so well known to viewers due in part to repeated disclosures on the shows, invite others to share their pain. And how the guests talk and talk and talk some more about their troubles! We see them shamed by the host, audience, and other guests, and we are reminded of what is considered right and wrong. The hosts are pop cultural moralists and the audience accepts them in that role.

Therefore, talk shows parallel nineteenth-century Protestant revivals. The host is the visiting preacher bent on offering salvation to all those who seek it. The guests are primarily sinners, and the audience is the ardent congregation goading, chastising, and cajoling the sinners and celebrating repentance. Guests not in need of conversion are the aggrieved victims, demanding change in the sinner-guest's behavior. All the televisual attention is directed toward creating a conversion experience. The music, the staging techniques, and the pace of the show all parallel the structure of revivals.

What mattered under the revivalist's tent is also what matters under the electronic tent of the talk shows—that people convert to a moral lifestyle. Turning away from sin is not a one-time event but something that has to happen every minute of every day. In the nineteenth century, the moral community of the local church was there for the former sinner. On talk shows, the host and the psychological expert, who appears at the end of many shows, share the conversion duties. The host and audience members diagnose and emotional experts certify the moral failings of the sinner-guests. Sinner-guests must earn our sympathy by admitting to sin and guilt *and* by agreeing to a process that will solidify their new status of convert. The experts show the way: therapy. Guests are chided until they agree to enter therapy or go to a 12-step program or some other support group. Like the sinners on the anxious bench, conversion on talk shows is understood as tenuous; backsliding is always a possibility. This is the *religion of recovery*.

We have come full circle: it is inaccurate to claim that there isn't morality on talk shows. Hosts, audences, and experts all have a moral perspective that shapes their performance. Conservative critics have missed this point. The question is not whether there ought to be a moral code on talk shows, but *whose* morality it should be. Talk shows are frequent visitors in American homes. We can be enveloped in their "electronic tents" 24 hours a day if we want to, for just about any time of the day some channel is carrying one. But when we watch, to what altar, to use revivalists' language, are the guests—and viewers—being called? I think it is important that we understand this newest form of American civil religion. What kind of moral code is being offered to viewers?

III
Constructing Conditions

Introduction to Section III

The preceding section focused on the people who make claims about problems. Now we can move to the actual work of claims-makers, the *social problems work* they do.

The backbone of this social problems work is *typifying*. Claims-makers must construct images of conditions, the victims who are harmed by it, and the villains (social structures, social forces, or individuals) who cause it. This is no easy task because, as we all know, social life is complex and defies easy summary. Yet from this real life complexity, claims-makers must construct typifications: What images come to your mind when you hear the term "pregnant teen"? Drug abuse? Poverty? Drunk driver? If you have images of social problems conditions, victims, and villains, these are *typifications* because it is not possible to know the unique characteristics of each drug abuser, each pregnant teen, and so on. Claims-makers construct these images. They define their terms and choose their examples. And, if they are successful, their social problems work will persuade audience members to evaluate the condition problem, just as it has been typified.

In typifying social problems, claims-makers must answer the questions often asked by audience members: What are the characteristics of the condition? How much harm does it create? What or who causes the condition? Who or what is harmed by it? Why is the condition intolerable? How can the condition be eliminated?

In answering questions about the size and harm created by the condition, claims-makers construct *grounds*, the basic "facts." They define terms such as "drug abuse" or "racism," they define the number and types of people who are harmed. Not surprisingly, claims associated with persuading audience members that the condition must be eliminated often emphasize the extreme magnitude of the harm, and the great number of victims the condition creates. Yet constructing the basic "facts" of the condition is not enough. Audience members want to know what causes the condition and why it cannot be tolerated.

In constructing their typifications, claims-makers construct *diagnostic frames*, claims that construct conditions as *types* of problems and explain what causes the condition. Any social problem condition can be constructed within many different diagnostic frames so, not surprisingly, there often are *claims competitions* among different ways to construct the meaning of conditions.

Consider, for example, the condition of "cigarette smoking." While this is accorded the status of a social problem in the United States, cigarette smoking is not a social problem in Japan, although Japanese people smoke more cigarettes than do Americans. In "Smoking Problems in Japan," Jun Ayukaya examines differences in how cigarette smoking is framed in these two countries. Because of pressure from the United States government to import more cigarettes, smoking in Japan is framed as a matter of international trade, rather than as a matter of health as in the United States. And while governments in the United States make a considerable amount of money on cigarette taxes, governments in Japan not only tax cigarettes, but control tobacco sales. Because they profit from the tobacco trade, they will not discourage cigarette smoking. And while nonsmoking Americans are quick to criticize people who smoke, nonsmoking Japanese do not want to appear impolite, so they do not criticize people who smoke; so there is little public outcry in Japan to ban cigarette smoking. In brief, any condition such as "smoking cigarettes" can be framed in multiple ways and these depend on characteristics of the larger social, political, and cultural environment in which the condition occurs.

Even within the same culture, any specific condition can be framed in different ways. In "Crime Frames and Their Sponsors," Theodore Sasson examines the multiple diagnostic frames for the condition of crime in the contemporary United States. Clearly, there is a great deal of competition among claims-makers constructing this problem. Some claims-makers construct crime as a problem of a "faulty system" that doesn't punish criminals so there is little cost for committing crime. Others construct crime as a problem of "blocked opportunities," others as a problem of "social breakdown," still others as a problem of "racism" or "media violence." Thus, the meaning of a condition such as crime depends on how claims-makers construct diagnostic frames.

In addition to constructing diagnostic frames, claims-makers must construct *motivational frames*, which are constructions answering audience members' questions about why conditions are troublesome. Or, more bluntly, why should audience members care that the condition exists? One way to motivate audience members to care is to construct conditions as violating one or more cultural themes—broadly circulating ideas about how the world should work. What is important? In the United States at the current time, for example, there are cultural themes such as the importance of healthy living and the well-being of children. Enduring cultural themes include beliefs such as nationalism (patriotism), capitalism, individual-ism, family, and religion.

One of the most common cultural themes at the present time is the importance of "fair play." Social movements on behalf of minorities, women, homosexuals, and people with disabilities all are framed within this cultural theme of the importance of equality of rights. For example, Gwyneth I. Williams and Rhys H. Williams examine "Framing in the Fathers' Rights Movement," social activists groups composed of divorced men who have been denied custody of their children. These men claim dis-crimination. In effect, they take the claims made by feminists about inequalities experienced by women and turn them around to argue that women are given unfair advantage in matters of child custody. Why should audience members care that men rarely are given custody of their children? Because the cultural theme of the importance of fair play is being violated. Audience members who believe in the importance of equality might be motivated to evaluate these claims as important.

Of course, Americans are not united in our understandings of the importance of particular cultural themes—many Americans believe the economic system of capitalism is good, a few believe capitalism is the root of all evil; many Americans believe families are important, but some peo-ple believe families are a relic of the past and should be discarded; some people willingly go to fight wars while others protest these wars, and so on. Claims-makers can't assume that audience members automatically will care about a social problem condition because it violates some partic-ular cultural theme.

One way that claims-makers can encourage more audience support is by constructing motivational frames involving multiple cultural themes. Consider, for example, the condition of "factory farming." This is a condi-tion where animals (pigs, cows, chickens) being bred and raised for food live their short lives in inhumane conditions. While these conditions can be graphically hideous in their details, framing the condition of factory farming as a problem of animal rights might not motivate many audience members in a country where the great majority of people eat these ani-mals. Karl R. Kunkel, in "Factory Farming as a Social Problem" examines how a social movement wanting to end factory farming changed over time from framing the condition as a problem of "animal rights" to one of "environmental ruin," to one of "human health." Each such framing of the same condition—factory farming—might serve to persuade more people that this is a problem. Individual audience members who don't particu-larly care about animal rights might be persuaded by claims that factory farming leads to too much environmental devastation; if they are not per-suaded by claims about environmental ruin they might be persuaded by claims that eating meat is not healthy for people. The important point is that it doesn't really matter *why* audience members are persuaded to care about a condition—all that matters is that they *are* persuaded to evaluate a condition as troublesome and in need of repair.

The social problems work of claims-makers involves typifying conditions in ways that answer audience members' questions: What are the characteristics of the condition (grounds)? What causes the condition (diagnostic frames)? Why is the condition intolerable (motivational frames)? The articles in this section demonstrate how claims-makers can answer these questions as they construct social problems as particular sorts of conditions with particular sorts of causes violating particular cultural themes.

9

Smoking Problems in Japan

Jun Ayukawa

Cigarette smoking in Japan displays patterns unlike those found in other industrialized countries. The consumption of cigarettes has been steadily rising in Japan due to the importation of cigarettes from the United States. In 1950, 65.3 billion cigarettes were sold, in 1990, 322 billion, and in 1995, 334.7 billion. This represents a 413 percent rise in the consumption of cigarettes from 1950 to 1995, while the population rose only 51 percent. In 1995, Japan's smoking rate was 58.8 percent among men and 14.6 percent among women. Compared to other industrialized countries, the percentage of male smokers is very high (28.1 percent of American males smoke cigarettes) while that of female smokers is low (23.5 percent of females smoke in the United States). In recent years, the smoking rate among men in Japan has decreased (down from 62.5 percent in 1986) while the smoking rate among women has increased (up from 12.6 percent in 1986). This was caused by an increase in the number of young female smokers greater than the small decrease in middle-aged and older female smokers.

We can see opposite trends occurring in the United States and in Japan. In the United States, regulations against tobacco were being advanced by the government in the 1980s and 1990s. In Japan, however, the number of cigarette vending machines on street corners, and the number of retail stores selling tobacco increased drastically during the same period. Although tobacco television commercials stopped in 1998, the number of such commercials had steadily increased in the previous years. Free cigarette samples also are distributed on the streets and in public spaces by young women dressed in very sexy costumes. Also, billboard advertising

This chapter is excerpted from Ayukawa, Jun (2001). "The United States and Smoking Problems in Japan." Pp. 215–42 in *How Claims Spread: Cross-National Diffusion of Social Problems*, edited by Joel Best. Hawthorne, NY: Aldine de Gruyter is common in Japan. While outside billboard tobacco ads were banned in the United States, you can see a lot of cowboys and surfers on top of Japanese buildings and at intersections. When TV commercials stopped, the advertising money spent for newspaper and billboard advertising increased dramatically.

Tobacco companies also offer gifts or premiums that are attractive to youngsters. When applying for gifts, applicants must write that they are at least 20 years old, but this information cannot be verified. Some gifts are simply ordered through a catalog: by sending a certain number of seals and a certain amount of money, you can receive the gift you want such as a Marlboro Zippo lighter, or a Marlboro duffel bag. Virginia Slims and Salem have been big factors in the rapid increase in young female smokers in Japan. Virginia Slims conducted a campaign in which the prize was an airplane ticket to the United States.

THE TOBACCO ENTERPRISE LAW AND THE MINISTRY OF FINANCE

In order to allow for the introduction of American tobacco companies into the Japanese market, Japan Monopoly, the government agency that monopolized the manufacturing and selling of cigarettes and salt, was privatized in 1985, becoming Japan Tobacco, Inc. (JT). Since privatization, JT has had three Chief Executive Officers; all were former high-ranking bureaucrats in the Ministry of Finance. The stock of JT was offered on the open market in 1992; however, two-thirds of JT stock is still held by the Ministry of Finance—that is, this "private" firm is largely owned by the government, which, therefore, has a direct stake in tobacco sales.

With the birth of JT, a new Tobacco Enterprise Law was introduced "to strive for the sound development of the tobacco enterprise and to contribute to the stability of income revenue and the sound development of the national economy." This law advocated promoting the consumption of tobacco without thinking about the health of the nation or its youth, and recommended that the Ministry of Finance promote tobacco sales in order to increase revenue from tobacco.

JT tries to keep the price of tobacco, the total sales of cigarettes, cigarette shares, and retailers' profits as high as possible. The Ministry of Finance refrains from imposing regulations on smoking and helps JT and American tobacco companies increase their sales of cigarettes. The Ministry tries to keep the revenues from the tobacco tax as high as possible. Cigarette-tax revenues total 2,800 billion yen ($24.3 billion), half of which goes to the national government and the remainder to local governments.

In the United States, tobacco companies were private from the very beginning. The U.S. government does not worry about the profit margins of these companies and it does not own stock in tobacco companies. Therefore, it is easier for the government to place restrictions on the companies.

U.S. INFLUENCE ON THE TOBACCO MARKET IN JAPAN

Due to the structure of Japanese society, the United States has influenced the tobacco market more than the opposition to tobacco. The U.S. government demanded an open market because it suffered from a trade deficit with Japan. This demand was met with the enactment of the Tobacco Enterprise Law in 1985. The Reagan administration handled the negotiation: it threatened to impose "Super 301" on Japanese imports (which would have had the effect of reducing Japanese exports to the United States) in 1986. In July 1986, Senator Jesse Helms (R-North Carolina) wrote a confidential letter to Prime Minister Nakasone calling for increasing America's share of tobacco imports to 20 percent within 18 months. In response to this pressure, Japan abolished the import tax on American cigarettes. In 1985, American tobacco's share of the Japanese market was less than 3.9 percent (7.5 billion cigarettes). Ten years later, in 1995, it had risen tenfold to 71 billion cigarettes—a 21.2 percent share of the Japanese market—accounting for most of the increase in Japanese cigarette consumption.

The threat of Super 301 led to significant changes. Before 1980, the import tax on cigarettes was 90 percent; it fell to 10 percent in 1983 before being abolished in 1987. Before the import tax was abolished, a retailer who sold Japanese tobacco got 10 percent of the sale price, compared to only 8.5 percent for American tobacco sales. Abolishing the import tax resulted in identical domestic taxes on American and Japanese tobacco, and the same profit margins for retailers. Once the Japanese government announced the abolition of all import taxes, Japanese TV commercials for American tobacco increased dramatically.

INSTITUTIONAL SUPPORTS FOR TOBACCO IN JAPAN

The Ministry of Health and Welfare has not made any strides toward reducing the number of smokers or discouraging the habit. It is more correct to say that the ministry cannot afford to promote a smoke-free society, given JT and the government policy to increase tobacco imports from the United States. When cigarette manufacturing was a government-owned enterprise, it was taboo to criticize it because of the huge amounts of income derived from it. After the Japan Monopoly was privatized, there was very little motivation for the Ministry of Health and Welfare to promote a smoke-free society because most JT stock was owned by the Ministry of Finance (which managed administrative matters concerning tobacco).

In 1964, the chief of public health within the Ministry of Health and Welfare made an announcement about the harmful effects of smoking on health. This announcement appeared in the same year as the first report on smoking by the U.S. Surgeon General and two years after a report on "Smoking and Health" was published by the Britain's Royal Academy of Medicine. However, in Japan, this announcement was sent only to the prefectural governors, and there was no substantive action required of the ministry. Only one local community office in the suburbs of Tokyo heeded this announcement by prohibiting smoking inside their city hall except in designated areas.

In 1987 a massive report, "Smoking and Health," edited by the Ministry of Health and Welfare, was published in Japan. However, this was not recognized as an official document. Finally, in 1997, permission was given to include smoking under the category of a "routine life disease" in the "White Paper" (annual report) of the Ministry of Health and Welfare. During this period, the Japanese government was suffering from a shortage of revenue, and needed the huge revenues from the sale of tobacco. The Ministry of Finance has the power to cut the budget for antismoking efforts by the Ministry of Health and Welfare. Moreover, if the Ministry of Health and Welfare persists in a policy that could threaten tobacco revenues, it has to fear budget cuts by the Ministry of Finance for items that it considers critical, such as care for the elderly.

When the Ministry of Health and Welfare started public awareness programs on smoking, it was able to secure a budget for them by restricting their application to settings it controlled. The Ministry ordered national hospitals, for example, to make their buildings no-smoking areas in principle and to separate smoking areas from ordinary air-conditioned spaces. Although this policy affects a very small segment of the population, it is similar to the strategy that was first taken in the United States of prohibiting smoking inside federal buildings.

In 1996, the Ministry of Labor published guidelines for the work environment. It announced that smoking should be prohibited in offices and in factories where people work and that separate rooms for smoking should be established. However, this rule was not complied with except in public office buildings. Although the guidelines were established, they are not enforced by private companies. For example, employees generally smoke freely in offices at my university, as at most private universities. If a person requests a non-smoking work space, that person might be moved to some unpopular section.

Local governments also are not active in nonsmoking campaigns because they get income from cigarette sales. Approximately 60 percent of the consumer price of cigarettes in Japan goes toward taxes. The revenue from cigarette taxes is indispensable, especially for small local governments. Thus, they hesitate to promote nonsmoking campaigns.

Medical and health-related associations are not active in antismoking campaigns in Japan. The Japan Association of Medical Doctors and Dentists for Tobacco Control was established in 1992. It is estimated that approximately 20 percent of Japanese doctors smoke. So, doctors themselves do not acknowledge the increasing risks of smoking on health.

The Tuberculosis Prevention Association, the Japan Cancer Association, the Mother-Child Health Association, the Cancer Research Promotion Association, the Making of a Healthy Strong Body Association, and the Japanese Eating-Life Association constitute the Tobacco and Health Program Council. They sponsor the conference on World No Tobacco Day. But their activities are not so vibrant as those of the American Cancer Association or the American Lung Association. One of the reasons why they are not so active in Japan is that these organizations are more professionally oriented than publicly oriented. Ordinary citizens seldom donate to these organizations or become members. Medical-equipment and pharmaceutical companies do donate. Ironically, the donors might profit if the number of people suffering from smoke-related cancer increases, thus increasing the demand for the equipment and the medicine being sold by the doctors.

Some labor unions try to promote the separation of smoking and nonsmoking workplaces. But, according to research by the Tobacco Problem Information Center, the percentage of smokers among union leaders is higher than that of ordinary union members. Also, as JT's labor union is well organized and powerful, the country's largest confederation of labor unions is not inclined to make claims or to appeal to politicians for laws regulating smoking.

OPPOSITION TO TOBACCO

The first Japanese antismoking group was the Circle to Protect Nonsmokers, established in 1977 by lawyers in Hokkaido, Japan's northernmost island. In the following year, two similar groups, the Circle of People to Establish the Rights of Nonsmokers and the Circle of Lawyers for the Rights of Nonsmokers were established in Tokyo.

The first action taken by antismoking groups was in 1979, when they gathered 35,000 signatures and petitioned the Japan National Railways for non-smoking cars and no-smoking areas. In April 1980, the Circle of Lawyers to Establish the Rights of Nonsmokers sued Japan National Railways in Tokyo to designate at least half of its Super Express coaches as nonsmoking cars. This led to one of the biggest trials on smoking in Japan, and it garnered huge mass-media attention. The trial lasted almost seven years. On March 27, 1987, a verdict was finally reached and the plaintiffs lost their case. The court ruled that the ill effects of smoking were tolerable; therefore the plaintiffs' suit was rejected.

There have been several suits filed demanding a separation of working space and smoking space. With the exception of two cases, all were defeated. In one case, an individual who filed a suit in 1992 succeeded in making his work space a nonsmoking area in 1994. In the other case filed in 1991, the individual agreed to move to another, nonsmoking working environment. It is interesting to note that the majority of people who filed suits were public employees, whose employment was insured by law.

People in Japan are less inclined to bring cases to court than in the United States. Thus far, there has been only one case in which a group of people who smoked and suffered from cancer brought a suit against a tobacco company. No family of a deceased person who smoked and died of cancer has sued a tobacco company in Japan.

CONCLUSION

Japan's unique social structure and culture shape the construction of tobacco as a social problem. Most important, through its ownership of a majority of Japan Tobacco Inc.'s stock and through the collection of taxes on tobacco sales, the Japanese government—and particularly the powerful Ministry of Finance—has a strong vested interest in the tobacco business. The Ministry of Health and Welfare and other government agencies that might be expected to promote antismoking policies therefore must proceed cautiously. At the same time, the Japanese legal system's tendency to move slowly, and the difficulties of mounting class-action suits, limit the courts' influence on tobacco policy. Perhaps because the antismoking movement has had difficulty influencing either the government or the courts, the movement remains small. And because the Japanese respect hierarchy and value harmony, reforms such as changes in workplace smoking rules depend more on decisions from the top than claims from below.

This does not mean that Japan's treatment of tobacco exists in isolation. The United States and other Western nations do affect what occurs in Japan, both encouraging and discouraging tobacco use. American tobacco companies have aggressively entered the Japanese market. The U.S. government used the threat of trade sanctions to open Japan to U.S. tobacco sales, and American firms have used a variety of marketing strategies to capture a growing share of the Japanese market. Much of this marketing plays upon the prestige of the United States, through the use of cowboy imagery, slogans about individualism, white models, and so on.

At the same time, the United States and other Western nations offer examples of effective antismoking efforts. Their governments—particularly public-health agencies—have been active claims-makers, first in detailing the health risks to smokers and later in constructing second-hand smoke as a social problem. A variety of regulations—restrictions on television commercials and other forms of tobacco advertising, restrictions on smoking in public places and the workplace, and so on—increasingly constrain smoking. In addition, the success rate of liability claims against tobacco companies is increasing. All of these tactics serve as models the Japanese antismoking campaign can consider adopting. Perhaps the most powerful of these resources is the idea of globalization—the concern that Japan's treatment of tobacco is increasingly out of step with policies in Western nations.

10

Crime Frames and
Their Sponsors

Theodore Sasson

In order to establish a catalogue of culturally available frames on street crime, I examined the speeches and publications of partisans on various "sides" of the issue. There are two advantages to this strategy: First, frame sponsors tend to express their views in an ideologically coherent manner, thus presenting relatively "pure" or unadulterated frames. Second, by first examining primary claims I could create a catalogue that comes close to including all culturally available frames rather than only those that enjoy prominence in the mass media.

My review of the activist and partisan discourse yielded a working catalogue of frames. I then tested the "fit" of this catalogue on the sample of media discourse assembled for the study. My aim at this stage was to make sure that the frame catalogue offered the right balance between precision (it should represent all of the important views and ideas in the crime debate) and economy (it should summarize and simplify the debate). The final, revised catalogue included five basic frames that I labeled *Faulty System, Blocked Opportunities, Social Breakdown, Media Violence,* and *Racist System.* Readers will note that I do not include "drugs and guns" as a frame. While in contemporary discourse, crime often is attributed to drugs and guns, these are things that demand explanation and not explanations in themselves. In what follows I describe the five basic frames of crime as ideal types.

This chapter is excerpted from Sasson, Theodore (1995). *Crime Talk: How Citizens Construct a Social Problem* (Pp. 13–16, 29, 55, 87, 105–6). Hawthorne, NY: Aldine de Gruyter.

FAULTY SYSTEM

The *Faulty System* perspective has its roots in what is commonly known as "classical criminology," most notably in the work of the eighteenth-century theorist Cesare Beccaria. Beccaria asserts the emerging Enlightenment notion that man is a rational actor whose behavior is governed by the desire to maximize pleasure and minimize pain. This premise concerning human behavior leads to the conclusion that crime stems from irrational laws.

The "law and order perspective" on crime is best captured in this frame that regards crime as a sequence of impunity: People do crimes because they know they can get away with them. The police are handcuffed by liberal judges. The prisons, bursting at the seams, have revolving doors for serious offenders. The only way to enhance public safety is to increase the swiftness, certainty, and severity of punishment. In the words of former President Richard M. Nixon, "The time has come for soft-headed judges and probation officers to show as much concern for the rights of innocent victims of crime as they do for the rights of convicted criminals." In this view, loopholes and technicalities that impede the apprehension and imprisonment of offenders must be eliminated. Adequate funding for police, courts, and prisons must be made available.

Faulty System is sponsored by Republican politicians, conservative policy analysts, and most criminal justice professionals. It can be symbolically condensed with the mug-shot of the convicted rapist Willie Horton, or by the images of inmates passing through a revolving door on a prison gate (both symbols courtesy of commercials aired on behalf of George H. W. Bush in the 1988 presidential campaign).

BLOCKED OPPORTUNITIES

The *Blocked Opportunities* perspective on crime has its social scientific roots in Robert K. Merton's 1938 essay "Social Structure and Anomie." Crime, Merton held, results from a disjuncture between socially prescribed goals and the institutionally available means for goal attainment. American culture, on one hand, inculcates a desire for material success—the American Dream—while American economic arrangements, on the other, render attainment of material success by legitimate means impossible for many.

The Blocked Opportunities frame depicts crime as a consequence of inequality and discrimination, especially as they manifest themselves in unemployment, poverty, and inadequate educational opportunities. People commit crimes when they discover that the legitimate means for attaining material success are blocked. In the words of former President

Lyndon B. Johnson, "Unemployment, ignorance, disease, filth, poor housing, congestion, discrimination—all of these things contribute to the great crime wave that is sweeping through our nation." The United States is unique among industrialized societies in both the extent of its income inequality and the weakness of its social safety net. Moreover, since the 1960s, the deindustrialization of American cities and attendant disappearance of well-paying blue-collar jobs has steadily worsened prospects for the urban poor. Growing desperation promotes violence as well as property crime. To reduce crime, government must eliminate the social conditions that cause it. In the words of former Minneapolis Police Chief Anthony Bouza, "Only the government can produce an educational plan that serves the poor, a welfare system that attends to the needs of the excluded and jobs programs that offer hope to all our citizens. The War on Poverty must be refought. The dilemma of racism must be attacked."

Blocked Opportunities is sponsored by liberal and left policy analysts and by some liberal Democrat politicians. It can be symbolically condensed through references to dead-end jobs reserved for inner-city youth, such as "flipping burgers at McDonalds."

SOCIAL BREAKDOWN

The *Social Breakdown* perspective has its social scientific roots in the work of the early "Chicago School" researchers Robert Park, Ernest Burgess, Clifford Shaw, and Henry McKay. In a number of studies extending from the 1920s to the 1950s, the Chicago sociologists examined the impact of rapid social change on various urban neighborhoods. They argued that rapid change destroys the prevailing normative order and thereby produces crime and delinquency.

This frame depicts crime as a consequence of family and community disintegration. Witness the skyrocketing rates of divorce and out-of-wedlock births. Witness the indifference of urbanites to the crime that plagues their communities. Family breakdown in the context of urban indifference has loosened the moral and social bonds that in better times discouraged crime. As President Bill Clinton explained in his 1994 State of the Union message, "In America's toughest neighborhoods, meanest streets, and poorest rural areas, we have seen a stunning breakdown of community, family and work—the heart and soul of civilized society. This has created a vast vacuum into which violence, drugs and gangs have moved." In this view, the remedy for the problem can be found in collective efforts to reconstitute family and community through moral exhortation, neighborhood associations, crime watches, and community policing. "Every parent, every teacher, every person who has the chance to influence children must force a change in the lives of our kids," urged President Clinton in a weekly radio address. "We have to show them we love them and we have to teach them discipline and responsibility." The frame can be symbolically condensed through laments over the decline of "family values," and by the figure of Kitty Genovese, the New York woman who was stabbed to death while her neighbors looked on passively.

Social Breakdown is typically expressed in a neutral, ostensibly non-ideological fashion, but the frame also has conservative and liberal versions. The conservative versions attributes family and community breakdowns to "permissiveness," and protest movements of the 1960s and 1970s (such as civil rights and feminism), and government-sponsored antipoverty initiatives (welfare). As Senator Daniel Patrick Moynihan put it, "Among a large and growing lower class, self-reliance, self-discipline and industry are waning. . . . [Families] are more and more matrifocal and atomized; crime and disorder are sharply on the rise . . . It is a stirring, if generally unrecognized, demonstration of the power of the welfare machine." The liberal versions, in contrast, attribute family and community breakdown to unemployment, racial discrimination, deindustrialization, and capital flight.

MEDIA VIOLENCE

Media Violence is rooted in notions concerning imitation that extend backward to the work of the American criminologist Edwin Sutherland who promoted a theory of "differential association." While the role of the primary group (family) was clearly most important to his theory, he also considered the mass media to be a potentially important agent of socialization into conformist and criminal values.

This frame depicts crime as a consequence of violence on television, in the movies, and in popular music. Violence in the mass media undermines respect for life. Testimony before the House Subcommittee on Communication asserted that by the time an average child reaches age 18, she or he will have witnessed 18,000 murders and countless incidents of robbery, arson, bombings, shooting, beatings, forgery, smuggling, and torture. Within this frame, to reduce violence we must first reduce it in the mass media because television has become a "school of violence" and a "college for crime."

Media Violence can be symbolically condensed through reference to violent television programs or musicians whose lyrics are said to promote violence. The frame is sponsored by citizen lobby organizations such as Action for Children's Television, and, periodically, by members of Congress and the Department of Justice.

RACIST SYSTEM

The fifth frame, *Racist System*, has criminological roots in both labeling and conflict theory. Labeling theorists such as Edwin Lemert and Howard Becker insist that criminal careers (what they call "secondary deviance") are the result of the successful labeling of particular youthful offenders as delinquent. Once successfuly attached to an individual the "delinquent" label influences both the individual's self-concept and how others behave toward him or her. The label creates a "self-fulfilling prophecy" impelling, for example, a youth guilty of only innocent hijinks into commission of more serious and more frequent crimes.

Racist System borrows this line of argument when it suggests that police harassment of minority group members—or society's general expectations concerning their alleged criminal propensities—are actual *causes* of crime. This frame depicts the courts and police as racist agents of oppression. In the words of Johnson Administration Undersecretary of State Nicholas deB. Katzenback, "We have in these United States lived under a dual system of justice, one for the white, one for the black." In this view, police resources are dedicated to the protection of low-crime white neighborhoods rather than high-crime minority ghettos. Black offenders are more likely to be arrested, convicted and sentenced to prison than whites who commit comparable offenses. And the death penalty is administered in a racist fashion. In some versions of this frame, the putative purpose of the criminal justice system is to suppress a potentially rebellious underclass.

Racist System is sponsored by civil rights and civil liberties activists and by left intellectuals. It can be condensed by reference to Rodney King or other well-known targets of racially motivated police violence.

REBUTTALS

Each of these five frames has a number of standard rebuttals. *Faulty System* for example, is frequently negated with the claim that imprisonment "hardens" offenders; *Blocked Opportunities* with the claim that most poor people are straight as an arrow; *Social Breakdown*, with the claim that rhetoric about the "nuclear family" is in fact thinly veiled hostility for feminism; and so on.

11

Framing in the Fathers' Rights Movement

Gwyneth I. Williams and Rhys H. Williams

Since the 1960s, enough changes have taken place in gender relations in American society to almost qualify for the much-heralded status as a "revolution." Debates over gender roles have become public and political. The women's movement, animated by an ideology of "feminism," has been a crucial player in these changes. As with many large-scale social movements, however, a significant countermovement has developed in response. This "men's movement" has tackled a wide variety of issues; in particular one segment has had a significant impact on family law.

In the past 15 years, a wave of reforms has washed over family law. Among the most notable changes are statutes that make joint physical and legal custody of children the preferred option in divorce settlements. One major group promoting joint custody has been the "Fathers' Rights Movement," a collection of organizations dedicated to ending what they view as gender bias in divorce and custody proceedings. Here we explore the rhetoric of the Fathers' Rights Movement (FRM). We contend that the FRM uses a particular interpretation of the "liberal feminist" rhetoric of *gender neutrality* to construct a "movement frame" that has the ironic consequence of privileging fathers' claims to child custody.

This chapter is excerpted from Williams, Gwyneth I. and Rhys H. Williams (1995). "'All We Want Is Equality': Rhetorical Framing in the Fathers' Rights Movements." Pp. 191–211 in *Images of Issues: Typifying Contemporary Social Problems*, 2nd edition, edited by Joel Best. Hawthorne, NY: Aldine de Gruyter

THE MEN'S MOVEMENT: AN OVERVIEW

The FRM is but one faction of the larger "men's movement" that has its roots in feminism. In the early 1970s, men who sought to break out of traditional male roles and experience personal growth began to form local groups. Informally, these men discussed the problems of males caught between societal expectations and the desire to become more caring, expressive individuals. Simultaneously, however, a different type of men's group was forming at the grass roots level. These organizations had a different agenda and a different constituency than the groups just described. They were composed largely of men who had gone through bitter divorces and custody disputes; they gathered to offer each other support and promote custody reform.

Like many social movements, the FRM is a coalition of small social movement organizations held together by a few particularly salient symbols and rhetorical frames. Within the movement there are many different understandings of men's primary problems, the best solutions to those problems, and the best strategies—both political and rhetorical—for attaining those goals. Thus, the movement overall is marked by frame disputes in its rhetoric. As a matter of analytic convenience, the FRM can be viewed as having both "liberal" and "conservative" wings. A slightly different version of the dominant fathers' rights ideology animates each wing. For both wings, though, the symbols of "gender discrimination" and the importance of the father to the child's "best interests" are the primary mobilizing and justificatory symbols. Importantly, these symbols borrow from liberal feminist framing of gender roles.

LIBERAL FEMINISM AND THE GENDER-NEUTRAL FRAME

Just as the early civil rights movement drew upon liberalism's individualistic premises and sponsored a rhetorical frame that emphasized "colorblindness" as a way of achieving a just society, liberal feminism sponsored a "gender-neutral" frame in its early years. Liberal feminism considered gender an "irrelevant" status to the full development of individuals' human potential. Reflecting its origins in the assumptions, lifestyles, and problems of the white middle class, liberal feminism has dealt primarily with reform of the public sphere of political and economic opportunities. However, the reasoning behind liberal feminism could be translated into the private sphere of domestic relations, particularly for domestic work and child care. Clearly women are not biologically predisposed to carry this burden. Men's nurturing sides can be developed as easily as women's achievement orientations could be. Feminists have argued, plausibly, that families would be better served by expanding women's opportunities. Not only would children benefit from having a more fulfilled and personally developed woman as mothers, but they would also benefit from having more direct parenting from fathers.

Despite the hopes that gender equality rested primarily on the removal of legal barriers, feminists have admitted that public remedies such as affirmative action are necessary to combat phenomena such as institutional discrimination and the entrenchment of gender stereotypes in social customs. These caused liberal feminists to abandon their requirement of "sex-blindness," the requirement that laws should be written in sex-neutral language and applied without regard to sex. Genuine equality of opportunity, feminists now believe, requires the state to take positive compensatory steps on behalf of women.

Key elements in the "liberal feminist" frame are as follows:

1. *Women are victims* of systematic discrimination and institutional arrangements that disadvantage them.
2. Human happiness and dignity depend on individual self-fulfillment and thus *external constraints on individual choice constitute discrimination*. Individuals should be judged not as members of social groups but as unique people.
3. *The differences between men and women are primarily cultural* rather than biological. While there is a sexual division of labor in reproduction, the "public man" of worldly achievement and the "private woman" of domestic nurturance are cultural constructions, not biological givens.
4. *Liberating women is in the best interests of everyone*, including children. Task sharing in the household leads to better relationships between children and both parents, and gives children healthier environments and role models.

THE FATHERS' RIGHTS MOVEMENT'S FRAMES

The FRM has taken these elements from liberal feminism, and, with significant changes, incorporated them into their frame of the joint custody issue. Claim 1 (with "women" changed to "men") and Claim 2 are embraced by virtually all fathers' rights activists. Claims 3 and 4 are disputed within the FRM, with the "liberal" wing cleaving tightly to them and the "conservative" wing challenging their validity at every turn.

Claim 1: *Men* Are Victims

The central theme in FRM rhetoric is the claim that men are victims of systematic discrimination in family law and the courts. Men are saddled with alimony and child support payments, and there is a maternal preference in custody decisions regarding children. The FRM claims that although the women's movement argues that gender should be largely irrelevant in the domestic division of labor, the courts continue to systematically favor mothers at the expense of fathers. Thus the FRM argues that a strict gender neutrality in child custody proceedings is necessary for equity between the sexes; it frames maternal preference in child custody as sexist and discriminatory against men.

Men's groups maintain that sole custody of children after divorce is a denial of equal rights. This is apparent in the names of many Fathers' Rights organizations: Dads Against Discrimination, Texas Fathers for Equal Rights, and Fathers United for Equal Rights in New Jersey. They believe that family law, and custody law in particular, is an area that routinely discriminates against men, depriving men of equal rights at virtually every stage of divorce proceedings.

Claim 2: External Constraints against Individual Choice Constitute Discrimination

FRM supporters often make their claim of victimhood in specific constitutional terms. For example, the FRM often refers to sole custody as a denial of the constitutional right to due process. The FRM also has argued that current custody practices violate fathers' equal protection rights. It is through the application of the 14th Amendment's equal protection clause that minorities and women have gained equality in many areas. If judges favor women in custody disputes for no reason other than their gender, then this denies men equal protection of the laws, according to men's rights activists.

More frequently than not, however, men's rights advocates simply make an ambiguous appeal for "equal rights" rather than spelling out the specific constitutional guarantees they believe have been violated. They perceive a basic unfairness, a general tendency of the legal system to discriminate against men during divorce proceedings by failing to apply laws in a gender-neutral way. In using this language, FRM activists, to an extent, yoke themselves to the rhetorical framing, and the political legitimacy of the women's movement. They equate what they want with what many liberal feminists want: a society in which the law treats individuals the same, regardless of sex. Men should be allowed to be custodial parents after a divorce the same way women are.

Claim 3: Differences between Men and Women Are Primarily Cultural and Claim 4: Liberating Women Is in the Best Interests of Everyone

These claims are, of course, closely linked. If one believes that gender roles are a product of nurture and not nature, then liberating women from restrictive social roles is both possible and desirable. Furthermore, such liberation will allow men to escape their own sex-role straitjackets. Conversely, if men's and women's biological differences are the cause of the different social and familial roles played by each sex, then any attempt to change these roles is foolhardy and destined to create problems for all.

The *liberal* wing of the FRM sympathizes with the liberal feminist ideal of absolute equality with regard to gender. They say they seek to share roles with women and to redefine what it means to be a man or a woman. Many of these men claim to have supported the Equal Rights Amendment and believe that gender does not determine what an individual's capabilities or potential might be. Therefore, they maintain that they have remained true to the original vision of feminism. They continue to want to free men and women from their stereotypical roles and from any type of legal discrimination. But because many feminists do not support joint custody, these men claim that the women's movement has become merely another special interest group, seeking advantages for its members alone.

Many feminists do oppose joint custody as a legal presumption; rather, they advocate awarding custody to the parent who has been the primary caregiver within the marriage. But according to the FRM, such a position reinforces the stereotype that women are innately superior nurturers and should not venture outside the home and thus sets the women's movement back. Joint custody to men in the liberal wing of the FRM, in other words, reaffirms the original feminist notion of both sexes being nurturers and breadwinners.

In comparison to the "liberal" wing, the *conservative* wing of the FRM uses a rhetoric that basically favors a "return to patriarchy." It is much more virulent in attacking women, especially feminists. These men decry the breakdown of the "traditional" family and clearly distinguishable sex roles. They hold feminists responsible for the destruction of patriarchy and the emasculation of men. According to men in the conservative wing of the FRM, feminists are wrong not because they have betrayed their ideals, but because their initial ideals were wrong. This faction of the FRM's anger goes beyond the issue of child custody to the entire range of male/female interactions. They often have little good to say about feminism at all.

Despite these differences, the movement's two wings do have a significant agenda in common. Along with portraying men as the victims of systematic discrimination, both wings of the FRM argue that joint custody is important for the "best interests" of the child. While this claim is important for both wings of the movement, they offer different rationales for making the claim. Again, the liberal branch of the FRM replicates much of the reasoning used by liberal feminism, that both men and women can be and should be caregivers to their children. Like liberal feminists, liberal members of the FRM sees the ideal family as one that excludes traditional gender roles.

The conservative faction premises its call for joint custody on the cultural tradition of two-parent families. These activists use rhetoric familiar to many "pro-family" positions in contemporary politics—that is, men and women are not interchangeable and the two-parent family is the best environment for raising children.

In sum, the Fathers' Rights Movement has used, in one form or another, most of the key elements contained in the feminists' master frame of equal rights and gender. Certainly FRM activists turn arguments gleaned from liberal feminism back on the women's movement with more than a little glee and often a great deal of anger. And their interpretation of the equal rights frames and the claims of liberal feminism often pays little attention to the intellectual or sociopolitical context in which they were first made. But the rhetoric of equal rights before the law, and a gender-neutral application of law in order to end systematic discrimination, are powerful tools in their political arsenal.

RHETORIC AND CLAIMS-MAKING IN SOCIAL MOVEMENTS

The politics surrounding joint custody reform are confusing because they do not fall along standard or easily recognizable fault lines. The issue can be interpreted as both "liberal" and "conservative"; both feminists and men's activists are split over the issue and its ramifications. Further, the rapidity with which joint custody became an issue in state legislatures left politicians without many of their normal guideposts, justifying rationales, or predetermined ideological slots.

Because normal constituency coalitions have not formed predictably around joint custody, legislators are left without the "cueing" that interest groups and lobbyists usually provide. In the absence of reliable interest group cues, the rhetoric and symbols of the joint custody issue are particularly important. The lack of hard data—gathered by independent sources—on the problems surrounding custody arrangements makes it difficult for any side of the joint custody debate to dominate discussion with statistics. The moral high ground becomes the most important turf. Therefore, individualized examples, anecdotes, and emotional symbols dominate many of the claims made in joint custody rhetoric.

Equal rights resonates in the cultural field of American politics and shaped the dominant frame of the early women's movement. Even as feminism has developed and fragmented the dominant frame of gender-neutral equality continues to "stick" to the movement and its claims. The FRM, by drawing on traditional liberal notions of equal rights, is able to accuse the women's movement of betraying its initial laudable principles.

The chief irony of the adoption of the same master frame used by liberal feminism, of course, is that the FRM uses it not only to oppose political positions many women's groups have taken, but often to attack feminists, and women generally. The language of equal rights is used by the FRM in a limited way, as support for a set of political arrangements that would promote men's interests at the expense of women's. By focusing on custody arrangements, and treating all other institutional statuses and social resources outside of the custody decision itself as irrelevant, the FRM's procedural equality would often give men an advantage in situations where custody is contested.

Many opponents of presumptive joint custody (particularly feminists) believe that men are advantaged under this arrangement because they become part-time primary caregivers of their children, even though they usually are not primary caregivers within intact marriages. Women are much more likely to have interrupted careers and/or to have taken low-paying jobs to give birth and rear children. Under presumptive joint custody, the caregiving roles within marriage have little standing when determining caregiving status in the postdivorce family. Further, sex discrimination in the marketplace means employed women are less likely to have the disposable income available to provide a middle-class lifestyle for a child. And these employed women are more likely to arouse suspicion as to their fitness as parents than are working fathers (almost a redundancy), particularly when the decision is in the hands of middle-aged, male judges. Thus, if one considers gender roles and gender discrimination occurring outside the custody case as irrelevant to the decision, and yet uses earning capacity as an important criterion for deciding the best interests of the child, women are systematically disadvantaged. Therefore we see that the rhetoric of the women's movement has been a major ideological weapon of the men's rights countermovement in pursuing policies that may be antithetical to women's interests.

We have analyzed the Fathers' Rights Movement's ideological frames and demonstrated their roots in the master frame of "equal rights." The master frame has become a *lingua franca* of American political discourse through the efforts of the women's, feminist, and civil rights movements. Thus our research has implications for the study of social movements generally and for understanding the nature of political culture and discourse. Processes of ideological interpretation, adaptation, and cooptation in social movements and countermovements illuminate the paradoxes of moralized political discourse in American culture and reveal the extent to which movements and countermovements are rhetorically linked even when they are politically opposed.

12

Factory Farming as a
Social Problem

KARL R. KUNKEL

Formed in 1981, the Farm Animal Reform Movement (FARM) claims that modern, rational, intensive farming techniques, referred to as "factory farming" are cruel to animals raised for human consumption.

FARM began as a grass roots organization and today has over 10,000 names on its national mailing list. FARM spokespeople say that 60 percent of those on the mailing list make financial contributions; the group's 1993 annual operating budget was nearly $102,000. FARM's ultimate goal is to eliminate the use of cows, pigs, and chickens as food for humans, but its short-term objective is to end factory farming because this would stop suffering for billions of animals. Throughout the 1980s, FARM experienced trouble generating mass public sympathy for the plight of farm animals. In response, the group expanded the domain of the factory farming problem beyond animal suffering to include threats to human health and environment.

Data for this study were derived from a content analysis of rhetoric as presented in FARM newsletters and other mailings collected from June 1990 through August 1994, and in books advocated by FARM as articulations of their position and arguments on factory farming. In addition, I was a nonparticipant observer at two animal rights conferences in June 1990 and November 1991, in which numerous speakers and seminars provided insights on FARM's rhetoric and strategy in advancing the rights of farm animals.

This chapter is excerpted from Kunkel, Karl. R. (1995). "Down on the Farm: Rationale Expansion in the Construction of Factory Farming as a Social Problem." Pp. 239–60 in *Images of Issues: Typifying Contemporary Social Problems*, 2nd edition, edited by Joel Best. Hawthorne, NY: Aldine de Gruyter

FARM'S ORIGINAL RHETORIC: CRUELTY TO FARM ANIMALS

FARM originated as an animal rights group. The organization's primary concern is ending what they see as pain, suffering, and murder of animals that are raised for food. Slogans appearing on bumper stickers, t-shirts, and posters distributed by FARM promote this position: "Meat is Murder," "I Don't Eat My Friends," "Farm Animals Never Have a Nice Day," "Farm Animals are Live *Not* Stock."

The books the organization recommends provide dismal and vivid descriptions of conditions under which cows, pigs, and chickens live on the modern factory farm. For example, this rhetoric claims veal calves are chained in crates that prevent movement because any form of exercise toughens and develops muscles, making the meat less tender. Pigs, according to FARM rhetoric, live in small cages with concrete floors for easy waste removal. Their lives are spent in environmentally regulated warehouses; the animals are not allowed to see sunlight or graze in fields. Critics of this farming method claim sows are viewed solely as pork-producing machines, forced to copulate with boars, and after giving birth are tethered on their sides so that piglets can nurse anytime. Layer hens allegedly are kept three to a cage, unable to spread their wings and forced to always stand on wire cage floors. According to FARM rhetoric, broiler chickens are housed in regulated warehouses that may contain hundreds of thousands of birds. Their beaks are burned off soon after hatching so that they will not peck each other to death in this chaotic living condition.

Factory farming and the treatment of animals in these environments are focal points of FARM claims-makers. Various demonstrations sponsored by FARM and performed by its members and sympathizers have occurred since the group's inception. In 1985, FARM picketed the United States Department of Agriculture (USDA), protesting factory farming. This protest was led by "Bobby," a veal calf "rescued" by FARM members and housed at a FARM sanctuary. Since 1982, FARM has held a veal ban campaign with "Veal Ban Action" held every year on Mother's Day. These actions include "informational" advertising in mass media, picketing restaurants serving veal, and advocating legislation that prohibits techniques used in veal raising.

FARM engages in acts of civil disobedience such as impeding truck entrances to slaughterhouses, obstructing the path of livestock trucks at auction yards, blocking the entrance to the USDA headquarters, and occupying the office of the Secretary of Agriculture. All of these events feature signs with various slogans and are designed to bring media attention to animal suffering on factory farms.

In its mailings, newsletters, and other rhetoric, FARM's original and primary concern is cruelty to farm animals. However, despite these activities and campaigns, the movement has not received enough support to implement policy changes. Even when people are sympathetic to issues of animal welfare and rights, it is easier to mobilize concern and action for mistreatment and welfare of dogs, cats, monkeys, even rabbits, in scientific research or the testing of cosmetics, than it is to generate sympathy for cows, pigs, and chickens. These animals typically are thought of as food in our culture, reflecting deep-seated cultural and personal dietary habits. Because claims that the treatment of animals on modern farms constitutes a social problem attract little support, groups such as FARM search for other arguments that might get the attention of consumers and policymakers.

EXPANDED FARM RHETORIC: HEALTH CONSEQUENCES

During the early 1990s, FARM began to advocate and adopt arguments designed for appeal to individuals' rationality and interest in personal survival. The group started to claim that meat and other animal product consumption causes such fatal or debilitating diseases as heart attacks, strokes, certain cancers, and even osteoporosis. Much of the rhetoric came from John Robbins's (1987) book *Diet for a New America*.

Robbins's book is widely discussed and advocated among FARM members. They refer to and quote from it at their conventions and seminars. FARM uses Robbins to claim that people should stop consuming animal products and switch to a vegetarian-based diet. Clearly his argument neatly fits the group's objective. FARM also points to Dr. Michael Klapper, an anesthesiologist, who is listed as an advisor for FARM, to demonstrate the unhealthy nature of an animal-based diet. Klapper attends FARM conferences and conducts seminars on the health consequences of consuming animal-food products, discussing medical phenomena in lay terms. FARM supplies its members with rhetoric and symbols to use in clarifying their claims. The organization sends numerous small "warning" stickers to its members featuring a drawing of a physician with the word "WARNING" written in large red letters; the sticker reads: "The Surgeon General has found that this product is hazardous to your health." Members are encouraged to place these stickers on animal-food products in grocery stores. FARM also distributes a drawing of a steak with various parts labeled "heart failure and stroke," "cancer," "hormones," "antibiotics," "premature sexual development," "vulnerability to infectious diseases," "fat and cholesterol," "kidney failure." This image is entitled "Here's the Beef."

FURTHER RHETORICAL EXPANSION:
ENVIRONMENTAL DEVASTATION

The final section of Robbins's book deals with the environmental consequences of mass animal production for any society, such as the United
States, that makes meat central to diet. Robbins discusses the large amount
of physical space necessary for animal production, arguing that 12
pounds of grain are necessary to produce one pound of beef. Thus large
amounts of acreage are devoted to growing grain to feed these animals.
This leads to deforestation, massive use of herbicides and pesticides necessary to grow mass amounts of grain, and depletion of fresh water for
irrigation of crops in areas normally too dry to sustain these fields. Numerous environmental perils are claimed.

Massive deforestation allegedly contributes to lower levels of oxygen in
the atmosphere, global warming, and changing weather patterns. Dangerous agricultural chemicals contaminate water tables, rivers, and
streams. Water that could be used for people in cities is allocated for growing grain in semiarid deserts. In addition, Robbins claims that large factory
farms produce an enormous amount of manure; since no modern sewer
system exists to deal with these stockpiles, mounds of manure grow
month after month, wind blows the residues into dairy products, and
nitrates contaminate drinking water. These are just a few of the environmental problems claimed by Robbins. He concludes that drastically lowering demand for animal-food products, and hence the need for factory
farming techniques, will reduce these threats to the environment.

DISCUSSION

Since FARM's origin in 1981, its claims-making strategy evolved from
emphasizing the single issue of animal suffering on factory farms to
expanding the rationales for its claims. FARM's early stance reflected the
emphasis on cruelty to farm animals; the group sought agricultural reform
through ending factory farming and returning to smaller scale operations
that allegedly involve more humane living and dying conditions for the
animals. Early FARM activities reveal this focus: its vigils, marches, pickets, civil disobedience, and demonstrations all centered around the ill
treatment of farm animals on the factory farm.

Given our long history of carnivorous dietary habits, it is difficult for
many people in a meat-consuming culture to feel enough sympathy for the
plight and treatment of farm animals to make them take action to change
the situation. For such sympathy to be meaningful, demand for animal-

food products must decrease; people must reduce significantly the amount of meat, eggs, and dairy products they consume. To gain additional support, claims of endangerment, based on personal health and longevity, and environmental well-being, became part of FARM's claims-making rhetoric. These expanded claims might have broader appeal. FARM needed to increase antifactory farm sentiment and attempted to do so through rational arguments supplementing the emotional and moral issue of cruelty to farm animals.

Initial studies of domain expansion focused on how claims about new problems were built upon established social problems. FARM's rhetoric reveals a different sort of domain expansion—rationale expansion—in which claims-makers expand their list of reasons for addressing a particular problem. Instead of arguing that their issue was the moral equivalent of some already established problem, FARM remained focused on a particular goal, the abolition of factory farming, but when its initial claims about animal cruelty on factory farms did not achieve the desired results, FARM offered new rationales for eliminating this mode of farming, expanding its rationales to include issues of personal health and environmental destruction. Thus, even if consumers are not concerned with emotional claims about living and dying conditions for farm animals, FARM believes they will respond to rational claims of threats to personal health and the environment. No matter which rationale elicits a response and behavioral change, FARM's objective, the abolition of factory farms, is achieved.

The strategy is one of linking people concerned with different issues. In this case, those concerned with farm animal rights join with others who have either a self-interest in health or a larger concern with the environment, in hopes of mounting a collective effort for a single policy, the eventual elimination of the factory farm.

The case study of FARM rhetoric suggests conditions under which rationale expansion may occur. When certain conditions are deeply embedded cultural practices, claims-makers are unlikely to generate widespread agreement that the condition constitutes a problem. Rhetoric centered upon a culturally unpopular theme may never be persuasive or successful in problem construction. Therefore groups perceiving these practices as problems need to concentrate on anticipated solutions while constructing other, more culturally accepted, reasons for favoring the same policy outcome. Rationale expansion thus provides an indirect attempt to solve the original problem. People who accept one of these added rationales, and take action for the cause, become advocates for the policy that solves the original problem. Even though they may not view the original condition as a problem, their activities do contribute to the solution. Rationale expansion requires that claims-makers be flexible, willing to make new, indirectly related claims.

In the case of FARM, these conditions are present. Viewing cows, chickens, and pigs as having rights and being capable of suffering is contrary to dominant cultural dietary custom. Claims along these lines will not convince enough people of the need to change their behavior to lead to the end of factory farming. But FARM found rhetoric calling for the same outcome and incorporated this rhetoric in an attempt to persuade those convinced by endangerment concerns to resist embedded dietary habit.

This study of FARM rhetoric reveals an attempt to use other, indirectly related claims to gain backdoor support for an outcome. When striving for solutions to perceived social problems, outcomes are more important than the rationales used in claims-making.

IV
Constructing People

Introduction to Section IV

The articles in the preceding section illustrated how claims-makers construct diagnostic frames for conditions and motivational frames that appeal to how audience members think the world should work. Still, such claims often are not enough to secure audience support. This is because we often *feel* about social problems every bit as much as—or more than—we *think* about them. Motivational frames can appeal to *emotion* in addition to—or rather than—*logic*; they might encourage audience members to feel in particular ways rather than to think in particular ways. For example, we can feel *anger* or *disgust* when we hear about social problems conditions. We also might feel *fear* or *anxiety* when we are persuaded that a social problem might hurt us or our loved ones. These emotions of fear or anxiety are very powerful in persuading audience members to support claims-makers' assertions that a condition must be eliminated.

Consider how many claims we hear about how social problems "randomly" produce victims. Who is a battered woman? According to many claims, any woman can be so victimized. Who might contact AIDS? According to claims, anyone. Who might unemployment strike next? Anyone. When claims-makers construct conditions as striking randomly, then it follows that nothing people do causes their victimization and, conversely, nothing can be done to prevent victimization. Joel Best considers "The Rhetorical Appeal of Random Violence." When crime is constructed as randomly producing victims, the threat is universal and audience members are motivated to take crime seriously because anyone can be the next victim. More subtly, constructing victims as "anyone" sidesteps the thorny issues of how, objectively speaking, race and class are very much involved in producing crime victims in real life. The rhetorical appeal of random victimization simultaneously encourages audience members to support claims because of fear while also discouraging audience members to think about perplexing issues of class and race.

In brief, constructions of grounds and diagnostic frames can encourage audience members' support because they encourage the feeling of fear. Claims-makers also can appeal to emotions in a second way. While grounds and diagnostic frames for social problems include constructions of the number and characteristics of victims (who or what is harmed) and villains (who or what creates this harm), claims often go far beyond simply tallying numbers or describing victims or villains in terms of bland generalities about their age, gender, income, and so on. Claims-makers often greatly expand their grounds and diagnostic frames by constructing full-blown typifications of the types of people harmed by social problems and the types of people causing these problems. Terms for social problem victims—such as "abused child" or "anorexic teen"—or social problem villains—such as drug addict or child molester—are constructed in ways yielding images of people that go far beyond demographic description. Emotions and typifications of people often come together as claims encourage audience members to feel in particular ways toward these types of people.

Claims-makers can encourage audience members to feel sympathy when they construct images of victims as *types* of people who deserve sympathy and help. This is complicated because of cultural feeling rules—general ideas about how we "think we should feel." In the case of sympathy, Americans do not automatically feel sympathy when a person is harmed. We tend to ask questions about the harm and about the person being harmed: Did the person do something to create the harm? If we consider the harmed person as responsible, then we do not categorize that person as a victim and we do not feel obliged to offer sympathy: Burglars who are shot by homeowners are not sympathetic characters. We also ask: Is the harm significant? If we evaluate the harm as minor we do not categorize the person as a victim, we do not feel compelled to offer sympathy: When Donald Trump lost several billion dollars in failed real estate ventures, few Americans felt he needed their sympathy. Finally, we tend to ask: Is this a good person? When bad things happen to bad people, we tend not to categorize the person as a victim, and we tend not to offer sympathy: How much sympathy is offered to drug dealers or gang members who are harmed? In brief, we tend to categorize people as victims when we evaluate them as morally pure people greatly harmed through no fault of their own. Not surprisingly, there are many claims-competitions over the constructions of types of people as either worthy or not worthy of sympathy.

Prostitutes are a case in point. Because prostitution always has been constructed as morally deviant, it is not surprising that prostitutes were implicated in the spread of AIDS from the homosexual to the heterosexual population. In "Prostitutes Respond to AIDS," Valerie Jenness examines how the social change group COYOTE (Call Off Your Old Tired Ethics) countered with claims that prostitutes were *victims* whose freedoms and rights were being violated by proposals to put them in jail simply because they were prostitutes. These claims also constructed prostitutes as moral by emphasizing how they are *better* than nonprostitutes in practicing safe sex. These are claims-competitions in which COYOTE's claims construct prostitutes as women who deserve sympathy, while others construct them as evil people deserving punishment.

At times, social problem claims about people also can encourage audience members to feel *hatred*. Diagnostic frames construct who or what causes the condition—the villain. Villains can be constructed as social structures (capitalism, the family, and so on), or social forces (racism, sexism, and so on), yet many villains are constructed as *people* such as drug dealers, greedy capitalists, or pedophile priests. By the logic of cultural feeling rules, these villains should be hated, condemned, and punished. But except in a few cases, such as terrorists or child sexual molesters, it can be difficult for claims-makers to encourage audience members to feel hatred and condemnation. It usually is far easier to encourage audience members to feel sympathy for victims than it is to motivate audience members to feel hatred for villains.

There is a tendency for claims-makers to pay far more attention to constructing images of victims than images of villains. Moreover, when claims-makers construct images of villains as people, they often do not construct them as people who should be condemned, hated, and punished. One construction that simultaneously blames people (rather than social structures or social forces) yet does not evoke hatred is the "medicalization of deviance." Why do alcoholics drink? They suffer from the disease of alcoholism. Why do some children fail to learn? They suffer from "learning disabilities." Medicalized constructions neatly circumvent the problem that American audiences are prone to blame people rather than social structures or social forces for problems, while simultaneously being hesitant to condemn all but the most evil people. When troublesome behavior is medicalized, the individual is constructed as the cause of the social problem but the blame is placed on an underlying disease or biological process.

In "Science Constructs PMS," Ann E. Figert examines the constructions of Premenstrual Syndrome made by scientists. As with the case of the *DSM* and homosexuality (Chapter 7), there were many back stage disagreements among scientists over whether a range of psychological troubles ("mood disorders") should be included in the PMS category; within medical and psychiatric practice there remain acknowledged problems of research and a lack of precise definition. Yet PMS now has the official stamp of "disorder," it is included in the *DSM*. Women experiencing a range of troubles—and sometimes causing troubles for others—can blame

PMS. Women can use PMS as an excuse to express their emotions or to explain their otherwise "strange" behaviors; others (husbands, children, doctors, coworkers, judges, juries) likewise can use PMS to explain women's behaviors. While medicalization of troublesome behavior appears, on the surface, to be humane because individuals are not blamed, Figert raises questions about other consequences that are not so positive.

The social problems work of persuading audience members to evaluate a condition as a social problem therefore involves constructing typifications of conditions and people, it is the meaning-making work of constructing the cause of conditions, of constructing who or what is harmed by those conditions, who or what causes those conditions. Yet our language of grounds, diagnostic frames and motivational frames is the language of people who study social problems. In comparison, audience members do not ask: What are the grounds? What is the diagnostic frame? Audience members are practical actors who see and hear social problems claims as a package. Often, successful claims—those that persuade audience members to evaluate the condition as a social problem—combine to produce a *social problems formula story*. This is a story of extreme harm done to pure victims with a moral that *something must be done!*

In "Multicultural Education as Moral Drama," Shan Nelson-Rowe examines the social problems formula story of multicultural education. Claims made by proponents of multicultural education construct pure victims (multicultural students) who suffer incredibly (they do not perform well in school and suffer from low self-esteem) and evil offenders (the "educational system"). Within this melodrama, the school system is constructed as organized in ways that all but ensure minority students will fail. At stake, according to these claims, is the very future of the United States: Although they are members of cultures that are outside the Anglo mainstream that dominates educational practices, people in these cultures soon will be the majority of Americans. The very future of the United States is at stake, so something must be done.

As the articles in this section demonstrate, claims-makers can appeal to logic and/or to emotion and they do so in order to persuade audience members to evaluate claims as believable and important. Public images of social problems are the consequences of successful social problems work.

13

The Rhetorical Appeal of Random Violence

JOEL BEST

BEWARE!

There is a new GANG INITIATION!!!

This new initiation of murder is brought about by Gang Members driving
around at night with their car lights off. When you flash your car lights to
signal them that their lights are out, the Gang Members take it literally as
"Lights out," so they follow you to your destination and kill you! That's their
initiation.

DO NOT FLASH YOUR CAR LIGHTS FOR ANYONE!!!

(flyer circulated in Chicago, 1993)

Tales of gang members driving around, planning to kill whoever flashed
headlights at them, spread from coast to coast during the fall of 1993.
Concerned citizens passed along the story via photocopies, faxes, and
of course, word of mouth. Employers warned their employees, law-
enforcement agencies alerted one another, and the press cautioned the
public. It seemed a plausible story: everybody knew that there were gang
members out there; the notion that gang "initiation rites" required members to commit terrible crimes was well ingrained; and cars and guns
seemed easy to come by. *It could happen*, people told themselves. *That's just
the kind of thing gangs do.*

This chapter is excerpted from Best, Joel (1999). *Random Violence: How We Talk
About New Crimes and New Victims* (Chapter 1). Berkeley: University of California
Press.

There was no evidence that the gang-initiation tale was true, yet it was widely believed. What explains this credulity? Concern about random senseless violence has become a central theme in contemporary culture. In addition to gang initiation rites, we worry about serial murders, carjackings, freeway shootings, sexual predators, hate crimes, kids with guns, stalking, drive-by shootings, copycat criminals, workplace violence, shootings in schools, and other unpredictable threats.

The notion that our society is plagued by random violence has surprisingly broad appeal. For example, the Federal Bureau of Investigation in 1994 warned "Every American now has a realistic chance of murder victimization in view of the random nature the crime has assumed." *Time* magazine in 1994 called random violence a "spiraling epidemic." In part, this concern with random violence seems grounded in a general sense that crime is both out of control and on the rise. But this generalized sense of dread is heightened by specific fears, fostered by what sociologists call "moral panics"—exaggerated, heavily publicized reports of sudden increases in particular sorts of criminal violence. Sociologists usually approach these topics through case studies of particular moral panics. I want to argue that such recent episodes of intense concern are a part of the broader, more general contemporary concern with random violence.

THE NATURE OF RANDOM VIOLENCE

Considering our readiness to talk and worry about random violence, we give surprisingly little thought to what the term means. Warnings about the threat of random violence rarely define the term; instead they illustrate the problem's nature with typifying examples. These examples can be highly melodramatic; there is an "ideal victim"—usually a respectable person engaged in some innocent activity—who suffers a sudden, unexpected, unprovoked, violent attack by an assailant with no connection to the victim, there is no good reason to hurt this person in this way.

Reports of terrible crimes committed by strangers are disturbing, but they do not justify broad generalizations about violence being random. The term "random violence" demands closer inspection. When statisticians speak of randomness they refer to independent events that occur by chance, in no identifiable pattern. Imagine a set of numbered balls used in a lottery drawing. The balls are stirred into an unpredictable arrangement, then five are drawn. In a random drawing, each ball has an equal chance of being drawn, as does each combination of balls.

What, then, do we mean by "random violence"? The term has several implications. Imagine a society in which some number of violent incidents occurs, each incident involving an attacker and victim. If this violence is truly random, then not only is each individual in that society at risk of being attacked, but all individuals run *equal* risks of victimization, and every individual also is a potential attacker and everyone is equally likely to attack someone else. Immediately, we recognize that this sort of chaos is not what most people mean when they speak of random violence. Although many claims about random violence imply that everyone is a potential victim, they do not assume that everyone is a potential attacker. Rather, they imagine that attackers are somehow different from their victims, that they are gang members, or psychopaths, or at least males. When most people speak of random violence they imagine a world in which the general population of potential victims shares the risk of being attacked by these likely attackers. Depending on the crime, the population of victims may be all women (vulnerable to sexual assault), all children (molestation), all gays (homophobic attacks), all drivers (carjacking and freeway violence), and so on. In this sense, we imagine that violence is *patternless*: all potential victims share the risks, so that victimization can happen to anyone.

What motivates these random attacks? We may acknowledge that violence can be deliberate and purposeful, as when a bank robber steals money. But other violence seems *pointless*, meaningless: the bystander shot in a drive-by; the rape victim selected apparently by chance; and so on. The notion of random violence refers to the risk that anyone might be attacked for no good reason.

In addition to patternlessness and pointlessness, the third theme running through claims about random violence is *deterioration*. Warnings about random violence imply that things are getting worse, that there are ever more violent incidents, that respectable citizens run greater risks of victimization than in the past. There are competing explanations for this deterioration: conservatives tend to blame a deteriorating culture ("the rising tide of immorality"), while liberals usually point to deterioration in the social structure ("the growing gap between rich and poor"). But regardless of which causal explanations they prefer, when people worry about random violence, they assume that things are worse today than they were yesterday, and they fear that things will be even worse tomorrow.

Those who speak of random violence rarely examine these three assumptions. For the most part, they assume—and their listeners take it for granted—that patternless, pointless violence is on the rise. However, even a cursory examination of the most basic familiar criminological evidence calls all three assumptions into question: most violence is *not* patternless; nor is it pointless; nor is it increasing in the uncontrolled manner we imagine. There are, for example, thousands of social-scientific studies showing that violence is patterned (by age, social class, racial/ethnicity, gender). Likewise, from the *perspective of offenders*, most violence is done for a "good reason." Most homicides are products of mundane motives. Yet they aren't all that newsworthy and they don't get much press coverage. And, recent changes in homicide rates do not tell a simple story of random, society-wide deterioration. The pattern is more complicated: declining risks for most adults, higher risks for many children, and terrible increases among nonwhite adolescents and young adults.

Most often, claims about random violence typify the problem with a horrific example, add a dramatic statistic or two, and mix them with the taken-for-granted notion that violence is on the rise throughout society. The resulting claim about the random distribution of risk in a society that is out of control seems so obvious that it needs no close examination. However, the evidence reveals that claims of society-wide deterioration are exaggerated and overly simplistic.

THE APPEAL OF RANDOM VIOLENCE

Although random violence has become a central image in contemporary discussions of crime, the notion of randomness distorts what we know about criminal violence. It exaggerates the degree to which violence is patternless, pointless, and increasing. It is an imagery calculated to promote fear rather than understanding.

Then why is this melodramatic imagery so popular? One answer, of course, is that melodrama is powerful. The idea of random violence is unsettling, disturbing, frightening; it challenges our most basic assumptions about social order. If violence is patternless and pointless, then anyone—women as well as men, children as well as adults, the middle class as well as the poor—might become a victim. If violence is random, then everyone is at risk, and anyone who is at risk—that is, everyone—has reason to be concerned and to demand action. Typifying a problem with frightening examples, and then democratizing the risk—defining the threat as universal—is a recipe for mobilizing social concern.

This widespread concern helps explain why warnings about random violence transcend the obvious ideological divisions within contemporary society. These warnings come from feminists and fundamentalists, liberal Democrats and conservative Republicans. The frightening imagery of random violence can be tailored to fit almost any ideological agenda. But there is another reason why rhetoric about random violence is so popular. By implying that pointless violence is a general, patternless threat to society as a whole, warnings about random violence gloss over the potentially awkward or embarrassing issues of class and race. There are dramatic racial differences in violence; in particular African-Americans are far more likely to both commit violent offenses and be victimized by violence than are whites. These racial differences, of course, reflect class differences:

rates of violence are highest among the poor, and blacks constitute a disproportionate percentage of the poor. Any discussion of patterns in violence must confront class and race—two of the most awkward topics in American political discourse.

Confronting race and class is awkward for both liberals and conservatives. Liberals fear they will have difficulty arousing sympathy for the poor and minorities, particularly if they propose publicly funded programs to benefit those groups. Opponents of these measures may argue that middle Americans have no stake in solving the problems of the poor, saying, in effect, "That's not our problem" or "We've already done enough to help the poor and we shouldn't have to do more." It is easier to finesse such potential opposition and arouse widespread concern by implying that a problem affects (and the programs to solve it will benefit) everyone. Because references to random violence imply that everyone is at risk, they can help mobilize such general concern. Depicting violence as random, and therefore patternless, also lets liberals circumvent potentially awkward questions about the patterns of violence. In particular, liberals are reluctant to call attention to evidence that blacks commit violent offenses at higher rates than whites. The subject of black criminality may invite all sorts of critiques, ranging from arguments that race somehow biologically fosters criminality to various critiques of black culture and institutions. Moreover, liberals fear both that minority criminality can be used as evidence that social programs don't work, and that focusing on the link between ethnicity and violence will result in a form of "blaming the victim." It is not that liberals lack rejoinders to these arguments—they can respond that social structure, particularly class and racial inequality, should be blamed for crime—but rather that the issue of race is volatile, and it seems easier to ignore it rather than confront it. Talking about essentially patternless random violence offers liberals a way to avoid raising this troublesome subject.

Warnings about random violence serve parallel purposes in conservatives' discussions of crime. For conservatives, it is class, rather than race, that seems awkward to address. Poor people are more likely to both commit violent crimes and be victimized by violence, but acknowledging this seems to invite arguments that more should be done to help the poor by improving job opportunities, increasing social services, and the like. Most contemporary conservative interpretations of the causes of crime locate them in culture. In this view, violence is part of a web of interlocking social problems, including broken families, teenage sexuality, premarital pregnancy, welfare dependency, substance abuse, delinquency and criminality, and gangs, all caused by and reflecting a damaged or dysfunctional culture. A potentially embarrassing counter to this argument, of course, is that all of these problems are associated with poverty, with social class:

might not these "cultural" problems have their roots in social structure? This is where references to random violence offer conservatives a convenient distraction. Random violence is patternless, and claims about patternless random violence gloss over the links between class and crime. Similarly, random violence is pointless, senseless. And pointless crime need not be understood as an act of frustration, rebellion, or some other more or less comprehensible reaction to the barriers of class. Rather, random violence, in its pointlessness, is just further evidence of the criminals' cultural pathology. In this view, random violence is a symptom of a sick culture, and talking about random violence helps conservatives keep the focus on culture, and play to the fears of the middle class by invoking the sense that no one is safe from predatory criminals.

In sum, there are two principal advantages to describing the crime problem in terms of random violence. First, the phrase "random violence" evokes rhetorically powerful imagery; it demands our attention and concern, because it questions the stability of the social order and makes us fear for our own safety, and for the safety of everyone around us. Second, defining the crime problem as one of ever-increasing, patternless, pointless—that is random—violence eliminates the need to explain the patterns in crime. Focusing attention on random violence allows ideologues to skip over embarrassing or awkward issues: liberals can avoid talking about race and culture, just as conservatives can avoid confronting issues of class and social structure.

It is easy to see the appeal of framing issues in terms of random violence but it is less clear that this is an effective way to think about crime problems. Defining violence as patternless not only discourages us from searching for and identifying patterns; it keeps us from devising social policies to address those patterns. Defining violence as pointless eliminates any need to consider and address the motivations for violence. Assuming that violence is increasing causes us to ignore patterns in change, and thereby fail to notice which policies are working.

THE LANGUAGE OF CRIME

The expression, "random violence," then, has become a commonplace in talk about contemporary crime, not because it accurately summarizes the nature of crime—it decidedly does not—but because it is rhetorically convenient, arousing intense interest in and concern about crime while diverting attention away from awkward questions of race and class.

The implications of describing violence as random suggest that the turnover in terms used to talk about crime and other social problems reflects more than a faddish attrraction to novel language. People invent new words to describe social problems sometimes quite deliberately, because those words evoke some connotations and avoid others. Consider the different implications of "crippled," "handicapped," "disabled," and "differently abled"; of "drunkard" and "alcoholic"; or "sexual deviate," "homosexual," and "gay." But it is not enough to create a word; some new words are ignored and soon forgotten. Successful terms get picked up, sometimes self-consciously at first, then used by more and more people, until they seem normal rather than novel. The example of "random violence" suggests that some terms may prove attractive to a broad range of users, and that this broad popularity encourages their adoption and widespread use.

The words we choose when we talk about crime and other social problems are consequential. Describing crime in terms of random violence has implications for how we think about crime, about criminals, and about prospective criminal justice policies. It becomes, therefore, important to stop taking our vocabularly of crime for granted. We need to explore the ways in which this language emerges, spreads, evolves, and influences.

14

Prostitutes Respond to AIDS

Valerie Jenness

The AIDS epidemic represents the most recent and the most dramatic change in the political environment of prostitutes' rights organizations. By the mid-1980s, the AIDS epidemic posed a recognizable health, social, and legal threat to prostitutes. As such, it represented a significant environmental constraint to the prostitutes' rights movement. As a result, COYOTE (Call Off Your Old Tired Ethics) and other sex workers' organizations have responded to the AIDS epidemic with considerable organizational activity. My focus is on the prostitutes' rights movement's efforts to respond to the many environmental constraints posed by the AIDS epidemic.

AIDS AS A SOCIAL PROBLEM

Although the media were slow to cover AIDS, once the issue finally became a story, the mysterious killer was constructed as a disease of *deviant sexuality*. As a way of accounting for the disease and the epidemic, the press focused not so much on the disease itself, as on groups whose life-style made them susceptible to AIDS. By focusing on the sociocultural characteristics of homosexual men, the largest group affected by AIDS, the press concentrated on the details of their life-style, claiming that it caused the spread of AIDS. By adopting a dual focus on deviant life-styles and the medical problem of AIDS, press coverage of AIDS tied the medical problem to a moral issue.

By 1985, however, AIDS was beginning to be understood as an explicit

---

This chapter is excerpted from Jenness, Valerie (1993). *Making it Work: The Prostitutes' Rights Movement in Perspective* (Chapter 5). Hawthorne, NY: Aldine de Gruyter threat to the heterosexual population. As the "gay plague" entered the general population, the AIDS epidemic was constructed as a fundamentally different type of social problem. Portrayed as a threat to the population at large, AIDS became a disease of the "normal" as well as a disease of the "deviant." As media attention turned to the emergent heterosexual threat, it began to focus on the issue of contagion with the same fervor it had previously focused on the lifestyles of those infected. As the danger of AIDS to heterosexuals attracted more media attention, the AIDS epidemic was redefined as a problem facing school children, married women, and college students. At the same time, concerns about halting the disease were heightened. Nonetheless, AIDS has not lost its original connection with deviants, deviant lifestyles, and promiscuous sex. The disease has been continually constructed as one implicating deviants in general and sexual deviants in particular.

The biological characteristics of AIDS, combined with the way in which the disease has been socially constructed, almost ensured that prostitutes would be implicated in the social problem of AIDS. This is not particularly surprising given that AIDS has been primarily conceived as a sexually transmitted disease, and that the historical association of prostitution with venereal disease, promiscuous sex, and moral unworthiness remains fixed in the minds of the public.

Prostitutes have been implicated in the AIDS epidemic as a primary bridge through which AIDS has been transmitted into the heterosexual population. The media contributed to making prostitution suspect as an avenue of transmission for the disease. For example, on a 1989 episode of the nationally televised *The Geraldo Show* entitled "Have Prostitutes Become the New Typhoid Marys?" the host offered the following introduction to millions of viewers:

> The world's oldest profession may very well have become among its deadliest. A recent study backed by the federal Centers for Disease Control found that one third of New York's prostitutes now carry the AIDS virus. If this study mirrors the national trend, then the implications are as grim as they are clear. Sleeping with a prostitute may have become a fatal attraction.

Supporting Rivera's introduction, a New York-based AIDS counselor appearing on the show argued:

> A high percentage of prostitutes infected with HIV pass it on to their sexual partners who are johns or the tricks, a lot of whom are married or have sex with a straight woman. I think this is how the AIDS epidemic is passed into the heterosexual population.

Throughout history, prostitution has been portrayed as a health threat as well as a moral threat. Many social historians have documented that, especially during the nineteenth century, female sexual organs—particularly those of prostitutes—were associated with disease and decay. Thus, it is not particularly surprising that legislators have once again turned their attention to prostitution as an avenue of transmission for an epidemic. In the name of preventing the transmission of the HIV infection, legislation that intrudes into private, consensual sexual relations has sprung up around the country. A number of proposals have been introduced that would, in one way or another, make it a crime for someone who is HIV-positive to engage in sex with anyone else, regardless of the degree to which the behavior is mutually voluntary and whether or not condoms are used. At the same time, jurisdictions that have no AIDS-specific criminal law have begun to rely on traditional criminal laws (such as attempted murder and aggravated assault) to prosecute HIV-positive individuals who engage in behaviors that put seronegative individuals at risk.

THE SCAPEGOATING OF PROSTITUTES FOR AIDS

Not surprisingly, prostitutes' rights organizations and their representatives were quick to respond to the multitude of threats posed by AIDS, as well as public officials' response to the epidemic. As early as 1984, when prostitutes met at the second Annual International Hookers' Convention, prostitutes wanted to talk about how to avoid AIDS. In addition to sharing information on how to prevent the contraction and transmission of AIDS, in the mid-1980s prostitutes and their advocates focused on the threat of being implicated in the transmission of AIDS into the general population. Many of COYOTE's more recent claims-making activities are in direct response to the popular notion that prostitutes represent a social problem because they constitute a threatening avenue for the transmission of AIDS into the general population. In a press release entitled "Women and AIDS/Prostitutes and AIDS," COYOTE made explicit the popular conceptualization of prostitution as a health problem connected to AIDS:

> Women who are infected with HIV or who have been diagnosed with AIDS are viewed its "vectors" for the transmission of AIDS to men or to children, not as people who get the disease and need services. Symbolic of this view is the frequent categorization of female prostitutes—in Africa, in Asia, in the United States—as "pools of contagion" or "reservoirs of infection." (*COYOTE Howls* 1988:1).

Similarly, Carol Leigh, an outspoken COYOTE member, argued in a 1987 *Oakland Tribune* editorial that "prostitutes become like other vulnerable victims of society, scapegoats and targets of backlash against this disease and the people who have it. Misfortune always hits hardest at those on the bottom." In response to prostitutes being viewed as "deadly pools of contagion," COYOTE has undertaken numerous campaigns to dismantle the conceptualization of prostitutes as contractors, carriers, and transmitters of the virus.

COYOTE counters conceptualizations of prostitutes as pools of contagion by constructing such assertions as the political scapegoating of stigmatized, thus vulnerable, populations. For example, as part of the Sex Workers/Outlaws in Civil Disobedience contingent of the National March on Washington for Lesbian and Gay Rights in 1987, COYOTE and its supporters pressed the following analysis:

> During the AIDS crisis, populations with little power, societal acceptance or political representation are extremely vulnerable to social and legislative scapegoating. Prostitutes are the most obvious targets of those who wish to control the sexual behavior of the general population, often serving as symbols of promiscuity and illicit sex and disease.

Consistent with the politics of other minority groups, COYOTE construes the AIDS crisis as one that has led to the political scapegoating of prostitutes. As Gail Pheterson, the co-director of the International Committee on Prostitutes' Rights (ICPR) explained in the introduction to her 1989 book, *The Vindication of the Rights of Whores*:

> The AIDS epidemic has reached alarming proportions and prostitutes are being scapegoated for spreading the disease. Like a hundred years ago during the syphilis epidemic, many governmental and medical establishments reacted to AIDS with increased regulation of prostitution.

COYOTE substantiates its assertions about prostitutes being scapegoated for the spreading of AIDS by pressing claims about prostitutes' HIV infection rates and by underscoring the civil rights violations involved in the forced testing of prostitutes.

RECONSTRUCTING CLAIMS ABOUT HIV INFECTION RATES

COYOTE has countered assertions that prostitutes represent a "pool of contagion" by claiming that prostitutes' rates of HIV infection are *lower* than other demographic groups. In the process, spokespeople for the prostitutes' rights movement invoke the use of many scientific studies and researchers to lend legitimacy to their claims. For example, at a press conference in 1988 ex-prostitute and COYOTE co-director Gloria Lockett claimed "Prostitutes test no higher for exposure to HIV than other women—when studies take into consideration IV drug use—since prostitutes use condoms."

In addition to asserting prostitutes' comparatively low infection rates, COYOTE has publicly explained that sex workers are not at risk for AIDS because of prostitution per se; viruses do not discriminate between those who exchange money for sex and those who do not. As Gail Pheterson claimed in her book, *A Vindication of the Rights of Whores*: "Prostitutes are demanding the same medical confidentiality and choice as other citizens . . . They are contesting policies which separate them from other sexually active people, emphasizing that charging money for sex does not transmit disease."

Claims similar to these culminate in suggestions that prostitutes practice safe sex, get regular health checks, and insist that clients wear condoms. From COYOTE's perspective, prostitutes do not constitute an "at risk" group because, at least in part, they *always* have been cautious about sexually transmitted diseases out of concern for their own health and their ability to work. By extension, what separates prostitutes from "women in general" is prostitutes' higher rates of condom use.

Related to this, COYOTE accounts for prostitutes who have tested positive for the HIV infection by pointing to intravenous drug use among some prostitutes. COYOTE concedes that to the extent that prostitutes have become infected, their rate of infection has paralleled the rate among intravenous drug users in their communities. As Gloria Lockett argued on *The Geraldo Show* in 1989: "You're focusing mostly on prostitutes when you should be focusing on drug use. *That* is the problem."

Through claims such as these, the focus on prostitutes and prostitution as vectors of disease is purported to be misguided, while a distinction between drug-using and non-drug-using prostitutes is enforced.

OPPOSING MANDATORY TESTING

In addition to promoting the notion that prostitutes do not represent a "pool of contagion," COYOTE has distributed public announcements, attended conferences, issued press releases, and staged protests to oppose legislation requiring the mandatory testing of prostitutes for the AIDS virus. COYOTE has protested on the grounds that selective forced testing is discriminatory and thus a violation of individuals'—in this case prostitutes'—civil rights. As the codirector of COYOTE argued in 1988: "prostitutes should not be targeted for measures which so patently violate our civil rights." Many of COYOTE's recent protests are in direct response to the threat of mandatory testing. Newspaper editorials and press reports reiterate the theme that mandatory testing is a violation of individuals' civil rights, including those of prostitutes. For example, in response to the introduction of a series of state bills targeting mental patients, prisoners, and prostitutes for mandatory AIDS testing, including one to repeal the guarantee of confidentiality of AIDS tests, a COYOTE spokeswoman offered the following plea in a 1987 guest editorial in the *Oakland Tribune*:

> Mandatory testing for the AIDS virus has been discredited by almost the entire medical establishment as counterproductive in the battle against the disease. . . . However, these plans are promoted by our president and legislators who say they want to reduce the public's fear of contamination by the undesirables of our society. On the surface, mandatory testing of prostitutes and prisoners sounds like it makes sense, representing an effort to control "lawbreakers." But, if we look below the surface, we see people who are already victimized by unfair laws and the discriminatory enforcement of them: gays, prostitutes, and people of color.

Remarks such as these remain fairly consistent with the advocacy work of other minority groups protesting on their own behalf in light of the AIDS epidemic. Like these other groups, COYOTE protests the implementation of mandatory AIDS testing on the grounds that it is a violation of individuals' rights, especially the right to privacy.

The prostitutes' rights movement's AIDS-related claims also point to the selective nature of mandatory testing as further evidence of civil rights violations. At a press conference held to discuss a mandatory testing bill that passed both houses of the California legislature, Gloria Lockett stated: "If, in the name public health, there is to be a law against people who are HIV positive having sex, let it apply to everyone, not just the most politically vulnerable groups." COYOTE's AIDS-related claims contain themes of their earlier claims about the law and its selective enforcement as the source of prostitutes' victimization and prostitution as a civil rights issue. However, the urgency of pressing AIDS-related claims required a circumvention of the movement's original primary goals.

ORGANIZATIONAL GOAL DISPLACEMENT

It is not uncommon for social movement organizations to modify, transform, and occasionally even to subvert the objectives for which they were originally established. Occasionally, they abandon the goals for which they were originally created, and adopt goals that facilitate the immediate and/or long-range survival of the organizations. In the latter part of the 1980s, COYOTE constituted an instance of this sort of organizational goal displacement. Namely, there was a demonstrable shift away from COYOTE's original primary goal of decriminalizing prostitution to a focus on responding to the scapegoating of prostitutes for AIDS, and by extension, on combating the increased social control of prostitution. This made sense.

According to one COYOTE leader: "We [COYOTE] don't have time for focusing on a concerted effort on decriminalization—we're worried about quarantining [of prostitutes]."

AIDS education efforts have taken primacy as the substantive organizational goal of COYOTE, even as it still advocates the decriminalization of prostitution. No later than the summer of 1985, COYOTE began focusing on the social problem of AIDS full force, often almost exclusively. At the Second National Hookers' Convention, for example, participants spent the majority of their time discussing AIDS at great length and developing statements and policies on mandatory testing, quarantining, risk reduction measures, and the need for public education.

CONCLUSION

Clearly, the AIDS crisis significantly reshaped the course of COYOTE's crusade. It has resulted in moving the prostitutes' rights movement away from feminist discourse and into public health discourse. The substance of its claims increasingly has been attentive to the way in which the AIDS epidemic has implicated prostitutes by constructing them as diseased women who are a danger.

COYOTE has been quick to respond to the emergent view of prostitutes as "deadly pools of contagion" and the policy proposals deriving from such a view. From the mid-1980s on, the prostitutes' rights movement has been preoccupied with dismantling the image of prostitutes as contractors, carriers, and transmitters of the HIV virus. In an effort to do so, COYOTE has undertaken numerous campaigns that target public health officials, as well as local and state legislators. These campaigns have challenged responses to AIDS by pressing claims about prostitutes' lower HIV infection rates, as well as prostitutes' historic attentiveness to monitoring their health and the health of their clients. Combined, these claims support the larger effort to construe public officials' response to AIDS as one of political scapegoating; in this case, it is the scapegoating of prostitutes and other marginalized populations. With this view of the problem in hand, COYOTE has become recognizable as a watchdog organization engaging in a defensive crusade to defend prostitutes against frequently proposed and increasingly adopted legislation.

15

Science Constructs PMS

ANNE E. FIGERT

Is Premenstrual Syndrome a mental illness? On June 23, 1986, after a year of bitter dispute, the Board of Trustees of the American Psychiatric Association said yes and placed a premenstrually related diagnosis in an appendix of the soon to be published revised third edition of its *Diagnostic and Statistical Manual of Mental Disorders* (*DSM*-III-R). The psychiatric manifestations of PMS became something called Late Luteal Phase Dysphoric Disorder (LLPDD). Since 1994, LLPDD has been known as Premenstrual Dysphoric Disorder (PMDD) and is listed in the main text of the *DSM*'s fourth edition. So, the short answer to the question is yes, a form of PMS is an official mental disorder. It is official because the *DSM* is seen as a basic reference book for all mental health professionals. It provides standardized diagnostic criteria used by most insurance carriers and is recognized by the federal government and the courts as the psychiatric profession's consensus over the diagnoses of mental disorders.

But deliberations to include this diagnosis in the *DSM* III-R—on their surface an obvious case of scientific consensus over a proposed diagnosis—quickly erupted into a major public problem. A campaign organized by women psychiatrists and mental health professionals to stop the inclusion was soon underway. The decision to include LLPDD in the *DSM*-III-R was so controversial and consequential because it concerned many people—not just women and psychiatrists—who were trying to define and claim ownership of PMS. This brief article will focus on the history of constructing PMS before it became reconstructed as LLPDD.

This chapter is excerpted from Figert, Anne E. (1996). *Women and the Ownership of PMS: The Structuring of a Psychiatric Disorder* (Chapter 1). Hawthorne, NY: Aldine de Gruyter.

IS PMS REAL?

The primary way in which new ideas or diseases achieve legitimacy or recognition in modern society is for scientists or physicians to call them "real." Scientists and physicians have the cultural authority in society to define realms of reality. When M.D.s or Ph.D.s in chemistry or biology believe something is real, the public in general usually goes along with them. This is what happened to PMS in its various forms and incarnations in the twentieth century: PMS became real as a medical diagnosis and condition.

An American gynecologist first published scientific studies about a condition he called "premenstrual tension" 1931. The list of patient complaints included "husband to be pitied," "psychoneurotic," "suicidal desire," and "sexual tension." Medical prescription for severe cases of premenstrual tension was either complete removal of or radiation therapy upon the ovaries to decrease estrogen production in the body and thus to restore order in both the home and the workplace.

Between 1931 and 1980 there were steady references to premenstrual issues in the medical literature. Authors generally constructed PMS as a medical condition requiring management and treatment by a physician or a psychiatrist/psychologist. However, PMS was *not* seen as a major problem for the majority of women at that time. Nor was PMS seen as a major research problem for most scientists.

PMS as a medical disorder received steady but relatively little attention until an English doctor, Katharina Dalton, began to investigate it. In 1953, Dalton coauthored an important article on PMS in the *British Medical Journal*. This article first introduced the term, "Premenstrual Syndrome," emphasizing that women need not accept the physical and emotional discomfort of PMS every month, and that modern medicine could help them.

Dalton has conducted research and written articles and books on PMS for over 40 years. She defines PMS as "any symptoms or complaints which regularly come just before or during early menstruation but are absent at other times of the cycle. It is the absence of symptoms after menstruation which is so important in this definition" (Dalton 1983:12). According to Dalton's research, PMS is responsible for decreased worker productivity (in both the sufferer and "her husband"), increased divorce rates, and even murder.

Dalton's own popularity, notoriety, and authority as a PMS "expert" heightened when she served as the chief defense medical expert in a 1981 murder trial in London, in which she successfully argued that the defendant was not responsible for murdering her lover because she suffered from a severe form of PMS. The publicity generated from this trial and Dalton's claims of successful progesterone treatments found many different audiences in the United States and brought publicity to PMS.

Due in part to the publicity generated by these trials, PMS and related diagnoses have been called the "disease of the 1980s." A disease that thousands of women previously had been told did not exist suddenly become a media event. More importantly, PMS also acquired medical legitimacy. A specifically biomedical orientation to PMS defines it as a medical problem requiring a specific type of scientific research, diagnosis, and intervention. The result is that PMS is real in the scientific and medical sense.

PMS AS A FEMINIST SCIENTIFIC ARTIFACT

It was feminist researchers (especially in nursing and psychology) who were responsible for conducting a significant portion of the scientific research done on PMS during the 1970s and 1980s. Since the 1970s, feminist scientists have actively worked within the field of science to study PMS and to make sure that the research was conducted. Feminist critics of traditional menstrual and premenstrual studies have long argued for different and better scientific methodologies, more appropriate research designs, and nonstigmatizing labels and assumptions. So, feminist scientists took responsibility for the majority of scientific research on menstruation in the 1970s and 1980s because they believed otherwise it would not be conducted. Thus, these early feminist researchers sought to "demystify" the negative stereotypical images of women and PMS by conducting "good" and "sound" science. These writers are quick to assert that the very use of the term "premenstrual syndrome" is an attempt by scientists to make premenstrual "tension" a more scientific term, and takes the control of women's bodies out of their own hands. These writers point out that the use of the word "syndrome" instead of "symptoms" itself suggests that there is an underlying disease process in women's bodies.

So, what scientifically constitutes PMS, and how PMS research should be legitimately carried out, were questions raised by feminists within the scientific profession in the 1970s and 1980s. The aim (and possibly its result as well) of feminist scientific work on menstruation was to use the tools and rhetoric of "science" to refute negative images of PMS. These feminists believed that changes in public perception and attitudes about the previously understudied topic of menstruation and PMS were achievable from within science.

Scholarly and Social Science Explanations of PMS/Menstruation

While physicians and scientists studied and tried to define PMS and other menstrual disorders in terms of *biology*, mainly feminist anthropologists, sociologists, and other scholars tried to place and account for PMS in its *social* and *cultural* context. Studies of the history of menstruation in human society point out that menstrual related disorders are often associated with the practice of labeling women and their behaviors crazy (dating back to ancient Greek writings).

Scholars have linked PMS to ancient descriptions of hysteria and other modern characteristics (lethargy, moodiness, and depression) previously attached to menstruation itself.

For example, in some cultures, menstruation has been portrayed as an evil spirit that invades women of childbearing age once a month. Cultural taboos and negative stereotypes—such as not touching a menstruating woman and physically separating her—also have existed. The ancient Greeks believed that the uterus "wandered" in women's bodies and caused all sorts of unusual behaviors—behaviors that today are attributed to PMS.

Other authors have tried to combat negative stereotypes of madness and PMS by tracing the diagnosis (as a cultural and political artifact) to capitalist patriarchal society. Some authors argue that PMS is historically located within the stresses of modern capitalism in western culture. Such authors might ask, how is it that a majority of all women are afflicted with a physically abnormal hormonal cycle? Within this view, it is not surprising that original interest in PMS arose during the economic Depression in the 1930s. Although women had made gains in labor force participation during World War I, the Depression led to women being forced to give up wage work because jobs were needed by men.

Post–World War II studies that emerged in the 1950s appear to fit into this traditional pattern of using medical rhetoric to diagnose and treat social and cultural problems in the home and workplace. These traditional medical studies have a distinct focus on the effect of a woman's PMS on her social roles of wife, mother, and worker. This early scientific work on PMS stressed how disruptive it is in the home, factory, and social order. By focusing on this "disruption," the medical community attempted to claim ownership over PMS and to medicalize women's bodies. In this respect, medicine attributes problems in families (unhappiness, arguments, and violence) to women in general and PMS in particular, and claims that these problems can be solved medically. Of course, this medical reasoning discourages us from looking at the social sources of problems.

Another author identifies the specifically male composition of the medical profession as the source of control and power over women's bodies and PMS. Still other feminist writers and health care providers have tried to communicate the need for every woman to take control over her body and its byproducts, such as menstruation and PMS.

The social, scientific, and feminist analyses suggest that the diversity of meanings assigned to PMS in contemporary Western culture (bitchy, moody, not responsible for behavior, uncontrolled emotional states) is related to the societies in which they are developed and is also indicative of the movement in modern society to assign a medical label or explanation for human behaviors. Within such constructions, PMS is a problem to be resolved socially and culturally, not medically.

In brief, what scientifically constitutes PMS, and how PMS research should be legitimately carried out were questions raised from within science itself as well as from political critics outside science.

The nature and content of pre-1980s PMS research is important. In 1983, one writer remarked that because PMS symptoms are behavioral, psychological, and physiological in nature, researchers have included biologists as well as social scientists. All types of scientific research (social science as well as biological science) were being conducted and funded by different types of researchers (biologists, gynecologists, psychologists, and psychiatrists). The major difference among PMS researchers was whether they held a purely biological/biomedical orientation or a feminist and thus more sociocultural orientation. A feminist or sociocultural perspective challenges traditional biomedical control of women's bodies and experiences, while a biomedical orientation to PMS considers it a medical problem requiring medical scientific research, diagnosis, and intervention.

THE 1983 CONFERENCE AND SCIENTIFICALLY DEFINING PMS

A marked shift in the PMS research community took place at a May 1983 conference sponsored by the National Institute of Mental Health (NIMH). This conference played a major role in bringing together a diverse group of research scientists, psychiatrists, and psychologists doing PMS-related research. The main product of this 1983 NIMH conference was a working scientific definition of Premenstrual Syndrome: "a diagnosis of premenstrual syndrome should be made when symptom intensity changes at least 30 percent in the premenstrual period (six days before menses) compared with the intermenstrual period (days 5–10 of the cycle) for two consecutive months."

The 1983 definition of PMS was seen as a scientific advance in a field in which no previous agreement or definition had been reached. A consistent definition could tighten research and clinical standards of evaluation. Yet the 1983 NIMH conference did not fully resolve all definitional and methodological issues of PMS research. Scientists still pointed to the lack of clarity and to the absence of solid scientific data to fully support it as a diagnosis. Given the increasing level of interest in PMS by the public and by other health and mental health professionals, more research was called for. For example, according to scientific and medical reports of the 1983 NIMH conference in the *Journal of the American Medical Association* (JAMA), panelists couldn't precisely define the disorder and they admitted that their research had many methodological problems. Even well-known and respected PMS researchers noted in the *American Journal of Psychiatry* that researchers did not agree on the definition of PMS, that they had not found specific biological correlates and that no one had demonstrated that any specific medical treatment worked better than no treatment at all. Another PMS researcher pointed out in an editorial in the *New England Journal of Medicine* in 1984 that there was much speculation but very little was actually understood about the pathophysiology of PMS.

Public interest in scientific research is generally perceived by researchers as vital. In fact, the impetus and pressure for PMS research came not from within the scientific community but from consumers or the public. A "proper" public image of PMS research was important for reasons both external and internal to the scientific community. If PMS research was seen as inconclusive and plagued by methodological or epistemological difficulties, it might not get funded by government agencies and other patrons, or published by scientific journals. If some scientists do not perceive PMS research as legitimate science, then the public might not believe PMS experts or seek out their advice and treatments.

Reports about methodological difficulties of scientific and medical research on PMS were indeed making their way into the popular press. *Ms.* magazine in 1983 and *Vogue* in 1984 informed their readers that there was little agreement on what causes PMS or how it should be treated. Yet this perception of scientific uncertainty conveyed by the public press was not necessarily a bad thing for scientists and PMS researchers. Because PMS was portrayed as the "new" disease of the 1980s, uncertainty meant that funding and more research were needed. Science and medicine had not yet come up with "answers" about PMS. But with proper support and attention from scientists and health professionals, science would eventually provide them.

Scientists' response to scientific and public accounts of PMS was important. Given the confused slate of symptoms and treatment possibilities, PMS attracted many "alternative" healers with "nonscientific" treatments and prescriptions. If PMS was indeed the "disease of the 1980s" then scientists needed to ensure that its study was "legitimate science," clearly demarcated from "quackery" or scientifically "unsound" treatments. One way to ensure scientists' control of PMS was to codify its definition and formally outline "legitimate" treatment protocols.

The 1983 NIMH conference and later interpretations of its guidelines played an important role in the controversy over LLPDD, a DSM category for the psychiatric manifestations of PMS. The apparent lack of scientific consensus about symptoms and treatments of PMS was played out by scientists in two different ways. First, beginning with the strategy supported by proinclusion researchers, efforts were made to push for a PMS-related psychiatric diagnosis in the revision of the DSM-III. Second, inclusion would ensure its scientific legitimation as a psychiatric disorder and was needed to secure funding for further scientific/medical research.

THE PMS INDUSTRY

While scientists continued to complain about the research underlying the "realness" of PMS, a PMS industry was being formed. One important aspect of this PMS industry involved the pharmaceutical industry, which began offering over-the-counter PMS drugs and more PMS-related products in the 1980s. At the time when scientists were arguing about whether or not to include PMS as a psychiatric diagnosis, total consumer spending in 1984 for menstrual pain relievers, including PMS products, was $111,132,000 a year.

What is the nature of the relationship of PMS-related products to PMS research in the scientific community? Simply stated, drug companies would not fund research unless PMS was accorded the status of a "real diagnosis" because they could not sell products to respond to a medical condition that didn't formally exist. But the relationship between the pharmaceutical companies and scientific researchers was more complex: There was much debate *within* the scientific community about whether to formally classify PMS as a *psychiatric* disorder. If PMS were classified only as a physical disorder then medical doctors would claim ownership; if LLPDD was included in the *DSM*-III-R then it would be a psychiatric disorder and psychologists/psychiatrists would claim ownership.

Chattem Pharmaceutical's advertisement in *People* magazine (June 30, 1986) represents a challenge to the scientific and medical expertise of psychiatrists over PMS. It portrays a psychiatrist's couch, with the words "Premenstrual Tension is not a psychological issue. It is a physical condition." The advertisement could be read as an effort to demarcate the boundary between physical treatment of PMS (which can be treated with products such as Premysyn PMS) and the "mental" treatment of PMS (which has no over-the-counter pharmaceutical products). It directly and not-so-subtly suggests to women that physical conditions such as headaches, bloating, and swelling can be taken care of with their products. Increased attention to the creation of PMS as a biomedical problem would appear to benefit drug sales. So, in the end, while the psychiatric manifestations of PMS were formally accorded a psychiatric diagnosis, the key for the pharmaceutical industry was defining PMS as something that can be helped with pills, diets, or other products offered in the PMS industry.

WHAT'S AT STAKE IN THE CONSTRUCTION OF PMS?

For some women, the publicity and legitimization of PMS and its symptoms as real, a natural part of their body and its processes, have led to a positive sense of control over this phenomenon. However, a more negative image of PMS as something that controls women once a month, that makes them "crazy" and subject to their hormones, is much more pervasive in our contemporary Western culture. This image has allowed women to use PMS as an excuse to express their emotions or to account for their otherwise "strange" behaviors. Other people (husbands, children, doctors, lawyers, judges, juries, coworkers) have also used PMS to explain women's behaviors.

How PMS is defined—and who controls or owns the diagnosis related to it—has been and continues to be a matter of social, political, and economic concern. The degree to which PMS has become a major issue is best understood in light of current estimates that anywhere between 20 and 90 percent of all women would qualify as having some of the more than 150 recognized symptoms of PMS.

PMS has been defined in a variety of ways (scientific, feminist, cultural, and economic) over the years, but there is no consistent or agreed upon definition. If the estimates given above are indeed true, and if almost all menstruating women do have at least some of these symptoms, then the "stability" of women's moods and behaviors can be called into question by scientists, doctors, politicians, bosses, and lawyers. What is considered "normal" for women itself is at the heart of the debate in the PMS controversy.

REFERENCE

Dalton, Katrina. 1983. *Once a Month*. Claremont, CA: Hunter House.

16

Multicultural Education as Moral Drama

SHAN NELSON-ROWE

Multicultural education is a social movement within education that seeks to transform the organization, practice, and ideological content of schooling. More specifically, the movement calls for greater cultural diversity in matters of curriculum, pedagogy, faculty, and other educational issues. Multicultural educators view themselves as representing subordinate cultural groups within schools in a challenge to the dominance of an institutional elite.

I examined 123 journal articles, books, and organizational position statements on multicultural education published in the United States between 1969 and 1991. Articles and position statements about educational reform in the United States were selected from *Education Index*. The documents sample multicultural rhetoric from a broad range of professional educators and their organizations. The sample includes articles by individual authors, as well as position statements by such professional organizations as the National Catholic Education Association, the National Council for the Social Studies, the American Association of Colleges for Teacher Education, and the National Coalition for Cultural Pluralism.

I examine the rhetoric of multicultural education as a melodrama. The melodrama is one kind of moral order typically constructed by social problems claims-makers, including multicultural educators. In the melodramatic moral order, the principal identities are those of victim, villain, and hero. Melodramas portray power relations, interests, values, and

This chapter is excerpted from Nelson-Rowe, Shan (1995). "The Drama of Multicultural Education." Pp. 81–99 in *Images of Issues: Typifying Contemporary Social Problems,* 2nd edition, edited by Joel Best. Hawthorne, NY: Aldine de Gruyter.

motives in terms of good and evil, weak and strong characters. Victims are completely powerless to confront the villain, and need to be rescued or protected by the heroes. Villains are unremittingly evil and heroes are paragons of virtue. Villains pursue their victims out of selfishness and malevolence. Heroes are altruistically motivated by their benevolent values.

THE RHETORIC OF MULTICULTURAL EDUCATIONAL REFORM

Multicultural education (MCE) means different things to different people. The root idea, however, is that the United States contains culturally diverse groups, each with its own traditions, customs, and ways of living. Rather than viewing cultural diversity as a problem to be solved by creating a unified national culture such as the "melting pot," multiculturalists see a resource to be preserved and celebrated. The problem, from their perspective, is that educational leaders in the United States traditionally have suppressed minority cultures because they viewed them as deficient next to the dominant Anglo-American culture. Multiculturalists claim the suppression of diversity leads minority pupils, who find their language and heritage denied, to develop negative self-images and perform poorly in school.

Casting "Culturally Different Students" as Victims

The most salient attribute MCE reformers assign to school children, especially those from ethnic and racial minority groups, is their powerlessness within schools. One monograph described "Negroes, Indians, and Mexican-American and other racial-cultural minorities as guinea pigs for experiments in monocultural, monolingual education." In 1983, the National Catholic Education Association criticized the failure of education to match "reality" and "ideals," particularly in its treatment of the poor and powerless.

According to MCE advocates, cultural imposition impedes the development of positive self-images among minority children. This is a crucial problem in American education, according to proponents of MCE, who tend to view self-esteem, ethnic or racial pride, and success in school as intimately bound together. Curricula, textbooks, and other school characteristics that exclude or denigrate racial and ethnic heritage send students a message that does not enhance their self-esteem. Indeed, one critic suggests that ethnic pride and self-esteem may decrease with increased time in schools. In 1976, the National Council for Social Studies claimed that the cost of assimilation was self-denial, self-hatred, and rejection of family ties. Minority students are doubly victimized by teaching styles and curricula that do not take into account cultural differences in how people learn. As a result, culturally different students become alienated from school, and display behaviors white, middle-class teachers incorrectly interpret as evidence of negative attitudes toward learning.

Multicultural education advocates believe minority students have an interest in altering the system of schooling, but their very powerlessness prevents them from doing so. In part, they are powerless because they do not recognize their victimization. According to MCE advocates, ethnic youth must be taught that they have been victimized by institutional racism so that they can learn to blame the system rather than themselves for their difficulties in school.

In short, MCE rhetoric constructs a collective identity of "culturally different students" as powerless, alienated victims of an educational system that either ignores or denigrates their cultural backgrounds, and crushes their enthusiasm for learning. Multicultural rhetoric also attributes to culturally different students an interest in changing how schools and other social institutions operate, and argues that MCE should empower those students to take action.

Casting "Anglocentric Schools" as Villains

The moral drama of multiculturalism casts "Anglocentric" schools as the villains. Multiculturalists' claims about schools criticize the melting pot ideology. This ideology claims that immigrants to the United States have all their cultural differences melted down and combined into a new and uniquely American culture.

This characterization of American schools attributes significant power to Anglocentric, or WASP (White, Anglo-Saxon, Protestant) educators, as they are often called. It does so by implication rather than by directly naming individuals or groups responsible for conditions in the schools. Attributing values to actors within biased schools is also indirect. MCE rhetoric attacks values embedded within Anglocentric schools rather than attributing values to specific individuals or groups. Without naming names, this assigns to schools (and the society that produced them) values opposed to democracy and individual freedom, and committed to suppressing minority heritage and enforcing conformity. The theme that American schools are antidemocratic and authoritarian recurs throughout the MCE literature.

Although MCE claims do not directly blame educators for creating a system that harms culturally different children, claims-makers do hold educators morally and professionally responsible for reforming the schools. For most multiculturalists, reform begins with changing teachers' training. But reform must also reshape the total educational environment, including the hidden curricula, institutional norms, school policy, assessment and testing, and teaching methods.

Multiculturalists also attribute inegalitarian interests and motives to educators who do not actively support MCE reforms. Taken together, these claims portray educators within Anglocentric schools as able but unwilling to promote more democratic schools committed to the freedom and individual expression MCE offers culturally different students.

Why do MCE claims-makers avoid directly identifying human villains in their rhetoric? And why do they fail to impute interests to human actors within the schools? In large part this may reflect the intended audience for the specific claims in my sample. Professional journals are read almost entirely by school teachers, principals, supervisors, and faculty of teachers' colleges. This audience includes some educators converted to the cause of MCE, some opposed to it, and some who may be persuaded to join the movement. By not directly blaming members of their audience, MCE educators may avoid alienating those in the third group whom they seek to enlist.

Casting "Multicultural Educators" as Heroes

Multiculturalists' collective presentation of self defines their identity in opposition to that of Anglocentric schools and educators. For example, MCE advocates claim to have the power to change how schools teach children and shape children's identities, and thereby to reduce social problems. Emphasizing the power of classroom teachers, one critic claims that sharp teachers can change the curriculum, implying that teachers who resist change are either dull or uncommitted to the goals of MCE.

Most of all, MCE advocates believe they have the power to reduce racial and ethnic hostility and promote harmony. Teachers of multicultural education can have these effects by promoting understanding and tolerance of cultural differences. This claim depends on a fundamental belief that racial and ethnic hostilities are based on ignorance that MCE can reduce.

Rhetorical claims about multiculturalists' power also reveal the values they impute to their collective identity. These values are defined in opposition to those imputed to Anglocentric educators. Multiculturalists' values, for example, include the value of the individual, a humanistic spirit, and a democratic heritage. More specifically, multicultural educators view their work in terms of values of cultural diversity, the importance of individual and cultural identity, the eradication of cultural biases and discrimination, and the promotion of intercultural harmony.

The rhetorical presentation of cultural diversity as a threatened resource, and MCE as the means of preserving and extending that resource, casts the multiculturalists as protectors. This protector identity receives further support from claims about the changing demographic composition of the United States. In general, multiculturalists argue that the United States, while always a multicultural nation, is becoming even more so as a result of immigration, birth, and death rates.

The combined power, values, and interests multicultural educators impute to themselves lead to very different conclusions about their motives in comparison with Anglocentric educators. Multiculturalists rhetorically construct schools as villains who are able but unwilling to help make MCE reforms. By contrast, multiculturalists impute to themselves the ability and willingness to act, and describe their motives in terms of MCE being a moral and ethical issue. They cast themselves as protectors, not only of cherished American values such as democracy, individual freedom, justice, and liberty, but also of the rights of children to receive an education that treats their cultural heritage with dignity. Multiculturalists give themselves the power to redefine how schools operate and to instill the value of cultural diversity in the curriculum.

DISCUSSION

For multiculturalists, the moral order is melodramatic. There are clearly defined victims, villains, and heroes whose identities and actions are unambiguous. Anglocentric schools are uniformly corrupt. Culturally different children are uniformly eager to learn, only to become alienated by oppressive schools. Multiculturalists are uniformly motivated by egalitarian and democratic values. Multiculturalists construct a world in which power is abused by a dominant cultural group to subordinate less powerful cultural groups, especially the children within these groups. As the heroes of this melodrama, multiculturalists propose to use the power they have within educational institutions to empower the victims (culturally different children) to seize control of their own lives.

Ironically, the multiculturalists' melodramatic rhetoric undercuts their claim of empowering culturally different students. The victim identity assigned to these students makes them ultimately dependent upon the multicultural educator-heroes for their liberation. Moreover, for students to gain their own power they must accept the multiculturalists' construction of their problems. That is, culturally different students must learn to view themselves as victims and multicultural educators as their protectors. Only by doing so will these students become effective political activists.

Claims and counterclaims by multiculturalists and traditionalists ignore the students' own construction of their identities. While educators on each side of the issue make claims about the effects of schooling on students' identities, neither group is particularly concerned with letting students speak for themselves. Allowed to do so, would culturally different students construct a moral order in which they claim the identity of victim? If so, would they identify their interests with multiculturalists or with tradition-alists? The silencing of the students on these questions speaks to the power educators of all ideological perspectives have over the students they claim to serve.

V
Constructing Solutions

Introduction to Section V

Claims-makers try to convince audience members both that a social problem is at hand and that something must be done to resolve it. We turn to the claims-making task of constructing solutions to social problems. These are *prognostic frames* answering the question posed by audience members: What should be done to eliminate the condition? What should be done to help and/or rehabilitate victims? What should be done to rehabilitate and/or punish villains?

In many respects, a social problems formula story, which is the package of claims typifying a condition and the victims and villains in it, almost automatically constructs a prognostic frame. Consider the perplexing question of what should be done about people who live on the streets. If the claims have a diagnostic frame blaming a "lack of housing," then it reasonably follows that what should be done is build more housing. If the claims construct "unsafe shelters" as the culprit then it follows that if shelters for homeless people were better then people would go to them rather than live on the streets. But in "The Homeless Mentally Ill and Involuntary Hospitalization," Donileen R. Loseke illustrates how the *New York Times* constructed people living on the streets as mentally ill. From that typification it follows that people on the streets because they are mentally ill should be forcefully removed "for their own good" and taken to mental hospitals where they can receive help. The social policy of involuntary incarceration in mental hospitals was justified by constructing people who lived on the streets as mentally ill and unable to make rational decisions. The prognostic frame constructing what should be done follows from the grounds and diagnostic frames constructing the condition and the characteristics of the people in it.

When there is claims-competition over diagnostic frames—and there often is—the claims that succeed will shape the response to the condition. The "War on Drugs" that began in the United States in 1986 is a case in point. In "Constructing a War on Drugs," Craig Reinarman and Harry G.

Levine offer another example of differences between objective conditions and subjective worry: According to their analysis of United States government data, there was *no* evidence that crack cocaine, the chief target of the War on Drugs, was a prevalent and increasing problem in 1986 when the War on Drugs started. But this policy started nonetheless and at this present time our prisons and jails are crowded with drug offenders. But why was crack cocaine constructed as a problem of *crime*? Why was it not constructed as a *public health* problem? Reinarman and Levine argue that the diagnostic frame of the problem of crack cocaine, and the accompanying social policy of a "War on Drugs" were the consequences of larger political issues in that historical era.

Many observers now question the appropriateness of framing drugs as a problem of crime rather than a problem of health. Yet it was this diagnostic frame that led to social policies that remain to this day. Indeed, aspects of the "War on Drugs" have been institutionalized in many private companies that test the urine of potential and sometimes continuing employees for evidence of drug use. William J. Staudenmeier examines these policies in "Urine Testing and Social Control." This article is fairly old—it was first published in 1989, yet we include it here because Staudenmeier's prediction that these policies would outlast public worry has been correct. Regardless of the multiple problems in implementing these urine-testing policies, regardless of the multiple questions they raise about how these policies violate the right to privacy, urine-testing policies have become an all but taken-for-granted aspect of employment. Private companies now do something the government could not do—they subject a wide variety of Americans who are not accused of criminal activity to invasive tests.

Social problems claims-makers at times achieve social change through changing *social policy*. New laws are enacted, or old ones struck down; new social services are started, or old ones are closed. Yet many other claims-makers do not seek social policy changes for reasons involving the political nature of social policy. For example, different political administrations are characterized by different policy climates—one group of politicians will be most concerned with issues of families or schools, and another will be focused on questions of economy, and so on. Some claims-makers will find their particular interests are "outside" these concerns so there is little chance of being successful in the public policy arena. In addition, social change through social policy is, almost by definition, a very gradual process. Claims-makers with prognostic claims promoting radical change likely will not be successful: Claims seeking to increase the minimum wage, for example, might be successful but claims that all Americans should be paid the same will not be successful.

Social change through social policy is not always possible. In addition, some claims-makers believe that it is not a good use of time and energy to focus on changing policy. These claims-makers seek social change through transforming the *cultural climate*: the ways behaviors or people are socially evaluated. Their logic is that social policy will not be effective unless people change the way they socially evaluate behaviors or people. We only need consider the Prohibition Era as evidence: Claims-makers were successful in changing social policy—buying, producing, and selling alcohol became illegal. Yet the policy was unsuccessful because it did not change the ways Americans think about alcohol. Hence, some claims-makers focus on transforming the cultural climate. For example, Jeffery Sobal examines "The Size Acceptance Movement." These are social change groups on behalf of people who use the term "fat" to categorize themselves. While these groups have sought changes in the physical world, such as larger seats on airplanes and in movie theaters, most of their attention has been on changing the cultural climate that prizes thinness and therefore leads fat people to experience prejudice and discrimination.

Social problems claims-makers therefore construct prognostic frames that answer audience members' questions about what should be done. While there often are multiple claims-competitions, successful claims can change the characteristics of the objective world and they can change the characteristics of the cultural climate. Some claims-makers are successful in changing both—drunk driving now is subject to more legal sanctions than in the past and it is also far less tolerated. Yet social change most often is partial—employed mothers are much more accepted than in the past but there remain insufficient day care and employers who do not offer flextime. Despite some successes, claims-making must continue.

17

The "Homeless Mentally Ill" and Involuntary Hospitalization

DONILEEN R. LOSEKE

What should the public do about a person who wants to live on the streets? What is the public's responsibility for this type of person? What can the public demand from such a person? These practical questions became central to controversies surrounding a policy of removing the "homeless mentally ill" from New York City's streets in the 1980s. I want to explore the roots of these controversies and examine how the *New York Times* (*NYT*) constructed the morality of the public policy resolution to them.

Two general social constructionist understandings about *all* social policy inform my analysis. First, central to my argument is the belief that socially constructed images of *types* of conditions and *types* of people underlie social policies of all types and that these images are important. Second, because my interest is in a social policy that allowed people to be removed from the streets and placed into mental hospitals against their will, it is important to note that any level of government in the United States can intervene in private lives for only two reasons: intervention must be justified as either necessary to protect the public by controlling those who violate social rules, or as necessary to help people requiring assistance.

This chapter is excerpted from Loseke, Donileen R. (1995). "Writing Rights: The Homeless Mentally Ill and Involuntary Hospitalization." Pp. 261–86 in *Images of Issues, Typifying Contemporary Social Problems*, 2nd edition, edited by Joel Best. Hawthorne, NY: Aldine de Gruyter.

Using data from 132 articles in the *NYT* between 1981 and 1992, I turn now to a perplexing question facing people living in New York City during that time. What should the public do about people who live on the streets? This controversy occurred within a historical backdrop: The 1960s and 1970s in the United States were characterized as a time when "mental illness" increasingly was accepted as a normalized response to poor environments, an era when most mental hospitals were closed, when powers of police, psychiatrists and other institutional representatives had been greatly curtailed in favor of self-determination for many types of people, including the "mentally ill." Yet during the 1980s in New York City a question arose: Did the public have the right to involuntarily commit to mental facilities the people who lived on the streets of the city? My argument is that answers to this question depend on images of both the problem, "homelessness," and the people, "the homeless."

CLAIMS-MAKERS AND PUBLIC POLICY

The pages of the *NYT* contain the voices of many claims-makers debating what to do about people who wanted to live on the streets of New York City. In historical retrospect, the victors in these debates were those promoting the policy of involuntary hospitalization. One person, then-Mayor Edward Koch, was identified by the *NYT* as the primary person advocating this policy. Yet while the mayor was the original, and the most vocal, spokesperson for policies of involuntary hospitalization, the pages of the *NYT* also can be read as containing a choir of supporting voices. For example, policies of involuntarily hospitalization were supported by *NYT* editorials as early as 1982; on these pages the policy of involuntary hospitalization was supported by such powerful claims-makers as a state senator, the president of the American Psychological Association, and city and state health officials. There also were supportive opinion editorials, letters to the editor, and reports that the plan won praise in "man-on-the street" polls.

The other side of this controversy, as constructed through the pages of the *NYT*, was twofold. First, many claims constructed practical, procedural, legal, or monetary problems associated with involuntary hospitalization policies. These were claims about practical problems of reversing changes in the 1960s and 1970s that made it very difficult to force hospitalization and which made hospital space itself very limited. My interest, though, is with claims constructing the morality of policy: *Should* policies promoting involuntary hospitalization be implemented? Although Mayor Koch often identified social workers, homeless advocates and civil libertarians as his moral opposition, this construction is both too broad and too narrow. First, it is misleading to claim that some groups always opposed policies of involuntary confinement or that they opposed these policies on moral grounds. For example, Robert Hayes, representing the Coalition for the Homeless, said that his group had "absolutely no objection" to proposals advocating involuntarily confinement when the weather was very cold. In the same way, another advocacy group, Partnership for the Homeless, endorsed policies of involuntary hospitalization as long as they were "compassionately implemented." And, social workers could agree that involuntary commitment should be easier.

Clearly, such policies promoting hospitalization reversed those of "community treatment" that had been very much in vogue during the 1960s and 1970s; policies making involuntary commitment easier reversed the prior trend of making commitment increasingly more difficult. Such changes did not come quickly or easily: Mental hospitals needed to be reopened and laws needed to be changed. Yet practical changes could be made only if the morality of policy was successfully constructed.

CONSTRUCTING IMAGES OF SANITY AND INSANITY

New constructions of *types* of conditions and people must compete with others already present in the social order. For the case in point, people who opposed policies of involuntary hospitalization constructed the problem as first and foremost one of a lack of *housing*; they constructed "mental illness" as a normal condition; they constructed the "mentally ill" person as a rational actor capable of self-determination. In other words, the types of constructions that had been the positive support for community mental health policies became defensive claims criticizing proposed new policies of involuntary hospitalization.

Some of these claims criticized the social order and constructed environmental explanations for the condition of people living on the streets. Within this construction, the problem was the lack of low-income housing creating "homelessness" in the first place, or the lack of "safe and decent" places for people to sleep once they were without homes. Claims constructed the city's shelter system as "big, barracks like quarters," that were "depressing" and sometimes "dangerous." According to these claims, people were on the street because they could not afford homes; they remained on the street because the city shelter system was despicable. Within this construction, people on the street would go to shelters willingly if shelters were better.

Constructing the social order as the problem yields an image of people on the street as rational actors no different from people who have homes.

After all, readers are reminded, the majority of Americans would not like the "long lines and regimentation" in shelters; most people might choose to live on the streets if their "only alternative was despicable, regimented, and downright dangerous shelters." Within this construction, the decision to remain on the streets rather than enter a city shelter becomes a "sign of mental health rather than of mental illness."

In addition, claims could produce what might be classified as indications of "mental illness" to rather be normal reactions to oppressive environments. Such claims warned readers to not confuse behavior realistically resulting from the experience of street living with "actual" psychiatric disorder. Even seemingly bizarre behaviors could be normalized. For example, while commonsense reasoning might judge "burning money" as an indication of "mental illness," one story told of a woman who burned money only when it was rudely thrown at her. "Burning money" becomes constructed as an act of "self-respect." This woman also "burned money" only when she did not need it for that particular day. This, according to a claims-maker promoting her normality, indicated her rational understanding that it is dangerous to have money and live on the street. Likewise, while urinating or defecating on a public sidewalk might be judged a sign of "mental illness," some writers constructed these as merely unfortunate consequences of a lack of publicly available toilets.

Constructions promoting the normality of such behaviors simultaneously promote the right to self-determination. Indeed, people who live on the street could be constructed as exemplary Americans who have a "fiercely independent lifestyle." Hence, a woman living on the street argued "I like the streets, and I am entitled to live the way I want to live." Another woman turned down an offer for transportation to a shelter because "I want to be independent." These can be read as comments of rational actors exemplifying the highly valued American love of freedom.

In brief, constructions of "mental illness" that were popular in the 1960s and 1970s associated with the community mental health policy did not simply disappear. They remained a part of the social scene in the 1980s and promoted the normality—or at least the rationality—of people living on the streets.

Within commonsense reasoning, it *should* be very difficult to take away the right to self-determination for rational actors who are not harming others. Hence, the morality of laws making involuntary commitment very difficult is accomplished by constructing the rationality of people living on the streets.

Yet if people living on the streets are *not* rational, then laws making commitment easier are justified. I turn now to a second construction of people living on the streets that supports policies promoting the morality of suspending their individual rights to self-determination. Within this construction, people choosing to live on the streets are not rational, so laws making it difficult to hospitalize them are morally wrong. Or, in the often-quoted opinion of Mayor Koch, "the law is an ass," and needs to be changed.

Claims constructed the commonsense *content* of the problem. According to these claims, normalizing mental illness and promoting unlimited rights to self-determination might lead to "stimulating dinner party conversation and Philosophy I discussions," but commonsense dictated that people living on the streets were not "normal." Within this construction, the "homeless mentally ill" was a person whose decisions and behaviors could not be normalized by practical reasoning.

First, claims promoting the need for involuntary hospitalization formed the unacceptability of living on the street as one knowable from the *practical experience* of *NYT* readers. There were articles about the large number of people living on the streets, and editorials claimed the number of such people "has sharply increased." Readers were informed by editors that "four out of five city residents said they saw such people every day." Hence, this was "one of the city's most visible problems." Readers were instructed to "trust the reality of your senses"; if they simply looked, they would see "craziness."

While claims forming the rationality of people living on the streets constructed behaviors in terms of their *causes* or *meanings*, "craziness" was constructed by purely *behavioral* descriptions. For example, readers learned of Rebecca Smith, a woman who froze to death in a cardboard box rather than accept a ride to a shelter, and Judy, a woman who sat docile all day but arose each and every night at 11:00 p.m. and spent the next several hours "screaming obscenities and intimate details about her life into the night." The "homeless mentally ill" were constructed as people who "stumble about addressing strangers . . . or unseen deities . . . , sometimes shouting obscenities or urinating against buildings"; they were "dirty, disheveled, and malodorous"; and they committed "filthy nuisances on streets and gutters." Such descriptions of appearance and behavior cannot easily be read as forming a "normal" citizen. The type of person known as the "homeless mentally ill" was rather constructed as a "wild presence on the streets of New York City."

But how do we know that a person living on the street is "mentally ill"? We know because the person is on the street. Within middle-class folk reasoning, problems with the city shelter system might lead rational people to live on the streets during summer months. But a person who continues to live on the streets in subzero temperatures when *any* choices are available is, by definition, not rational. Therefore, in response to claims-makers who argued that people made rational choices to remain on the streets in the winter, Mayor Koch replied: "baloney, baloney." According to the mayor, people remained on the street because they were "deranged."

By commonsense logic, a deranged person is not normal. Readers are told such people "don't have their wits about them," suffer from "disorientation and impaired judgment," are "incapable of logical thinking," "incapable of taking care of themselves," and "incompetent." The act of being on the street is constructed as a sufficient sign of incompetence: "Anyone who chooses to be on the streets in the cold when we offer that person . . . a shelter, that person is not competent." "Incompetence" is doubly constructed. First, this type of person is not competent at *self-diagnosis*: They are "too sick to know they are sick," "so sick they imagine they need no help." It follows that such a person also is incapable of making *rational decisions*. "A person who is seriously mentally ill often doesn't realize that he's sick. He will deny that he is ill and refuse to be treated." Such a person "often resists treatment precisely because he [is] mentally ill." Therefore, it goes without saying that others must make decisions because such people "can not be held competent to choose beds of stone and to resist help."

The value of the right to self-determination, of course, is challenged by this construction of the "homeless mentally ill" as a mad person who is, by definition, incompetent. Within middle-class logic, "the freedom to sleep in doorways is no freedom at all." The right to self-determination for people living on the streets becomes constructed as the "freedom to die in the streets," the freedom to "remain wrapped in their agonies of illness of the mind," the "freedom to be left enslaved to madness." Freedom becomes constructed as slavery.

What, then, constitutes freedom for this type of person? According to claims-makers, this was the "freedom from the prison of mental illness." Involuntary commitment was a "rescue" allowing people to "regain rationality." Involuntary commitment could "save the homeless from themselves." So, although the U. S. Supreme Court ruled that involuntary incarceration in a mental institution was a "massive deprivation of liberty," for the "homeless mentally ill" such hospitalization was freedom.

These obviously are moral constructions; they justify hospitalization as the only conceivable policy toward a type of person who, if allowed self-determination, would die. Because policy was justified in terms of how it literally saved lives, it follows that failure to support this policy was constructed as *immoral*: As readers are reminded, "Government cannot be forgiven for letting them just lie there"; a "civilized society has an obligation to help those so deranged that they are likely to die if left alone on the streets." Failure to treat "mental illness" is constructed as "a cruel neglect on the part of society." This was not simply a civil obligation—it was a "*human* obligation to intervene" (emphasis added). Hence, the humanity of the policy of involuntary commitment was constructed as "beyond challenge."

As in earlier eras, claims-making justified practical changes in the social environment. As compared with the early 1980s, by the end of the decade it was procedurally easier to involuntarily commit people to mental hospitals, and there were now many more facilities. But claims-makers promoting more involuntary commitment constructed such change as insufficient. By the early 1990s, readers were told that people living on the streets had become an "unmanageable presence." When the public expressed sympathy for a man who had killed an aggressive homeless person, the *NYT* claimed such sympathy reflected the "community's disgust, and fear, about a continuing assault on public decency posed by people living on the streets." The "homeless mentally ill" now was constructed as a type of person who "befouled private and public property," a type of person whose "very presence devalued everything in the city." Citizens were described as "increasingly irritated," neighborhoods were constructed as "living in absolute terror." While claims in the early- and mid-1980s emphasized *helping* people living on the streets, by the late 1980s, the *NYT* claimed that the public mood had "soured," and that compassion from earlier years had been "replaced with a simple desire to get them out of here." The condition was constructed as "madness in the streets," and "madness is not an acceptable alternative lifestyle to sanity."

The scales of tolerance had tipped, and so, too, had the scales balancing the rights of a public with the rights of individuals. Stated bluntly by a radio talk show host: "What about the rights of people like me who walk past the people who urinate on the sidewalk? I'm a taxpayer. What about my rights?" An editorial bemoaned: "when and why did this country accept madness in the streets as a part of the city scenery?" Concern about the rights of the public—defined implicitly as people who have homes—now became central. Rhetoric shifted to justifying policy in terms of social control: Involuntary commitment was necessary to protect the public from the contagion of madness. But shifting from a rhetoric of help to one of social control did not pose a moral dilemma: By the late 1980s it was simply taken for granted that involuntary confinement was good for the "homeless mentally ill." If policies also were constructed as good for the public then all was as it should be—the policy was beneficial for all and detrimental to none.

SOCIAL CONSTRUCTION AND PUBLIC POLICIES

What should the public do about people who want to live on the streets? What is the public's responsibility for such a person? What can the public demand from such a person? While this examination certainly has not answered questions about what *should* be done, exploring how moral justifications are constructed has practical implications.

My major argument is that images of what the public *should* do depend on our images of types of people. So, for example, a policy of "community mental health" is sensible given an image of "mental illness" as a more-or-less "normal" condition, and the "mentally ill" person as a more-or-less rational actor. Policies of involuntary confinement in mental hospitals are justified by images of the "mentally ill" person as dangerous to self and/or others. Differing images justify different types of public responses toward types of people.

Changes in laws in New York City during the 1980s that made it far easier to involuntarily commit to mental hospitals people who lived on the street came after much public dialog about the characteristics of those people who lived on the street. What should be done about people who live on the streets? The answer to that question depends on constructed images of who these people are.

18

Constructing a War on Drugs

CRAIG REINARMAN AND HARRY G. LEVINE

In the spring of 1986, American politicians and news media began an extraordinary antidrug frenzy that ran until about 1992. During this period, newspapers, magazines, and network television regularly carried lurid stories about a new "epidemic" or "plague" of drug use, especially of crack cocaine. Politicians from both parties made increasingly strident calls for a "War on Drugs." It is certainly true that the United States has real health and social problems that result from illegal and legal drug use. But it is also certainly true that the period from 1986 through 1992 was characterized by antidrug extremism.

Crack was not a new drug, for its active ingredient is entirely cocaine. Nor was it a new way of using cocaine; smoking cocaine freebase had been practiced since the mid-1970s. The National Institute on Drug Abuse (NIDA) found that by 1985 more than 22 million Americans in all social classes and occupations had reported at least trying cocaine. All phases of freebasing, from selling to smoking, tended to take place in the privacy of homes and offices of middle-class or well-to-do users. Yet in 1986, cocaine smoking became visible among a "dangerous group," and the drug scare began. Crack attracted the attention of politicians and the media because of its downward mobility to and increased visibility in ghettos and barrios. Crack was sold in small, cheap units, on ghetto streets to poor, young buyers who were already seen as a threat.

This chapter is excerpted from Reinarman, Craig, and Harry G. Levine (1995). "The Crack Attack: America's Latest Drug Scare, 1986–1992." Pp. 147–90 in *Images of Issues: Typifying Contemporary Social Problems*, 2nd edition, edited by Joel Best. Hawthorne, NY: Aldine de Gruyter. 1995.

THE FRENZY: COCAINE AND CRACK IN THE PUBLIC EYE

From the opening shots in 1986 and through all the stories about "crack babies" in 1990 and 1991, politicians and the media depicted crack as supremely evil—the most important cause of America's problems. For example, in April 1988, ABC News "Special Report" termed crack "a plague" that was "eating away at the fabric of America." According to this documentary, Americans spend "twenty billion a year on cocaine"; American businesses lose "sixty billion" dollars a year in productivity because their workers use drugs; "the educational system is being undermined" by student drug use; and "the family is disintegrating" in the face of this "epidemic." This program did not give its millions of viewers any evidence to support such dramatic claims, but it did give them a powerful vocabulary of attribution: "drugs," especially crack, threatened all the central institutions in American life: families, communities, schools, businesses, law enforcement, and even national sovereignty.

The media frenzy continued into 1989. Between October 1988 and October 1989, for example, the *Washington Post* alone ran 1,565 stories—28,476 column inches—about the drug crisis. In 1988 and 1989 the drug war commanded more public attention than any other issue. The crack scare continued in 1990 and 1991, although with somewhat less media and political attention. By the beginning of 1992, the War on Drugs in general, and the crack scare in particular, had begun to decline significantly in prominence and importance. However, even as the drug war received less notice from politicians and media, it remained institutionalized, bureaucratically powerful, and extremely well funded. Because the policy consequences of the drug war have become enduring features of our social environment, it is important to ask: Upon what evidence was the drug scare based?

OFFICIAL GOVERNMENT EVIDENCE

On those rare occasions when politicians and journalists cited statistical evidence to support their claims about the prevalence of crack and other drug use, they usually relied on two basic sources, both funded by the National Institute on Drug Abuse (NIDA). One was the Drug Abuse Warning Network (DAWN), a monitoring project set up to survey a sample of hospitals, crisis and treatment centers, and coroners across the country about drug-related emergencies and deaths. The other was NIDA's national surveys on drug use among general population households and among young people. Because they are still considered by experts and claimsmakers to be the most reliable evidence available, we review what these two NIDA data sources had to say about crack in 1986, the beginning of the drug scare.

The Drug Abuse Warning Network

DAWN collects data on a whole series of drugs—from amphetamine to aspirin—that might be present in emergencies or fatalities. These data take the form of "mentions." A drug "mention" is produced when someone tells attending medical personnel that the patient recently used the drug, or, less often, if a blood test shows the presence of the drug. These data provided perhaps the only statistical support for the crack scare: Cocaine was "mentioned" in an increasing number of emergency room episodes in the 1980s. During 1986, as the scare moved into full swing, there were an estimated 51,600 emergency room episodes in which cocaine was "mentioned." In subsequent years, the estimated number of such "mentions" continued to rise, providing clear cause for concern.

While this might seem to be clear evidence of the increased use of cocaine, it is not so clear because the meaning of a "mention" is ambiguous. In an unknown number of these cases cocaine was probably incidental to the emergency room visit. Such episodes include routine cases in which people went to emergency rooms, for example, after being injured as passengers in auto accidents or in home accidents. Moreover, in most cases, cocaine was only one of the drugs in the person's system; most people also had been drinking alcohol. Finally, the DAWN data do not include information about preexisting medical or mental health conditions that make any form of drug use riskier. For all these reasons one cannot properly infer direct cause from the estimates of "emergency room mentions." Certainly, cocaine did play a causal role in many of these emergency cases, but no one knows how many or what proportion of the total they were.

The DAWN data on deaths in which cocaine was "mentioned" by medical examiners also must be examined closely. When the crack scare got underway in 1986, coroners coded 1,092 deaths as "cocaine-related." But cocaine was "mentioned" as the *only* drug in a fraction of these deaths—in less than one in five. In most cases, cocaine had been used with other drugs, again, most often alcohol. Although any death is tragic, cocaine's role in such fatalities remains ambiguous. "Cocaine-related" is not the same as "cocaine-caused," and "cocaine-related death" does *not* mean "death due to cocaine." There is little doubt that cocaine contributes to some significant (but unknown) percentage of such deaths. But journalists, politicians, and most of the experts on whom they relied never acknowledged the ambiguities in the data. Nor did they commonly provide any comparative perspective. For example, for every *one* cocaine-related death in the United States, there have been approximately 200 tobacco-related deaths and 50 alcohol-related deaths. Seen in this light, cocaine's role in mortality was substantially less than media accounts and political rhetoric implied.

Interpretive and empirical difficulties increase when the DAWN data are used to support claims about crack. Despite all the attention paid to the crack "plague," the DAWN data for 1986 contained *no specific information on crack* as distinct from cocaine. Thus, while it is likely that crack played a role in some of the emergencies and deaths in which cocaine was "mentioned," the data necessary to accurately assess crack's impact *did not exist* when the crack scare began.

NIDA Surveys

The NIDA surveys of drug use produce the data that are the statistical basis of all estimates of the prevalence of cocaine *use*. One of the core claims in the crack scare was that drug use among teenagers and young adults was already high, and that it was growing at an alarming rate. While politicians and the media often referred to teen drug use as an "epidemic" or "plague," the best official evidence available at the time did not support such claims.

NIDA's national surveys of over 8,000 randomly selected households showed that the number of Americans who had used any illegal drug in the previous month began to decline in 1979, and in the early years of the crack scare drug use continued to plunge, cocaine most sharply of all. Lifetime prevalence of cocaine use among young people (the percentage of those 12-25 years old who had "ever" tried it) peaked in 1982, *four years before the scare began* and continued to decline after that. Between 1986 and 1987 the proportion of both high school seniors and young adults who had used cocaine in any form in the previous year dropped by 20 percent. Further, two-thirds of those who had ever tried cocaine had not used it in the previous month. Although a significant minority of young people had tried powdered cocaine at some point, the great majority of them did not continue to use it.

It is important to note that there had been a few signs of increasing cocaine use. The proportion of youngsters who reported using cocaine at least once in the previous month had increased slightly over the years, although it never exceeded 2 percent of all teens in the seven national household surveys between 1972 and 1985. The 1988 NIDA household survey found an increase in the number of adult daily users of cocaine, presumably the group that included crack addicts. But this group constituted only about 1.3 percent of those adults who had ever used any cocaine. NIDA also estimated that about 0.5 percent of the total U.S. adult population (5 out of every 1,000 people) had used cocaine in the last week.

But aside from these few slight increases, in almost every category of drug use, the trends in official drug use statistics had been down *before the scare began*. The figures for cocaine use in particular were dropping sharply just as crisis claims were reaching a crescendo.

NIDA Survey Data on Crack

Tom Brokaw reported on "NBC Nightly News" on May 23, 1986, that crack was "flooding America," that it had become "America's drug of choice." An ordinarily competent news consumer might well have gathered the impression that crack could be found in the lockers of most high school students. Yet at the time of these press reports, *there were no prevalence statistics at all* on crack, and no evidence of *any* sort showing that smoking crack had become even the preferred mode of cocaine use, much less of drug use.

The first official measures of the prevalence of teenage crack began with NIDA's 1986 high school survey. It found that 4.1 percent of high school seniors reported having *tried* crack at least once in the previous year. This figure dropped to 3.9 percent, in 1987, and to 3.1 percent in 1988, a 25 percent decline. This means that at the peak of the crack scare, 96 percent of America's high school seniors had *never* tried crack, much less gone on to more regular use, abuse, or addiction. Of course, any drug use among the young is certainly worrisome, particularly when in such an intense form as crack. However, at the start of the crusade in 1986 to save a "whole generation" of children from death by crack, the latest official data showed a *national* total of eight "cocaine-related" deaths of young people 18 and under for the preceding year.

In general, the NIDA surveys indicate that a substantial minority of teenagers and young adults experiment with illicit drugs. But as with other forms of youthful deviance, most tend to abandon such behavior as they assume adult roles. Politicians, the media, and antidrug advertisements said that cocaine is inevitably addicting, but that crack is still worse because it is "instantaneously addicting." However, according to the NIDA surveys, two-thirds of Americans in all age groups who had ever tried cocaine had not used it in the past 30 days. It is clear that the vast majority of the more than 22 million Americans who have tried cocaine do not use it in crack form, do not escalate to regular use, and do not end up addicted.

In sum, the official evidence on cocaine and crack available during the crack scare gave a rather different picture than Americans received from the media and politicians. The sharp rise in "mentions" of cocaine in emergency room episodes and coroners' reports did offer cause for concern. But the best official evidence of drug use never supported the claims about an "epidemic" or "plague" throughout America, or about "instantaneous addiction." As media attention to crack was burgeoning, the actual extent of crack use was virtually unknown and most official measures of cocaine use actually were decreasing. Once actually measured, the prevalence of crack use turned out to be low to start with and declining throughout the scare.

THE POLITICAL CONTEXT OF THE "CRACK CRISIS"

If the many claims about an "epidemic" or "plague" endangering a "whole generation" of youth were at odds with the best official data, then what else animated the 1986–92 War on Drugs? The crack scare must be understood in terms of its political context and its appeal to important groups within American society.

The New Right and Its Moral Ideology

During the post-Watergate rebuilding of the Republican Party, far right-wing political organizations and fundamentalist Christian groups set out to impose what they called "traditional family values" on public policy. The New Right formed a core constituency for Ronald Reagan. Once he became President in 1981, Reagan and his appointees attempted to restructure public policy. Through the lens of this ideology, most social problems appeared to be simply the consequences of *individual moral choices*. Programs and research that had for many years been directed at the social and structural sources of social problems were systematically defunded in budgets and delegitimated in discourse. Drug problems fit neatly into this ideological agenda and allowed conservatives to engage in sociological denial—to scapegoat drugs for many social and economic problems. For the right wing, American business productivity was not lagging because investors spent their capital on mergers and stock speculation instead of new plants and equipment. Rather, conservatives claimed that businesses had difficulty competing partly because many workers were using drugs. In this view, U.S. education was in trouble not because it had suffered demoralizing budget cuts, but because a "generation" of students were "on drugs." The "drug problem" served conservative politicians as an all-purpose scapegoat. They could blame an array of problems on the deviant individuals and then expand the nets of social control to imprison those people for causing the problems.

Political Party Competition

The primary political task facing liberals in the 1980s was to recapture some of the electorate that had gone over to the Right. Most Democrats responded by moving to the right and pouncing on the drug issue. Part of the early energy for the drug scare in the spring and summer of 1986 came from Democratic candidates trading charges with their Republican opponents about being "soft on drugs."

Crack could not have appeared at a more opportune political moment. After years of dull debates on budget balancing, a "hot" issue had arrived just in time for a crucial election. In an age of fiscal constraint, when most problems were seen as intractable and most solutions costly, the crack crisis was the one "safe" issue on which all politicians could take "tough stands" without losing a single vote or campaign contribution.

CONCLUSION

Even if all the exaggerated claims about crack had been true, it would not explain all the attention crack received. Poverty, homelessness, auto accidents, handgun deaths, and environmental hazards are also widespread, costly, even deadly, but most politicians and journalists never speak of them in terms of "crisis" or "plague." Indeed, far more people were (and still are) injured and killed every year by domestic violence than by illicit drugs, but one would never know this from media reports or political speeches.

That said, it remains that crack *is* an especially dangerous way to use an already risky drug. Despite all the exaggerations, heavy use of it has made life more difficult for many people—most of them from impoverished, urban neighborhoods. If we agree that too many families have been touched by drug-related tragedies, why have we bothered criticizing the crack scare and the War on Drugs? If even a few people are saved from crack addiction, why should anyone care if this latest drug scare was in some measure concocted by the press, politicians, and moral entrepreneurs? Given the damage that drug abuse can do, what's the harm in a little hysteria?

First, drug scares do not work very well to reduce drug problems and they may well promote the behavior they claim to be preventing. For all the repression successive drug wars have wrought (primarily upon the poor and the powerless), they have yet to make a measurable dent in our drug *problems*. Indeed, hysterical and exaggerated antidrug campaigns may have increased drug-related harm in the United States. There is the risk that all of the exaggerated claims made to mobilize the population for a "War on Drugs" actually arouse interest in drug use. Along with statements about "instant addiction" the media also reported some very intriguing things about crack: "whole body orgasm," "better than sex," and "cheaper than cocaine." For TV-raised young people in the inner city, faced with a dismal social environment and little economic opportunity, news about such a substance in their neighborhoods may well have functioned as a massive advertising campaign for crack.

Further, advocates of the war on drugs and the crack scare explicitly rejected public health approaches to drug problems that conflicted with their ideology. The most striking and devastating example of this was the total rejection of syringe distribution and exchange programs by the federal government. By the end of the 1980s, the fastest growing AIDS population was intravenous drug users, primarily heroin addicts. Because syringes were hard to get, or their possession criminalized, heroin injectors shared their syringes and infected each other and their sexual partners with AIDS. In the early 1980s, activists in a number of other Western countries had developed syringe distribution and exchange programs, first to deal with an outbreak of hepatitis, and then with the far more deadly AIDS. There has been mounting evidence from major cities in the Netherlands, England, Australia, Switzerland, Germany, and other Western countries that subsidized needle exchange programs work to reduce the spread of AIDS. But the U.S. government rejected such harm reduction programs on the grounds that they conflicted with the policy of "zero tolerance" for drug use.

The crack scare, like previous drug scares and antidrug campaigns, promoted misunderstandings of drug use and abuse, blinded people to the social sources of many social problems (including drug problems), and constrained the social policies that might reduce those problems. The crack scare routinely featured inflated, misleading rhetoric and blatant falsehoods. At best, the crack scare was not good for public health; at worst, by manipulating and misinforming citizens about drug use and effects, it perverted social policy and political democracy.

19

Urine Testing and
Social Control

WILLIAM J. STAUDENMEIER, JR.

In 1986, President Ronald Reagan and his senior advisers submitted urine specimens to be screened for the presence of illegal drugs. While few Americans suspected the president and his cabinet of using "crack," their tests symbolically encouraged employers' use of urinalysis testing of employees, and aimed to reduce employees' opposition to being tested. This rather bizarre footnote in American history only begins to make sense in the context of the drug crisis that emerged in 1986 with claims about drug abuse harming the quality of work and the health of employees (see Reinarman and Levine, Chapter 18). In this context, employer urine testing of employees emerged as a solution to the drug crisis, and this solution had strong federal support as illustrated by the testing of the president and his cabinet.

The 1986 drug crisis was characterized by extensive media attention, extensive political attention during the 1986 campaign season, and growing public concern. In times of crisis, people look for solutions, and employer-mandated urine testing was a solution receiving strong emphasis. Urine testing had been around for well over a decade, but prior to the 1980s, its adoption was limited primarily to the military and to the screening of job applicants by some large companies. Over time, cost competition led to the development and marketing of cheaper, but less accurate,

This chapter is excerpted from Staudenmeier, William J., Jr. (1989). "Urine Testing: The Battle for Privatized Social Control During the 1986 War on Drugs." Pp. 207–22 in *Images of Issues: Typifying Contemporary Social Problems*, 2nd edition, edited by Joel Best. Hawthorne, NY: Aldine de Gruyter.

tests. As awareness of testing increased through media attention and marketing, as the government promoted it as a solution to the drug crisis, and as costs for testing fell, more employers were encouraged to adopt urine testing. By January 1987, over 20 percent of the companies responding to a national survey used drug urine testing, and an additional 12 percent reported they were developing a testing program. By late 1986, urine testing had become an estimated $300 million per year growth industry.

There are four major categories of employee urine testing conducted by employers: (1) applicant screening (often a part of the medical examination required by large companies); (2) selective screening based on a suspicion of drug impairment on the job; (3) random urine screening (unannounced testing of employees chosen randomly); and (4) periodic testing of all employees (either at fixed intervals or unannounced).

What makes this policy especially interesting is that urine testing is an example of privatized social control. Sociologists usually assume that claims-making influences public policies; the impact of claims on private policy is a neglected topic. Who are the claims-makers promoting privatized social control? How are private policies affected by these claims-making activities?

CLAIMS-MAKING, COUNTER CLAIMS-MAKING AND EMPLOYER POLICY

During 1986, claims in support of testing employees came from several sources, including employers, employer groups such as the Chamber of Commerce, drug testing service providers, politicians running for office, President Reagan and members of his administration, and the President's Commission on Organized Crime. Testing supporters dramatized the scope of the general drug problem, the scope of the work-related drug problem, and the effect of testing on these two problems. According to testing supporters, millions of workers abused drugs; drug abuse affects productivity, absenteeism, and work accidents; medical problems of drug users affect insurance use and premiums; and worker drug use can lead to customer and coworker lawsuits for the employer. Yet these claims did not go unchallenged.

The reaction to the proposals for widespread drug urine testing was vociferous. The core opposition came from organized labor and the American Civil Liberties Union (ACLU). In May 1986, for example, the AFL-CIO Executive Council adopted a policy on urine testing that included the following: "We deplore the recent efforts by many employers, in the hysteria of the moment, to bypass the collective bargaining process and require mandatory screening or impose punitive programs which ride roughshod over the rights and dignity of workers and are unnecessary to secure a safe and efficient workforce." Both employee unions and the ACLU have used court challenges to urine testing. The opposition to urine testing also is felt at the organizational level. Many employers have been challenged on specific test results as well as on the testing programs in general.

THE CONTROVERSIES OVER URINE TESTING

There are three major issues regarding urine testing: the effectiveness of the urine testing process, the nature and effects of drug abuse, and employees' privacy rights.

The *effectiveness* of urine testing is a major point of controversy. There are concerns about every stage of the testing process: selection; notification; actual specimen collection; the administration and control of samples prior, during, and after testing at the laboratory; and the technology of urine testing at the laboratory.

Selecting and notifying the individuals to be tested poses problems. Any form of selection or notification allowing individuals to anticipate the approximate date or time when they will be tested allows knowledgeable drug users to reduce their chances of testing positive. There are several ways in which anticipating testing can influence the results. For example, an individual can simply stop taking drugs for a short time prior to the testing date; illegal drug use can be masked by obtaining and publicly using a prescription drug or over-the-counter product known to yield test results similar to their drug of choice; an individual can find a reason for missing work on the testing date or can make arrangements to have a substitute take the test using false identification.

The *point of specimen collection* also is problematic. First, it is not sufficient to let an individual go to the restroom and provide a specimen, because drug users might substitute clean urine. Therefore, there is a need for both male and female observers. Second, the observers' position must allow them to directly observe the genitalia of the individual who is urinating in order to block more sophisticated switching strategies. In practice, it is difficult to get observers to do this. Observers and employees often manage their mutual embarrassment through unobtrusive positioning, looking away, or focusing on some other body location or restroom fixture. Third, some switching strategies are very hard to detect without a prior body search even if there is direct observation (running a tube under the penis that is connected to a container of clean urine). Some testing laboratories have suggested as part of the proper procedures to prevent switching that the employee be required to change into a hospital gown prior to testing.

The *administration and control of samples* also can influence testing effectiveness. A "chain of custody" must occur from the time the sample is taken, through testing and reporting to ensure that the sample being tested is the same as the one collected. Commonly, however, this chain of custody is not ensured and administrative mistakes can lead to one employee being linked with the positive test result of another employee.

The area of testing effectiveness most often called into question is the *technology of urine testing*. Here, the major concerns are false negatives (failing to detect drugs in a sample that includes evidence of drugs) and false positives (finding evidence of drugs in a sample that does not include such evidence). One study from the Centers for Disease Control found that the average correct response rate on positive samples of urine (those containing evidence of drug use) ranged from only 31 percent to 88 percent depending on the type of drug in the sample. This is the problem of false negatives. Conversely, there are "false positives." At times, individuals who had been in a room with marijuana smoke register positive even if they did not themselves smoke. On the average, the correct response rate for negative samples (those containing no evidence of drug use) is 88 percent to 100 percent depending on the drug.

Not surprisingly, the technology used to test urine samples significantly affects the false positive rate. Relatively inexpensive screenings have a higher rate of false positives than more expensive laboratory screenings. The difference in price, however—$5 for the inexpensive test, up to $100 or more for laboratory screenings—often leads employers to adopt cheaper, less reliable testing technology. In these inexpensive screenings, Advil and Nuprin register as positive for marijuana; Vicks inhaler, Contact, and approximately 150 other over-the-counter drugs containing phenylpropanolamine register as positive for amphetamines.

In addition to the multiple controversies surrounding questions about the effectiveness of urine testing, there are other controversies about the *nature and effects of drug abuse*. To critics, urine testing represents an unwarranted invasion of the employee's right to privacy, but others see it as merely employers looking out for their proper business interests. A key definitional point separating the two positions is whether all illegal drug *use* is drug *abuse* that is harmful or potentially harmful to the employer. Advocates claim that all drug use—whether or not it occurs at work—is abuse that directly affects the employee's productivity and reliability. But research shows that for a large class of drug users, illegal drug use does not impair their work or social relationships. Such use often is occasional rather than continuous, recreational rather than dependent, private rather than public. Paradoxically, urine testing seems most likely to detect these users because their lives are not centered around drug use. Individuals whose drug use is daily and dependent commonly have drug-centered lifestyles. They are more likely to know myriad ways to beat the urine-testing system and to have access to the necessary props to do so.

The controversy over urine testing also centers on the extent to which mandatory urine testing is an unwarranted extension of employer power into employee's *private* lives. There are four basic elements to this debate: (1) the intrusion of taking a person's urine; (2) the intrusion of observing a person urinate; (3) the intrusion by an employer into an employee's off-the-job behavior; and (4) the identification by the employer of not-work-related legal drug use and stigmatized diseases or conditions.

EMPLOYERS' RESPONSES TO DEVIANCE

Employer urine testing is part of the greater social response to drug abuse in American society. Employers can respond to social problems in several ways: (1) setting policy for employees, such as requiring urine testing; (2) committing resources directly to address a social problem, such as hiring a consultant on drug abuse prevention; (3) aiding a third party in its efforts to address a social problem, such as directing contributions to a social service agency for drug prevention activities; and (4) using their influence to change or support the policies and practices of other institutions, such as lobbying for new federal legislation on drug abuse.

Given these choices we must ask, why this response by employers at this time? The answer relates to the type of social problem; this social problem involves attributed employee deviance. A deviant act believed to occur at the workplace or harm workplace performance is generally considered to be the employer's concern, for which some sort of policy response is justified. But the question remains; since employers have policy alternatives that appear both more effective and more humanitarian (employee assistance programs), why adopt urine testing?

In part, the answer lies in the claims-making activities and employers' perceptions of these claims, their self-interest, and the threat posed by counterclaims. Successful claims influence and legitimate the adoption of new policies and practices by employers. Claims to support urine testing include that there are grounds for action (drugs pose a serious problem), and that employer action is warranted because the workplace is involved. At the same time, the choice of policies is mediated by beliefs about the effectiveness of particular actions (the technology issue) and beliefs about the proper limits of employer power (the privacy issue).

For employers to gain legitimacy for controversial policy, such as urine testing, they need both to receive the support of other powerful interests, such as government agencies and political leaders, and to neutralize the predicted opposition of competing interests, such as organized labor. In short, employers do not have unlimited power to respond to social problems as they see fit. The acceptability of their responses reflects others' beliefs about the nature of the problem, the appropriate employer response, public and political interests, and the proper limits of employer power. These concerns interact to constrain employers' responses to social problems. Claims-making can affect these concerns and, when an issue is being treated as a crisis, opportunities emerge for employers to adopt types of policies that otherwise might be rejected as inappropriate.

THE SOCIAL NATURE OF EMPLOYERS' URINE-TESTING POLICIES

Whether or not urine testing deters illegal drug use remains to be seen, but clearly it is having other significant social effects. Many individuals face discrimination in hiring decisions that are based on test results, often without their knowledge. Current employees have to choose between being fired or giving up their privacy by submitting to testing, often against their will, under the close observation of another employee, with the possibility of their employer discovering nonbusiness-related drug use and/or legitimate drug use related to an existing medical condition of which the employer previously was unaware.

For thousands of employees, stigmatized conditions such as epilepsy will have to be identified to their employers in order to explain the legitimate nature of their positive result on drug urine tests. Such employees may subsequently face reduced opportunities in their employment. Statistically, millions of drug urine tests likely will yield tens of thousands of false positives.

For those who have illegal drugs in their urine and test positive, the results will be the same. Yet many of the drug users that are identified will not be drug dependent or have drug-related ill effects at work or in their social lives. That is, *their* "drug problem" starts with their identification as illegal drug users and criminals. The effects of employer identification may be disastrous for the individuals identified. What will be the effect on employee assistance programs and rehabilitation programs when they are "rehabilitating" individuals who do not use illegal drugs or whose drug use is not dependent or addictive?

Even in times of moral outrage there are limits on the state's exercise of power. The state, for example, cannot require all citizens to provide urine samples. Yet this is precisely what many employers require as a condition of employment. We find the President of the United States appealing to employers to use their power to accomplish what the state cannot: widespread urine testing of American citizens. Thus, ownership of social policy is transferred to the economic sector where constitutional safeguards do not protect workers from employer power. Social control therefore is privatized. Without the countervailing force of government legislation to restrict or prohibit it, the institutionalized vestiges of this practice will remain long after the current war on drugs fades in our memories.

20

The Size Acceptance Movement

JEFFERY SOBAL

Social problems are often tightly intertwined with organized social movements that work to define, draw attention to, and change the conditions associated with those particular problems. This chapter will examine how a social movement that opposes the stigmatization of obese individuals has played a role in the way body weight is constructed as a social problem in the United States and other postindustrial societies.

Over the course of the twentieth century an increasing emphasis on slimness has emerged and developed. The emphasis on thinness has broadened and intensified since the 1960s, with weight concerns salient and even obsessive among women. The rise in emphasis on thinness was accompanied by a parallel rejection of fatness. Obesity became a stigmatized condition, a discredited characteristic that was perceived as a moral failure of fat people. Prejudice against fatness led to labeling large people as deviant.

The cultural focus on slimness in recent decades led to the development of a system of weight industries that developed vested social, economic, and political interests in portraying high levels of body weight as a social problem. These included the weight loss, medical, pharmaceutical, fitness food, dieting, apparel, fashion and insurance industries, all of which operated in the role of moral entrepreneurs who have vested interests in promoting slimness and rejecting fatness.

This chapter is excerpted from Sobal, Jeffery (1999). "The Size Acceptance Movement and the Social Construction of Body Weight." Pp. 231–49 in *Weighty Issues: Fatness and Thinness as Social Problems,* edited by Jeffery Sobal and Donna Maurer. Hawthorne, NY: Aldine de Gruyter.

THE EMERGENCE OF THE SIZE ACCEPTANCE MOVEMENT

The size acceptance movement focuses on advocating for fat people who are stigmatized and discriminated against. Many movement participants use the term *fat* to describe themselves, and attempt to neutralize its connotations. Body size dimensions other than weight could be, but have not been, dealt with by a size acceptance movement. Thin people are typically admired and have not developed a social movement to advance their acceptance. Tall people are also socially valued, although short people are negatively evaluated, but they have not been part of the size acceptance movement.

Size acceptance did not begin to emerge as a social movement until the late 1960s and early 1970s. Before then, a few individual pioneers spoke out for size acceptance, but a broader consciousness about the problem and organization around the issue did not exist. Understanding the development and growth of the size acceptance movement requires consideration of its social location with respect to other precursor and parallel social movements and particular social conditions related to the movement.

Precursor Movements

Postwar society in the United States bred skepticism and opposition to many established social patterns and institutions. A variety of social movements developed, many challenging inequalities in the way particular segments of society were treated. Civil rights, women's rights, age rights, gay rights, and other movements emerged, mobilized resources, and changed social identities. Social movements of the 1960s and 1970s captured the attention and imagination of the public, and led to a climate of protest that generated a variety of oppositional movements that dealt with other causes, such as the antiwar, antinuclear, and antipollution movements.

The size acceptance movement was a product of race, gender, age, sexuality, and other precursor movements that blazed the trail, established methods for creating social change, and served as a training ground for some size activists. However, few fat feminists have come from or been tied to the mainstream women's movement and often feel alienated by the lack of recognition and attention to size acceptance issues.

Nondieting as an Allied Movement

In addition to larger precursor movements, an alliance with another movement catalyzed attention and resources for body weight. What was widely called the nondiet movement became a close ally of size acceptance, even though the two movements draw from different populations of leaders and participants. The nondiet movement was a backlash against dieting and a reaction to public concerns about thinness and eating disorders, which fit well with size acceptance ideas, although people associated with nondieting may not actually endorse acceptance of very large people.

By the 1980s there were increasing attacks on the emphasis on thinness and dieting. The orientations of these challenges ranged from feminist to sociological. Dieting to lose weight had become almost obligatory among many women, but was plagued by a terrible lack of reported success in achieving and maintaining weight loss. Backlash against stringent thinness standards, compulsive aspects of dieting, low weight loss success rates, and fraudulent and even harmful side effects of some diets fueled the nondiet movement. The nondiet movement is partially a reaction to overmedicalization of eating and weight.

Social Conditions

Demographic changes that resulted from the aging of the baby boom cohort contributed to conditions that facilitated the earlier culture of thinness and later reactions of size acceptance. During the 1960s an accelerating emphasis on thinness was based in the growing focus on the youth culture of the baby boom, with thin adolescents adopted as ideals for body shape. Mass media and mass marketing in the fashion industry blossomed to emphasize thinness during this period. The general aging of the population as the baby boom matured and the rise in fatness in the United States in the 1980s moved many away from the earlier youth culture and its focus on appearance.

THE STRUCTURE AND PROCESSES OF THE SIZE ACCEPTANCE MOVEMENT

Size acceptance ideas developed in the United States in the late 1960s as reactions to pervasive stigmatization and discrimination against fat people. The movement grew and developed a structure that included a loose collective of organizations, groups, and individuals connected through interpersonal relationships and more formal communications channels such as publications, and, more recently, the Internet. The underlying ideology of the size acceptance movement focused on exposing, combating, and preventing fatism, weightism, and sizism; promoting size diversity and tolerance; and developing a size-accepting, size-neutral, and size-friendly society. Size acceptance became a new conceptual model that was used in the broader construction of body weight, opposing the moral and medical models that dominated discourse about fatness and thinness. The major strategies of the size acceptance movement were to use political changes to collectively challenge mainstream beliefs and practices and, at the same time, create cultural change in ideas about weight in their emphasis on fat pride, fat liberation, and fat power.

Like most social movements, several organizations have played a crucial role in advancing the size acceptance movement. The National Association to Advance Fat Acceptance (NAAFA) was founded in 1969. The Association for the Health Enrichment of Large Persons (AHELP) held its first conference in 1991 as an organization for health professionals, including psychologists, dieticians/nutritionists, nurses, exercise professionals, social workers, educators and researchers tied more to the nondieting movement than the size acceptance movement. Many other allied groups have existed in the size acceptance network, including diverse small activist groups (Fat Underground, Fat Liberation Front, Council on Size and Weight Discrimination) and other types of groups (Abundia, Ample Opportunity, Body Image Task Force, Largesse). The structure of the size acceptance movement has been and continues to be highly diffuse. NAAFA, the largest organization, has forty local chapters, which all have considerable autonomy.

The number of people involved in the size acceptance movement is relatively small. NAAFA is the largest and only national organization, claiming approximately five thousand members. This is only a tiny fraction of the estimated third of the U.S. adult population defined by health researchers as overweight. Size activists who form the size acceptance movement's leadership, act as crusaders, and serve as experts probably number only in the hundreds.

The size acceptance movement includes two major components: (1) political activism that attempts to reform the values and practices of society about body weight, and (2) social support that provides a refuge for large people from the intolerance of a thin society through assistance and companionship.

Political Activism

The size acceptance movement organizes and engages in a variety of political activities to promote its causes. Several types of protest events are employed, including rallies (the Million Pound March was held in 1998), boycotts (of Coca-Cola, Southwest Airlines, and other companies), and other forms of civil disobedience like protests and picketing. Other strategic tactics include activism to gain attention to size issues by designating events (International No-Diet Day, Size Acceptance Month), support groups, letter writing, educational services, and programs.

An important component of the size acceptance movement is producing materials to communicate its concerns and ideas. These include popular books describing the problems of being large and promoting size acceptance, self-help books offering practical and instrumental support for large people, and glossy magazines for large people. Formal size acceptance organizations and informal groups also distribute newsletters. Numerous computerized Web sites, listservers, and other electronic services function to promote the movement and facilitate communication among those who are involved but scattered across various locations.

Social Support

As an organized social movement, size acceptance offers several forms of social support to its participants. Emotional social support is an important resource. In the broader society thinness is the reigning value, but the size acceptance movement offers its large-sized participants who may weigh 300, 400, 500 or more pounds a refuge from a world organized for thinner people. By offering large people acceptance and positive evaluation, the movement can become a functional "family" for individuals oppressed because of their size.

Another function of the size acceptance movement is to provide instrumental social support for its members. The women's fashion industry has largely emphasized extreme slimness and is seen by many in the movement as a barrier or even an opponent to size acceptance. Obtaining clothing is a problematic experience for large people, particularly for women. However, a segment of the fashion world is recently beginning to cater to larger women, and members of the size acceptance movement offer important marketing opportunities.

SIZE ACCEPTANCE AND THE SOCIAL CONSTRUCTION
OF BODY WEIGHT

The size acceptance movement has struggled to gain acknowledgment in the body weight arena, and appears to have gained a place on the agenda. In the weight arena, size activists and size acceptance organizations have broken into the circle of sources that the news media seek out. This may not have led to large changes in the way most of the general population deals with weight, but has influenced some individuals and groups. Most significantly, size acceptance has gained sufficient attention to offer a political counterpoint to the largely medical and moral discussion of body weight.

The impacts of size acceptance on the public construction of body weight reflect the size and structure of the movement, with the relatively small and diffuse organizations, groups, and individuals influencing a variety of specific and local decisions, but not leading to sweeping social changes. The power of the movement tends to be cultural, rather than economic and political, with few financial or governmental resources to draw upon. While there are powerful moral entrepreneurs that profit from encouraging thinness, such as pharmaceutical companies, there is less overt profit to be made in promoting size acceptance. That has led to difficulty in producing allies with financial and political power.

VI
Social Problems and Everyday Life

Introduction to Section VI

Constructionist perspectives focus on the process whereby claims-makers seek to persuade audience members that an intolerable condition exists that must be changed. Regardless of all the claims-competitions, successful claims can change the world in two ways.

First, successful claims can change the characteristics of the objective world around us. Compared with the fairly recent past, we now live in a world that is more accessible to people in wheelchairs, and this is a consequence of successful claims about the needs of people with disabilities. We also live in a world where an increasing number of companies demand that potential employees have their urine tested for drug use, and this is the consequence of successful claims about the evil of illegal drugs. Because of concern about terrorism, flying on airplanes has become far more time-consuming than in the recent past, and so on.

Second, successful claims can change *cultural climates*: The ways we think about our world, our selves, and others around us. In the not so distant past, for example, cigarette smoking was generally evaluated as an acceptable behavior, help-wanted ads in newspapers were categorized as "Help Wanted," "Help Wanted, Colored," and "Help Wanted, Women." Also in the not so distant past, men who failed to be the sole economic support of their families were criticized, and cohabitation outside marriage was evaluated as sinful. Changes in how we evaluate both behaviors and people change as a consequence of successful social problems claims-making.

Our cultural obsession with eating "low-fat food" is a case in point. According to S. Bryn Austin, scientists and physicians concerned with issues of public health worked with food producers to stage massive marketing campaigns in "Constructing the Need for 'Low-Fat' Food." We can note cynically that this has been very good for the companies that produce "low-fat food" because this public health campaign created a public demand for this food, so companies that manufacture it have benefited financially. Yet it really doesn't matter how the importance of eating low-fat food became a cultural theme. What matters is that many Americans now believe that eating low-fat food is critical to health and well-being. Successful claims-making in this instance changed our cultural climate by adding a new cultural theme: The importance of eating low-fat food.

We also can examine how pregnancy has been turned into a social problem. To be more precise, according to Carol Brooks Gardener, magazines for pregnant women construct "Pregnant Women as a Social Problem." These claims warn women that any misstep during pregnancy—engaging in the wrong activity, eating the wrong food—will damage their babies. Women now are expected to produce "perfect" children and if they do not, their behaviors during pregnancy will be blamed. Such claims linking the conduct of pregnant women with social problems, such as children who don't learn quickly enough or who are disruptive or delinquent, certainly can influence the experience of pregnancy: Pregnant women who don't follow experts' advice face social condemnation from others.

Successful social problems claims can change our daily lives by encouraging us to think about particular behaviors—eating low-fat food, the conduct of pregnant women—in different ways. Successful social problems claims also can change the ways we evaluate our selves and those around us. Indeed, quite a bit of claims-making now is associated with what are called "new social movements" or "identity movements." These social movements—on behalf of socially discredited people such as minorities, homosexuals, women—focus on changing public perceptions of *types of people*. In comparison to social movements in previous historical eras that focused on changing public policy, social activists in identity movements seek to change the cultural climate by increasing the social regard accorded to types of people.

For example, in "Constructing Sexually Marginalized Catholics," Donileen R. Loseke and James Cavendish examine the claims made by a social change group called Dignity. This group seeks to construct a new image of identity; the "homosexual Catholic," as a person who should be highly evaluated by others, who should have a high evaluation of the self (high self-esteem), and who should be accorded full membership in the Catholic Church in particular and the social order in general. This group offers counterclaims to traditional evaluations of gays and lesbians as outsiders, as people who should not be respected because they defied the cultural theme promoting the goodness of heterosexuality. To counter these negative evaluations, this social change group constructs the homosexual Catholic as a good family member (although their families do not resemble heterosexual families), a good citizen, and a good and faithful believer in Catholicism. If individual homosexual Catholics evaluate themselves in this way, their self-evaluations will improve. If others around these people evaluate them in this way, discrimination and prejudice will decrease. This is social change through constructing new *collective identities*, images of types of people.

Finally, successful social problems claims can change the ways we evaluate our own troubles and the troubles of those around us. In American society, many people feel uneasy about our lives and our futures; there often is uncertainty about what is really important in life and what is not. How do we make sense of these unsettling emotions that we can experience in our daily lives? People in the past often turned to religion, and so, too, do many Americans in the present. According to Kathleen S. Lowney, one of the currently most popular ways to make sense of personal trouble is to evaluate that trouble as "codependency," and to seek trouble resolution through "recovery." She examines "The Beliefs of Recovery Religion" and argues that it emphasizes the cultural theme of individualism that promotes putting the self first above all others. Within this perspective, promoted by countless self-help groups to resolve the problems of "codependency," other people, especially families, hinder the development of the self. "Recovery" is a religion because, like other religions, recovery is a set of beliefs about the world that can be deeply held by adherents. The cultural belief in the power of "recovery" is the consequence of successful social problems claims-making. It has changed the ways many people make sense of their selves and their troubles.

When social problems work is successful, claims can change the world around us, they can change the ways we evaluate ourselves and others, as well as the ways we make sense of our personal troubles. This is why competitions among claims-makers can be so heated: Successful claims can change the world. And, when they do that, it matters little that rarely—if ever—do all Americans agree that the change is beneficial. It does not matter, for example, if an individual believes that cigarette smoking should be an individual choice; smoking now is prohibited in many places, and people who smoke cigarettes can be openly criticized by strangers. The cultural climate has changed. Or, an individual who objects to being searched before entering a plane has only a choice of not being allowed on that plane. Social policy has changed.

One of the lessons in examining social problems as constructions is that the claims-making process always is characterized by claims-competitions, claims-makers who direct public policy at times are the most politically connected rather than those with the claims that are most beneficial for the public good. Yet successful claims can change the characteristics of the world around us, they can change how we make sense of that world, they can change how we think about our selves.

21

Constructing the Need for "Low-Fat" Food

S. BRYN AUSTIN

As far as I can tell, the commercial side of health is both legitimate and socially beneficial. After all, medical care has always been a business and a profitable one at that. So let's not get upset that money is being made in the health biz. Climb aboard. (Levin 1987:60)

Some may consider these words from a Yale professor of public health, Lowell Levin, to be a voice of pragmatism: Profit-making is a given in our capitalist society, so public health professionals should not waste efforts resisting and instead should come along for the ride. While this linkage between health and business may appear normative, by what standard have we established its social or health benefits?

My aim is to delineate the structure of the industry-health promotion linkage and its consequences today for both commercial profits and societal patterns of health risk. The end result of this pairing, I will argue, has been far better for the diet industry's profit than for the public's health.

LIGHT FOOD AND NUTRITION

Until the late 1960s, food manufacturers maintained a small niche market for dietetic foods. At that time, a dietary counterculture garnered a small

This chapter is excerpted from Austin, S. Bryn (1999). "Commodity Knowledge in Consumer Culture: The Role of Nutritional Health Promotion in the Making of the Diet Industry." Pp. 159–82 in *Weighty Issues: Fatness and Thinness as Social Problems*, edited by Jeffery Sobal and Donna Maurer. Hawthorne, NY: Aldine de Gruyter.

but enthusiastic following and the dietary counterculture's association of "light" foods with health and holistic living gave manufacturers the foothold they needed to reposition diet foods and broaden their appeal by emphasizing their relationship to health. In the process, however, the dietary counterculture's meaning of "light" was stripped of its more subversive sentiments: The movement previously had been distinguished by its opposition to processed foods and food additives and its promotion of chemical-free (so-called organic) foods.

The concept of "light" food was first made popular with a mass audience with the 1975 introduction of the low-calorie beer Miller Lite. The term then took on a broader definition by the early 1980s to include any processed foods that had less of an ingredient that was perceived as negative.

By recasting the formerly unsavory image of dietetic products, manufacturers were able to increase profits appreciably, with new lines of light foods, charging more for these specialized "health" foods and expanding their market—originally targeting primarily middle-class, educated, white consumers, especially women. But more importantly, by offering less in the way of calories and fat, manufacturers were able to solve a unique biological dilemma facing the food industry: The typical adult can eat no more than 1,400 to 1,500 pounds of food per year. By circumventing biological constraints, light products facilitated increased consumption, particularly of highly profitable snack foods.

From the late 1960s through the 1970s, diet products steadily proliferated, and grocers began to mainstream the low-calorie foods that for decades had been cordoned off in special dietetics sections. The industry boomed in the 1980s. In that decade, the diet soda market grew at a 20 percent annual rate, and G. D. Searle and Company earned $585 million in 1984 from its newly approved artificial sweetener aspartame. Nonprescription weight control drug sales exceeded a 20 percent annual growth rate in the same decade, after the FDA approved phenylpropanolamine as an appetite suppressant. The first diet fast food chain, D'lites, opened in 1981. Light foods made up more than 40 percent of the $10 billion market in snack foods in 1982. Through the 1980s, frozen low-calorie dinners were the fastest growing segment of the food industry.

PUBLIC HEALTH AND SOCIAL MARKETING

This boom period for the industry selling diet products occurred at a time when public health campaigns focused increasing attention on diet and obesity and widened the reach of promotional messages through the mass media. The volume of publications from the federal government and major health organizations offering nutritional recommendations has ballooned since the 1960s. In 1969, for example, the National Academy of Sciences warned that recommended levels of daily calorie intake be lowered by between 100 and 300 calories, and in 1974 the American Heart Association raised the pitch of its antidietary cholesterol crusade. In 1977, the Senate's Select Committee on Nutrition and Human Needs advised that Americans should cut fat intake by 10 percent or more.

In brief, public health campaigns took on the task of consumer education. Since the late 1960s, *social marketing*—an approach to education that borrows extensively from commercial marketing techniques—has been enthusiastically adopted in the field of public health. Following commercial marketers, government agencies and nonprofit organizations have sought to adapt industry techniques to the "sale" of social and health issues.

Social marketers promote a *lifestyle model* of health behavior. This lifestyle model assumes that personal habits can be changed and that people can choose to change their habits. By the late 1970s, the lifestyle model had become the leading framework in health promotion and continued to hold this position through the 1980s and 1990s, especially in nutritional health promotion. For example, Louis Sullivan, secretary of the U.S. Department of Health and Human Services under President George H. W. Bush, lauded the kickoff of the federal health promotion crusade, Healthy People 2000, from a decidedly lifestyle model perspective when he said "We need a nationwide priority placed on personal responsibility and choices," "[to] enhance our individual independence. . . . We need a clear, serious, and constant acceptance of personal responsibility."

A special issue of the *Journal of Nutrition Education* in 1995 contained a review of national and regional nutritional health promotion programs that had been launched in the United States over the past two decades in response to the evolving nutritional guidelines. Many of the programs reviewed were social marketing based and a number involved supermarket and vending machine point-of-purchase campaigns. The authors describe health promotion campaigns that identify specific brands and are located in grocery stories and restaurants as "highly effective." A number of other studies find increased product sales following nutrition education interventions. I examine the relationship between public health campaigns and the food industry in relation to nutritional guidelines for "low fat."

THE AGE OF LOW-FAT

The contempt for dietary fat was—and still is—consistently endorsed by government agencies. In 1980, Americans saw the first edition of *Dietary*

Guidelines, issued jointly from the U.S. Department of Health and Human Services and the U.S. Department of Agriculture, which instructed people to avoid dietary fat, especially saturated fat and cholesterol. The latest edition of *Dietary Guidelines*, published in 1995, continues to promote the recommendations of 30 percent of calories from fat and 10 percent of calories from saturated fat. Nonetheless, one intractable problem remains: The scientific evidence is far from clear about what health risks are associated with dietary fat and exactly which of the many types of fat can be blamed.

The 30 percent calories from fat and 10 percent from saturated fat guidelines are largely arbitrary, and there is very little medical significance to the popularized cutoffs. The cutoffs were chosen chiefly because they were modestly below the nation's estimated mean dietary intake and, therefore, considered reasonable goals for change. They are not representative of any type of threshold above which the risk of disease or obesity increases appreciably. While the absence of a threshold does not in principle negate the merit of recommending safe limits for risk exposures, the insistence on specific values—such as the 30 and 10 percent limits—evokes the assumed authority of scientific precision in a situation where there is none.

A more important issue is that the sizable health risks associated with dietary fat inferred from animal and ecological studies have not been borne out in research. After animal studies had found evidence of an association between tumor growth and fat intake, some researchers took center stage in the scientific community by making international comparisons of human cancer rates and per capita fat consumption and claiming a causal relationship. These studies, based on what is referred to as ecological analyses, have been widely challenged on methodological grounds. More analytically rigorous studies have not corroborated the assertions of a clear increased risk of breast, colon, prostate, or other cancers posed by dietary fat.

For obesity research, the story unfolded similarly. Following up on some plausible hypotheses generated from metabolic and animal studies, international comparisons were made using ecological data on per capita fat consumption and prevalence of obesity. When nonindustrialized nations were compared with industrialized nations, where both dietary fat intake and obesity prevalence tend to be higher, researchers inferred a causal relationship from what is clearly only associational data. Again, these conclusions have been critiqued for their serious methodological weaknesses. Reviews of decades of epidemiological and experimental studies have found results to be inconsistent at best, with no indication that fat consumption is a cause of the increasing prevalence of obesity in the United States.

Results from studies on coronary heart disease and dietary fat are more suggestive of a relationship, though again the evidence is not clear cut. Studies through the 1980s were largely conflicting, and studies from the

1990s have found only mild or no association between total dietary fat or saturated fat intake and coronary heart disease.

The dilemma of the dearth of evidence was not a secret to food processors. In a 1989 issue of *Prepared Foods*, a writer acknowledged that the scientific evidence on the relationship between dietary fat and illness was far from conclusive. Nor was it unknown to nutritional researchers. A 1980 National Academy of Sciences publication on dietary guidelines for the nation asserted that, based on the scientific evidence of the day, there was no need for healthy people to lower their intake of cholesterol or fat. By 1989 the National Academy of Sciences had changed its recommendations to be more in line with the dominant public health opinion on dietary fat, but it nevertheless acknowledged that the supporting evidence was less than conclusive.

PROJECT LEAN AND HEALTHY CHOICE: PUBLIC HEALTH AND THE FOOD INDUSTRY

After a decade of mounting animosity toward dietary fat, the crescendo culminated in 1989 with the arrival of an unprecedented and ambitious public health social marketing campaign and an unexpectedly profitable line of low-fat frozen dinners. In early 1989, Project LEAN (Low-Fat Eating for America Now), a national nutrition education campaign initiated by the Henry J. Kaiser Family Foundation, kicked off its first major media drive. Also, in January of that year, ConAgra Inc., a food manufacturer based in Omaha, Nebraska, launched its Healthy Choice brand of low-fat and low-cholesterol frozen dinners and entrees. The timing of the Project LEAN nutritional program could not have been more fortuitous for ConAgra.

Project LEAN

"The latest effort to get Americans to cut down on their biggest edible vice" is how one *Washington Post* reporter described Project LEAN, a national social marketing initiative dedicated to the mission of persuading Americans to cut dietary fat intake from a national average of 37 percent to 30 percent of daily calories by 1998. The term edible *vice*—with connotations of a moral crusade more than an informed health campaign—seems appropriate given the lack of strong evidence on the risk of disease or obesity posed by dietary fat or the health benefits of dietary fat reduction.

With a $3.5 million grant from the Kaiser Foundation, Project LEAN was up and running in the fall of 1988 with plans for a major national media drive beginning in early 1989. The project acronym, LEAN, no doubt was meant to tap into the connection in most people's minds by that time between lean food and lean bodies. Through public service advertising, print and broadcast press publicity, and point-of-purchase programs in stores, restaurants, and cafeterias, the national nutrition education campaign targeted consumers, government, and the food industry. Ten regional projects also were set up to intensify efforts in some areas. Local programs worked closely with grocery chains such as Sloan's Supermarkets in New York and Safeway in California.

From its inception, Project LEAN was established as a partnership between public health and the food industry—part of its stated mission was to increase availability of and consumer demand for low-fat products. In addition to the grant from Kaiser, Project LEAN received nearly $100,000 in the first three years from corporate sponsors, including funds from food giants Procter and Gamble, Kraft, General Foods, and Campbell Soup Company. The project's advisory board, called Partners for Better Health, was a coalition of thirty-four public agencies and private associations and industry groups. The members included the American Cancer Society, U.S. Department of Agriculture, American Public Health Association, American Dietetic Association, Centers for Disease Control, and American Heart Association, alongside industry groups such as the Food Marketing Institute, National Fisheries Institute, National Food Processors Association, and National Turkey Federation. The Food Professionals Working Group, made up of forty chefs, nutritionists, and journalists, advised the project on low-fat recipes.

Although the project began with a policy to not allow product endorsements, the Project LEAN instructional manual for health educators was paid for by a grant from Nestlé's Stouffer's Lean Cuisine division and comes with a cover letter cosigned by representatives from the American Dietetic Association and Stouffer's. The project's educational video kit, "Lean 'n Easy: Preparing Meat With Less Fat and More Taste," was coproduced with the National Cattlemen's Beef Association.

Healthy Choice

ConAgra chairman and CEO Charles Harper astutely predicted in the late 1980s that low fat foods would be a lasting trend, and in January 1989 launched a new brand of frozen meals. The company announced that any products under the Healthy Choice label would be low in calories, cholesterol, and sodium, and, plainly linking the new product profile to the de rigor health promotion language, the products would contain no more than 30 percent of calories from fat or 10 percent from saturated fat.

Within months, Healthy Choice had taken nearly a quarter of the $700 million market in frozen dinners, earning an estimated $150 million in sales in the first year. Earnings more than doubled in 1990, making Healthy Choice the top-selling brand. Healthy Choice became one of the most successful upstart food brands in recent decades. For the fiscal year beginning June 1992, ConAgra slated $200 million to promote its expanding Healthy Choice brand. Healthy Choice entrée and dinner sales alone were $341 million in the year ending April 1992. Within four years of its launch date, Healthy Choice had taken a 40 percent share of the market in frozen dinners and entrees.

ConAgra's decision to parrot the much publicized public health nutrition goals—no more than 30 percent of daily calories from fat and 10 percent from saturated fat—clearly paid off for the corporation. A new line of Healthy Choice entrees was introduced just weeks after a February 1990 report from the National Cholesterol Education Program (endorsed by Project LEAN), reiterating the recommendation that all Americans reduce dietary fat and cholesterol.

The Project LEAN and Healthy Choice social marketing campaigns were wildly successful. The Food Marketing Institute's annual surveys of household shoppers documented an upward trend in consumer concerns with dietary fat throughout the 1980s. In 1983, 9 percent of consumers reported concern about dietary fat, and in 1988, the number rose to 27 percent; by 1990 fully 42 percent of those surveyed reported dietary fat as a major concern. In turn, American's concern with fat fostered by Project LEAN translated into consumer demand for products. A series of surveys conducted for the Calorie Control Council, a food industry group, found that 45 percent of adults in 1986 consumed low-calorie, reduced-fat, and other light food products. By 1993 the percentage had almost doubled, rising to 81 percent. And within three more years, consumption of these products by adults was virtually universal, rising to 92 percent—a figure representing 179 million Americans. The food industry offered these products to consumers: In 1989, 626 reduced-fat foods were launched—an increase of 127 percent over 1988, and 962 calorie-reduced products were introduced—more than double those of the previous year. And this was very good for the food industry: Low-fat processed food sales for the industry as a whole reached $29 billion in 1990 and rose to $32 billion in 1991. By the mid-1990s, the market in light food products had expanded to $35.8 billion and accounted for more than half of the so-called health foods sector.

CONCLUSION

In open partnership with the food industry, nutritional health promotion has privileged a conception of health that is compatible with the needs of the marketplace and educated modern consumers about how to seek commodity solutions to real and anticipated health problems. The stalking of dietary fat in public health promotion has been pursued with a zeal well beyond that justified by the field's own scientific research. This unprecedented consolidation of "expert" opinion has been buttressed, I maintain, by the logic of the marketplace when a logic of scientific evidence alone would not have proven sufficient.

The uncritical promotion of a dietary fat reduction message was accompanied by a comparative neglect of fruits and vegetables. In contrast to the lack of evidence about the importance of dietary fat, evidence fairly consistently has shown that a diet high in whole fruits and vegetables is inversely associated with cancers of the colon, lung, stomach, and other sites and coronary heart disease. Promotion of the consumption of fruits and vegetables, however, has not been emphasized in public health campaigns until relatively recently. Not coincidentally, raw fruits and vegetables in most cases do not present a profit potential for producers anywhere near that of processed foods. Importantly, while national nutrition surveys have documented a downward trend in total fat and saturated fat consumption by Americans in recent decades, there has been no evidence of an accompanying increase in the consumption of fruits and vegetables.

A small but vocal minority in public health has complained about the preeminence of the lifestyle model and social marketing in health promotion efforts. Critics have pointed out the tendency to decontextualize health, ignoring significant social and economic forces shaping patterns of risk, and to focus instead on individual responsibility. This case of "low fat" might serve as an object lesson regarding the consequences of the presumption of commodity logic over alternative ways of conceiving illness and health.

REFERENCE

Levin, L. S. 1987. "Every Silver Lining Has a Cloud: The Limits of Health Promotion." *Social Policy* 18 (1):57–60.

22

Pregnant Women as a Social Problem

CAROL BROOKS GARDNER

Although not an exclusively modern concern, fetal harm, resulting in the presumed warping of a child to be born, is a concern with modern dimensions that have been reflected in fiction and film. It did not take the scientifically engineered horrors of the *It's Alive* movie series or the morally hybrid birth of *Rosemary's Baby* to worry prospective parents, although fiction and film often depict melodramatic situations where the wrongs of parents or the parents' generation have been visited on hapless embryos and often on the societies into which those embryos have been born. In this generally circular trajectory, parents or "society" irresponsibly create or injure a fetus that, when born, returns the harm—a retribution that gives parents, as well as others, incentive for closely toeing the line.

PREGNANCY, PERCEIVED DEFECTS, AND HISTORY

For centuries, the physical state and the social situation of pregnancy have been used to explain physical and mental traits considered undesirable in children. In past centuries, children with disabilities were considered reliable evidence of divine pleasure or displeasure. Modernism shifted

This chapter is excerpted from Gardner, Carol Brooks (1994). "Little Strangers: Pregnancy Conduct and the Twentieth-Century Rhetoric of Endangerment." Pp. 69–92 in *Troubling Children: Studies of Children and Social Problems*, edited by Joel Best. Hawthorne, NY: Aldine de Gruyter.

responsibility from gods to parents. Much popular (even at times medical) advice literature is reminiscent of advice literature of the previous century, which advised progressive nineteenth-century Americans to understand that children are made by their parents, not sent from heaven. Parents, especially mothers, should devote themselves to preparing for children and to preparing children who are themselves capable of preparing for the future.

The traits that erring mothers are now believed to visit on the malleable fetus include flaws of temperament, mental aptitudes and gifts, as well as minor physical characteristics, such as birthmarks, minor allergies, an unhealthy constitution, and personal unattractiveness. Taken together, these qualities are the opposite signifying the many requirements that the "perfect" child is now expected to have, the need for parental efforts to imbue these qualities, and the mother's ultimate responsibility for effecting them.

I examined all issues of *American Baby* from 1983–93. *American Baby* is a mass-circulation magazine geared toward middle-class women that reaches about 1,300,000 readers with each monthly issue. Of course, it is impossible to know if these articles stimulate feelings or behavior in their readers, or, indeed, if the particular articles I have cited have ever been read at all. Yet, there are good reasons for using these sources. Specialized magazines such as *American Baby* are among the few venues for the collected and organized expression of beliefs and advice about pregnancy, both popular and scientific.

A FETUS-CENTERED FETAL ENDANGERMENT RHETORIC

Legitimate Activity and Pregnancy

Nineteenth- and early twentieth-century writing on activities during pregnancy amounted to counseling a woman to remain quiet and at home. Nowadays, this is rarely advised explicitly. Yet activities, even those inside the home, and the pregnant woman still seem to exist in an uncomfortable relationship. Although most pregnant women work outside the home as well as within it, pregnant women are advised simultaneously to avoid any activities that might strain the fetus and to engage in activities that are mundane or boring or blot out thought.

Yet even women ordered by doctors to complete bed rest (as few are these days) are told to maintain their activity level. They should, for example, dedicate themselves to keeping "your eyes on the prize" by thinking positively, moving cheerfully from room to room to brighten their spirits, phone catalogue-shopping, and decorating their "space" with attractive objects "on the same level as your head on a pillow." If they work outside the home, perhaps a loaner fax or modem can be arranged. In short, even if a woman is confined to bed for nine months, she is still to fulfill role requirements, whether as future mother, attractive wife, current house-keeper, or worker at an outside job.

Ingestion as Conscious Activity

Articles from 1983–93 identify two principal causes of harm to a fetus: imprudent exertion, such as too-ambitious exercise, activity at work, or even sexual intercourse; and—by far most common—unwise ingestion of food, drink, or other substances. Ingestion has long had a special moral valence for women, pregnant or not.

It is somewhat unusual to think of food ingestion as a conscious activity, given that it is one needed to sustain life and thus unavoidable. During pregnancy, however, what usually can be accomplished without great thought is to be constantly on a woman's mind: Some advice books are little more than lists of foods and drinks, vitamin supplements, and over-the-counter and prescription drugs. Women are to compare ingestibles they choose with these lists. The catalogue of ingestibles women are to approach with prudence is impressive. Together, this catalogue suggests that were a woman to try and conscientiously take every instance of potential harm into account while pregnant, she would need to consider the impact of virtually every thought and deed and certainly every bite of food and sip of drink.

As a woman reads popular sources, she discovers that basically no ingestible is reliably safe, so that even eating is difficult to perform without tremendous thought. At the same time, she has a wealth of detail about common substances to learn and relearn. What seems innocuous for non-pregnant women becomes a possible killer of the fetus. Scientific studies published in 1985, which have only now come under question, suggested that consuming several sodas a day made a fetus at risk for growth retardation, microcephaly, or death by miscarriage. According to another article, even "light drinking" (which, is defined here as four alcoholic drinks per month) can cause a fetus to become a child "deficient in pre-academic, as well as math and reading skills . . . [and] showing attention and behavioral problems." By educating herself about ingestibles and faithfully putting what she learns into practice when pregnant, it seems that a mother-to-be can affect a child's educability.

Suspicion of the familiar and the need for re-education about food are hallmarks of pregnancy advice that might disorient or perplex a pregnant woman. Another is that advice tells women that old habits, patterns, and ingestibles must be rigorously examined anew: a woman who believes she has heretofore understood calcium requirements may simply be told that she must now think of "providing for baby" in a way that will enrich her or his entire life, too.

Getting To Know the Hidden: Information Gathering about the Fetus

One legitimate activity for the pregnant woman is a conscientious information gathering, a sort of first step in becoming acquainted with the child presumed to be on the way. At the most basic level, women are encouraged to amass all evidence of and about the physical fetus that they can: they are, for example, to familiarize themselves with the fetus's schedule of developmental milestones (much as they will be urged to do for their infants and children) and observe quickening, movement and kicking schedules, turning, and so on. Taking advantage of quite recent technology, women are advised to keep hard copies or videotapes of amniocentesis readings, X rays, and sonograms. A wide variety of "pregnancy diaries" are available, many advertised in *American Baby*. These often encourage a woman to write her daily thoughts and feelings concerning the fetus that she imagines within her, as well as measurable changes of her weight—a reflection of the fetus's growth—and other physical changes.

Mental and Emotional Harness: Against Worry, in Favor of Acceptance

Recommendations about maintaining the proper attitude and eschewing anxiety occur again and again. It seems to me that much of the other advice about activities is complexly related to the pregnant woman's *mental* and *emotional self-management*. Thus, writers have long presumed that the anticipated experience of pain, which we still understand childbirth to include, will color preparation for that experience. Advice in the United States about pregnancy has long contained a rock-solid conviction that women's emotions during pregnancy can cause anything from death of a fetus to the birth of an "anxious" child, and this assumption continues. We now charge pregnant women with creating harmed fetuses, then flawed children, because of mental or emotional weakness while pregnant.

During pregnancy, women are often told to avoid "thinking too much," "being anxious," "worrying," or "introspecting" for a variety of reasons. Today, the litany is to advise a woman to shun thought that will lead to worry, even though this seems a difficult thing to do given the extent of the prescriptions and proscriptions we have for pregnant women. Advice writers link thought with worry and worry with lack of acceptance of the pregnancy itself. Any chink in a pregnant woman's devotion to the fetus is deeply suspect, because maternal effects could have a poor effect on the child once born.

Legitimate Concern with Appearance: The Pregnant Appearance and Its Connotations

Yet another legitimate activity is maintaining one's appearance while pregnant. Some of this appearance maintenance is said to be for a woman's husband but much of the advice on appearance maintenance is also written with attention to the woman's emotional health: A fat or sloppy pregnant woman, these articles say, is depressed or anxious, a resistant pregnant woman. Rather than attending to the root cause of depression or anxiety, advisors recommend diets, exercise, and slimming clothing.

Our standards for appearance for pregnant women compare them to an ideal of never and nonpregnant women. The greatest compliment a woman can receive while pregnant is that she looks just like her prepregnant self, albeit with a small embryonic bolus traveling somewhere in front. Similarly, we do not cherish—indeed, we have créated plastic surgery to outwit—the physical evidence that a woman has been pregnant. A woman is advised to keep to an ideal timetable: For example, after delivery she should return to her prepregnant appearance as quickly and precisely as possible, preferably without drooping breasts, scarred abdomen, stretch marks, or weight change.

Students of Pregnancy

Another legitimate activity is to become a student of pregnancy. A woman may be advised to study many topics while pregnant, such as the stages of pregnancy and labor options. Of immediate concern to a woman may be preparation for delivering a baby. Selecting a pediatrician, through an extensive series of visits to many different doctors if need be, and learning about labor are two topics the pregnant woman should study . Even a bed-resting woman can manage these, through phone calls to physicians or hiring a private tutor or watching videos to learn about labor. Before a baby arrives, a mother may be advised to educate herself about the first few months of her child's life, the local school system, and her own family history, or to revamp her home with an eye to the safety of the child who will live there.

Of course, all these activities bespeak a woman's concern for the health of the future child she envisions. Sometimes, however, advice seems to encourage over-preparation. A woman may be told, for example, that she should envision the child's friendships with other neighborhood children. To best prepare her fetus to have friends and herself to be friendly with the mothers of other children, she should, while pregnant, take neighborhood walks, preparing herself to smile in a friendly manner and introduce herself (and, presumably, allude in some way to her fetus as well). Such measures will pay off later.

DEVELOPING THE RHETORIC OF FETAL ENDANGERMENT

Even when activities are not specifically linked with fetal endangerment, there are many suggestions and requirements for the modification of a woman's activities, modifications that might, in fact, occupy much of a woman's pregnancy and become to seem as necessary for the good of the fetus. Pregnancy conduct advice is of a piece, and cautions about fetal endangerment exist in the fuller context of advice about looking good, getting organized, and getting to know one's fetus by conscientious information gathering. In fact, although modern pregnancy conduct advice with regard to fetal health pertains most to ingestion, there is some aspect of every other activity advised that reflects on fetal health, too.

Furthermore, pregnancy advice claims-makers invoke an expanded retrospective timeline, sometimes cautioning prospective mothers to monitor their behavior for years in advance of actually becoming pregnant, as when they speak of slimming down or setting aside poor eating habits in service of becoming pregnant—and fetus-ready. Thus, nonpregnant women are also subject to measures to ensure fetal health. For women, an expanded timeline would result, if put into practice, in pregnancy careers reaching far beyond the actual nine months of gestation. Indeed, some writers suggest periods of one, two, or even three years of "preparation" for pregnancy: gynecological assessments, fertility workups, weight loss when needed, an exercise program that will increase a mother's chances of passing through pregnancy and childbirth easily, and attainment of job status that will facilitate a stress-free pregnancy or a pregnancy with job benefits. Pregnancy thereby becomes a long-range and deeply involving process, one that speaks at every turn and twist of the pregnant woman's devotion to her fetus and of the fetus itself as a profoundly social being toward whom one must behave responsibly. It is significant, however, that prospective fathers have not been similarly targeted. Ignoring men in pregnancy advice literature diminishes their roles in the lives of their born children, too.

RHETORICS OF ENDANGERMENT AND
THE PRICE OF DISAGREEMENT

The limits of the contemporary rhetoric of fetal endangerment are significant. Every rhetoric names responsible parties, and the responsible party overwhelmingly named in the rhetoric of fetal endangerment is the pregnant woman. It is she, for the most part, who controls events in her womb, and she also is given a wealth of other tasks to perform, among them paying attention to official experts and maintaining a bond with her husband. In this, our current rhetoric of fetal endangerment does not emphasize the responsibility of others such as physicians, the scientific community, partners, other relatives, fate, or laws of genetic averages. In short, this rhetoric points out whose interests may be risked or overlooked when weighed against who else's: a pregnant woman's may be overlooked when compared to a fetus's. In its details, the rhetoric shows what exactly can be sacrificed, namely, a pregnant woman's peace of mind, activity pattern, fit body, career, and preferred diet can all easily be sacrificed for the good of the future child.

Why would a pregnant woman be motivated to adhere to the many suggestions of our present rhetoric of fetal endangerment? The price of disagreeing with this moral idiom is high. The pregnant woman who disagrees with our rhetoric of fetal endangerment must take a position against aiding the most helpless children, those yet to be born. She must argue with the wisdom of thinking of the future good of the nation. She must support her own right to put her personal satisfaction of seemingly petty wants and desires against the physical and mental health of a fetus soon to be child. Finally, she must do all this while knowingly contradicting those "expert" enough to write articles, even volumes, detailing the subtle and blatant damage that can result.

Having problematized certain physical and mental traits or conditions apparent in children, claims-makers use this rhetoric to evaluate and judge the prospective mother, fetus, and child. To say that a child has an "attention problem" and is failing in school may indict the caffeinated soda-drinking mother while ignoring the rest of the family, the school and the teacher, as well as all other interaction a mother has with that child. Through the exercise of this rhetoric, the thoughts, feelings, and actions of a future parent—most often, of a pregnant woman—are deemed acceptable or unacceptable because of their alleged effect on the fetus. In addition, the rhetorical idiom implicitly judges a child's physical and mental disability, as well as a child's undesirable personality traits and physical appearance: The rhetoric of fetal endangerment does not simply warn pregnant women of unacceptable or harmful acts; it also creates and sustains categories of unacceptable and undesirable children, among them children with disabilities. The "successful" outcome of a pregnancy is not merely a live birth, it is a "perfect" child. Therefore, children with shortcomings, large or small, can be read as evidence of parental moral failure during pregnancy.

23

Constructing Sexually Marginalized Catholics

Donileen R. Loseke and James C. Cavendish

On a personal level, stories circulating in the social world are available for social actors to use as a narrative model; stories can furnish moral identity roles for people attempting to make sense of self and others; they can be an important resource for creating an internal, private sense of self; they can be used by social actors as supports for identity change. In addition, storytelling is a *political* phenomenon whereby contending stories can be understood as political contests. The constructed characteristics of types of people—story characters—lead to commonsense folk reasoning that such types of people deserve sympathy or condemnation, rights or punishment, inclusion or exclusion.

In this paper we are concerned with what Ken Plummer (1995) calls a sexual story, a narrative of the intimate life of sexual minorities. We are particularly interested in sexual stories of people who have seemingly contradictory identities because they are both members of sexual minorities and devout Catholics. Our focus is on how an *organization* called Dignity rhetorically constructs a type of narrative character who simultaneously is proudly sexually marginalized and devoutly Catholic.

This chapter is excerpted from Loseke, Donileen R. and James C. Cavendish (2001). "Producing Institutional Selves: Rhetorically Constructing the Dignity of Sexually Marginalized Catholics." *Social Psychology Quarterly* 64:347–62.

CONSTRUCTING THE SEXUALLY MARGINALIZED PERSON

In his examination of the social and political reasons for sexual stories circulating at the end of the twentieth century, and the consequences of such
stories, Plummer notes that "the western world has become cluttered with
sexual stories" and that the "grand message keeps being shouted: *Tell me
about your sex*" (1995:3–4, author's emphasis). Although some sexual stories concern child sexual abuse, rape, sexual harassment, and sex addiction, many others are about people whose sexual identities and/or sexual
practices do not conform to the culturally preferred model of the heterosexual actor. Even while these sexual stories revolve around the erotic—
what these people sexually *desire* and what they sexually *do*—they
simultaneously construct types of *characters*: what these people *are*. Hence
our world is populated by sexual types of people: heterosexuals, gays, lesbians, bisexuals, transgendered. Sexual behavior in these stories becomes
the central organizing device for constructing people as particular types of
story characters.

The sexually marginalized person, as a distinct type of person, is a
social construct that begins with sexuality but ends with an image of
a total person. We need not repeat here the well-known complaints of sexual minorities who find that, within a world organized around heterosexuality, their very selves can be condemned because of their sexual
orientations and practices. Observers therefore note that cultural images
of sexual minorities contain few positive characteristics and tend to be
focused on negative attributions. Furthermore—a critical point—this story
character can be read through another cultural narrative surrounding
moral evaluations of worthiness and citizenship: In folk reasoning, a type-
of-person construct justifies social and political outsider status. Therefore,
because sexual minorities are constructed as deviant, it follows through
this cultural narrative that they do not deserve inclusion as full members
of society.

Stories are the way in which people make sense of lives; thus it follows
that when sexual minorities use this broadly circulating cultural story to
understand their selves, an array of personal troubles can follow. Again,
we need not elaborate because these troubles are well known. Observers
claim sexually marginalized people often lack self-respect, they often suffer from excessive guilt and self-hatred as a result of judgment passed on
them by society.

We might expect such troubles to be more severe when members of sexual minorities are strongly Catholic in their religious identification. In secular movements on behalf of lesbians and gays, the Catholic Church often
serves as an example of institutions criticized for advancing the cultural

story of sexual minorities as deviant. With its model of nonheterosexual orientation as "objectively disordered," and its proclamation that any sexual practices outside heterosexual marriage are sinful, Catholic Church doctrine constructs sexual minorities as deviant in sexual orientation and as sinful in sexual practices.

Not surprisingly, academic observers have examined the particular plight of lesbians and gays who identify strongly with a religion that condemns them. Most common in these studies is the finding that compared with their nonreligious counterparts, gay Christians experience a greater sense of alienation and a higher degree of anxiety about their sexuality and its exposure. Vivid contradictions between sexual and religious identities also can lead to cognitive dissonance, the inability to integrate seemingly contradictory identities. How are such people to understand their selves when their identities are contradictory?

There are two obvious ways to reconcile identity. First, if religious identity is not strong, it can be discarded. For example, members of sexual minorities can opt out of Catholicism or other nonaccepting religions and embrace a religion more accepting of their sexual orientations and behaviors, or they can disregard religious identity entirely and understand their lives through the secular "gay is good" story. Second, sexual minorities can attempt to change their sexual orientation: A support group called "Exodus" promotes this. Also, because only nonheterosexual practice within the Catholic Church is a sin, sexual minorities can remain celibate and a support group called "Courage" promotes this.

But what about people who prize both their Catholic and sexual identities highly, and somewhat equally highly? These people live in a space between two worlds. They are shunned by the institutional Catholic Church, but because they identify so strongly with Catholicism, they are not particularly drawn to worship in other places. Similarly, sexual minorities who identify strongly with the Catholic Church can find secular rights organizations that support their marginalized sexualities but ignore, or even condemn, their Catholic identity. Offering a narrative that reconciles seemingly incompatible identities can be read as a service of an organization called "Dignity."

THE ORGANIZATION OF DIGNITY

Dignity was founded in 1969 and has two missions. First, it is a social change organization with a political mission to work for the reform of the Catholic Church and for justice and equality. Its second mission is our focus here: from its beginnings, Dignity has been an informal ministry to troubled gay Catholics. Dignity envisions itself as a support group with a mission to promote self acceptance and dignity within individual gay, lesbian, bisexual, and transgendered Catholics; it seeks to help members integrate their spirituality and sexuality.

While Dignity gatherings of all sorts furnish support to their members, we will focus here on the rhetorical production of a sexual story: a story of a type of person who simultaneously is sexually marginalized and an exemplary Catholic. We call this type of person the "Dignified Self." Our data for this analysis are the nine Dignity/USA newsletters (each between 25 and 40 pages long) published between fall 1997 and autumn 1999/winter 2000.

CONSTRUCTING THE DIGNIFIED SELF

Constructing Spiritual Sexuality

In Catholic doctrine, the stories of all sexual minorities can be read as sexual stories because, regardless of what gays, lesbians, bisexual, and transsexual people do *not* share, either as unique people or even as types of people, their stories are the *same*: within Catholic doctrine, each is a person whose sexual identity and/or sexual practices are other than the heterosexuality approved by the Church. Not surprisingly, Dignity's story, integrating sexuality and spirituality, also can be read as a sexual story. It begins by constructing the sacred importance of both sexual orientation and sexual behavior.

Sexuality as a God-given gift. Dignity newsletters differ from secular constructions in that these newsletters typically construct God as the ultimate source of sexual identity. Hence a speaker tells readers, "My friends, this is who we are. We are the children of God. We are the Lord's creation. We are a part of the Christian family;" a supportive Catholic bishop says "[G]ays and lesbians have suffered simply for being the people God created them to be"; readers are told they must publicly support GLBT people as created by God, as part of Christ's mystical body.

A God-given sexuality, however, is not the most important construction because, within the Catholic Church, an orientation other than heterosexual is "objectively disordered" but not a sin. The sin is other than heterosexual *behaviors*. Although separating sexual orientation from sexual behavior leads to the possibility that sexual minorities can be "good" Catholics as long as they remain celibate, the president-elect of Dignity in 1997 is clear that the distinction between homosexual orientation and homosexual acts makes no sense. These pages construct the goodness of sexual *practice*. Again using rhetoric with reference to the sacred, Dignity members are informed that "sex and gender are divine gifts, intended to be celebrated, bring pleasure, and be shared." This mandate to practice sexualities condemned by the Catholic Church comes from none other than God, as readers are told that "God gave us our sexuality as a gift and he wants us to use it."

Although Dignity constructs both sexual orientations and sexual practices as God's gifts, these newsletters make it clear that not all sexual practices are acceptable.

The ethics of sexuality: love, commitment, family. In sharp contrast to the secular "glad to be gay" story often characterized by an obsession with sex, and in contrast to the cultural story of gays focusing on sexual promiscuity, dignified sexuality is constructed as characterized by love and commitment. Members are informed, for example, that "love is natural, and homosexuality has far more to do with loving someone of the same sex than it has to do with having sex with members of the same sex." Newsletters are filled with discourse applauding "commitment," which is constructed as none other than sacred because it has a scriptural basis. Each newsletter applauds members who demonstrate this commitment.

While the Catholic Church in particular and secular society in general tend to focus on the physical practices of marginalized sexualities, dignified sexuality is constructed on these pages as distinctly social: it is about love and commitment. Furthermore, Dignity promotes family. True, Dignity families defy Catholic Church prohibitions against other than heterosexuality; yet the rhetoric of family is ever-present. Dignity holds national couples celebrations, the national organization designates National Couples Month, and has established a couples registry so that coupled members can affirm their relationships.

Dignified sexuality is about love, commitment, and family. Furthermore, dignity requires that sexuality be integrated with spirituality. The goal of Dignity is to promote spiritual/sexual integration. The defining characteristic of all types of sexual stories is their focus on sex: the erotic, the gendered, and the relational (Plummer 1995:4). The sexual story constructed by Dignity is clearly about gender and relationships; yet the erotic remains in an often unspoken and never dramatized background. Rhetorically, sexuality has been spiritualized.

Constructing Sexual Spirituality

Although their sexual behaviors are condemned by the Catholic Church, members of Dignity are told that they should be proud of their spirituality, that "it is time to pull spirituality out of the closet." As constructed, this is a distinctive Catholic spirituality. Yet it is simultaneously a sexual spirituality because it is constructed as a spirituality unique to sexually marginalized people.

These newsletters construct the ongoing importance of religion and the particular importance of Catholicism. The Dignity newsletters contain many indications that distinctly Catholic rituals and symbols are very important to members. Reports of national and individual chapter events, for example, center on the importance of Catholic spirituality and ritual in members' lives: Dignity national conventions include a liturgical event every day, a healing service on Friday, a Eucharist liturgy on Saturday. Yet even while these newsletters clearly seek to maintain Catholic tradition and rituals, they simultaneously can be read as producing a distinct spirituality for sexual minorities.

Dignity's newsletters can be read as constructing a special spirituality held by sexually marginalized Catholics. A magazine is described in an advertisement, for example, as a monthly newsletter reflecting on Christian spirituality from a *gay perspective*; Dignity members attend social change conferences in order to add their own *unique* perspective.

This special spirituality is sexual because it is constructed as a consequence of sexual marginalization. As constructed, sexual marginalization does not mean that sexual minorities have been abandoned by God. Readers rather are instructed to "see even the God of the Old Testament as the source of love without limits who is concerned with those outcasts who are victimized or marginalized." Indeed, the Dignified Self becomes comparable to "the prophets in the Bible [who] rarely enjoyed official status, but rather lived on the margins of society." When combined, these constructions yield an image of the Dignified Self as no less than favored by God, as declared in the Dignity anthem called "Celebrate": "Yes! We are chosen! Yes, we are a sign! Destined for a prophet's role, a sacred trust."

In brief, the contents of Dignity newsletters can be read as producing a particular type of person, the Dignified Self. This is a collective identity of a type of person whose sexuality is spiritual and whose condemned status in the Catholic Church leads to a sexual spirituality that leads to being chosen by God.

DISCUSSION

Our primary argument is that rhetoric on the pages of Dignity newsletters can be read as a sexual story forming a particular type of narrative character. Although innumerable stories of sexually marginalized people now are circulating in our social world, this particular story is unique. First, in contrast to characters in secular "gay is good" stories, the Dignified Self is organized around both sexual marginalization and religious identity. Second, in contrast to characters in stories constructed by groups such as Courage or Exodus that praise Catholicism and condemn sexual marginalization, the Dignified Self praises both Catholicism and sexual marginalization. Third, in contrast to characters in narratives associated with secular support groups for those with troubled identities, the Dignified Self is not weak, does not require personal transformation, and is made stronger by adversity.

Because this narrative character is constructed by the organization, we can ask how it can be read as supporting the organizational mission to support the identity of sexually marginalized Catholics. Dignity's support group mission is to promote self-acceptance for individual sexually marginalized Catholics; our assumption is that the Dignified Self narrative is constructed in service of this mission. Clearly, many stories circulating in our culture potentially speak to sexually marginalized people. The story of such people as deviant competes with the "glad to be gay" story, stories told through television talk shows, stories promoting celibacy, or stories promoting the transformation of homosexuality into heterosexuality.

Such an array of possibilities raises a very practical question: To what extent is the narrative constructed by Dignity likely to be evaluated by individuals as a credible model for the self? Because people will be drawn to narratives that seem to make sense of their unique biographical experiences and understandings, we can speculate that the Dignity narrative might be compelling to sexually marginalized Catholics who are unwilling to deny, transform, or minimize either their sexual or their religious identities. At the same time, we would speculate that the Dignified Self story would not be compelling to other sexually marginalized people. For example, sexual minorities without strong Catholic identity or those who are not drawn to an image of spiritual sexuality might decide that the narrative character of the Dignified Self does not speak to them.

In brief, sexually marginalized people now can find many stories with which to make sense of their selves; the Dignified Self narrative, with its emphasis on Catholic identity, inclusion in the Church, and sexual ethics, logically will be compelling to only a subset of those people. Such people, however, may be most in need of this narrative because other stories deny or minimize either sexuality or Catholic identity, and the audience for Dignity is unwilling to do either.

Finally, in focusing on how Dignity newsletters produce a type of person rhetorically, we gain further insight into the construction of justifications for social change in general. For example, prior research demonstrated how the mandate for equality for gay Christians, gay Catholics, and Jewish feminists can be accomplished by constructing the immorality of religious doctrine or the immorality of traditional interpretations of religious scripture. Although Dignity rhetoric in these newsletters also rejects the moral framework of the Catholic Church, we ignored that theme in order to explore how the rhetoric also can be read as constructing a type of person. We argue that Dignity rhetoric can be read as justifying social inclusion by constructing the *morality* of sexually marginalized Catholics. With the only exceptions of sexual identity and practices, the Dignified Self is an exemplary Catholic, family member, and citizen. According to folk reasoning, such an exemplary type of person deserves inclusion in the Church and in the social order. Hence observers examining how mandates for social change are justified for minorities of all types might do well to note how inclusion can be justified by constructing narratives where characters are particular types of people whose social exclusion is not warranted, whose inclusion is deserved.

REFERENCE

Plummer, Ken. 1995. *Telling Sexual Stories: Power, Change and Social Worlds.* New York: Routledge.

24

The Beliefs of
Recovery Religion

KATHLEEN S. LOWNEY

Salvational talk shows testify to the benefits of recovery religion. Hosts ask guests, the studio audience, and those watching at home to believe in the power of being in recovery. With their shows, hosts proclaim that most Americans are "lost souls" and then prescribe talk—recovery talk, that is—as the solution. The movement offers its converts a new way to live, freed from behaviors considered troublesome. But recovery discourse is much more than just talk about getting clean and sober from drug or alcohol addiction. Unhealthy relationships—those that thwart individuals from being the best that they can be—are even more harmful than the physical effects of addiction. Indeed, relationships are the very essence of recovery discourse. Here I will analyze the movement's basic tenets—its faith statements, if you will. Recovery religion affirms five central beliefs: (1) that one's own needs must come before the demands of society; (2) that families emotionally and spiritually wound children during the socialization process; (3) that those scars carry into adulthood, causing us to be stuck in debilitating behavioral patterns; (4) that to heal, we must let go of these private wounds by sharing them with others; and (5) that these patterns are symptomatic of the disease that ails us—codependency. Talking to others similarly hurt, who have "been there," can break the hold of the past that has had such power over the individual and permit the miracle of recovery to commence.

The Recovery Movement is a broad yet diffuse social movement. Defining it is difficult. I will use the term to include information on personal dis-

This chapter is excerpted from Lowney, Kathleen S. (1999). *Baring Our Souls: TV Talk Shows and the Religion of Recovery* (Chapter 4). Hawthorne, NY: Aldine de Gruyter.

covery and self-help as well as the narrower topics of addiction and code-pendency. The movement is religious, with certain beliefs one must hold sacred. Information about its beliefs is readily available to the public in a ever-growing variety of ways, including books, radio programs, videos, infomercials, seminars, and, of course, talk shows. The movement has an always-changing list of experts whose popularity ebbs and flows based primarily on whose book is most recently published. Membership in the movement is nebulous, for although many participate in the ritual of attending a group to "work a program," not everyone who is influenced by its beliefs will do so. A significant number voraciously will read the literature or watch talk shows and they will apply what they have learned to their lives, but they will do so in relative isolation, without the sustenance of like-minded others. For someone not involved in the movement, reading some of its literature or talking to someone who shares its views can be quite disconcerting. It can seem as if members are speaking a different language. And in a way, they are.

FREEDOM TO BE ME: VALUATION OF SELF OVER SOCIETY

The Recovery Movement is a recent phenomenon, but its roots are intricately woven from the social fabric of American culture. The nation was founded, we are taught as children, by a group of strong individuals who rejected being under English control. Individual freedom was their rallying cry, independence the culmination of their hard-fought struggle. But freedom is a complicated concept, involving the interplay between society and its members. There is a delicate balance that each nation must find between the role of the social group and the rights of individual people. Americans have valued, from the nation's inception, freedom *from* control by larger entities—the King, religious organizations, and so on. Freedom, however, was a culture-bound concept for our early leaders. Freedom from control by larger social groupings was a right offered primarily to land-owning white men; few, for instance, thought it should include indentured servants, Native Americans, slaves, or women. Such freedom also entailed responsibilities. When others' rights are at risk, citizens must rally in defense of the national interest. Such an understanding of "freedom from" acknowledges that the social order has legitimate power over individuals' lives, but calls on citizens to be watchful for unnecessary and illegitimate impositions of such a power.

But there has long been another way of conceptualizing freedom in our nation, one that emphasizes that citizens have the freedom *to* make choices. This view stresses the role of the individual, arguing that the social order impedes people's ability to shape their destinies. Such a conception of freedom regards most any means of social control as illegitimate, for it imposes collective norms onto individual citizens. Such a use of power is considered harmful, even abusive, for it places limits on the self in the process of becoming.

One of the principal tasks of cultural discourse is to construct and then maintain the connection between self and other, especially the society as other. When a significant number of citizens no longer share the same convictions about how self and society are linked, an opportunity for cultural change arises. Broadly speaking, there are three main responses to social change. The society can resist the change, reaffirming the old values as still meaningful, or the society can opt for reformation, changing some values now understood as out of date, but affirming others as still significant. The third option is revolution; the society completely reorganizes its basic understandings. For most of us, these phrases bring to mind the arena of politics. We think of revolution when a dictatorship becomes a representative democracy or visa versa. But a nation's culture—its values, ways of understanding, and the like—can also experience change. The success of the Recovery Movement is evidence that America has undergone cultural change; more and more Americans are choosing new ways of defining the connections between self and others. Increasingly more and more Americans use therapeutic discourse—the language of the Recovery Movement—to talk about themselves, their families, and relationships with others. Some even use such language to analyze our nation itself. Such a transformation in how we talk about ourselves and others has been, for better or worse, an enduring legacy of the Recovery Movement.

Leaving aside for the moment judgment about the effects of this recovery revolution, this triumph of the therapeutic, it is clear in its affirmation that the self is more highly valued than society. The shift to therapeutic discourse is undergirded by the "ethic of self-actualization," which assigns ultimate moral priority to the self, over and against society. To affirm the belief that there ought to be a balance between self and society is at best, in the discourse of the Recovery Movement, to misunderstand; at its worst it is to be an instrument of abuse toward others who are searching for their true selves.

FAMILY: THE TIES THAT BIND

While the Recovery Movement is anti-institutional, it is the family as an institution that suffers its most severe condemnation. The "old" discourse claims that it is within the family's socialization process that children learn about social norms and social structure. Social order exacts a price for membership, however: the child must learn self-control and self-denial. But the tradeoff is more than fair—in exchange, the child learns the skills needed to negotiate successfully in the adult world. But the second belief of the Recovery Movement contradicts this view of childhood. It considers the family as an instrument of repression, within which children are taught toxic rules that stress obedience to the more powerful parents rather than the freedom to be who one can be. To compound the damage, American culture—shaped by generations of adults who were socialized into these very same norms—reinforces these harmful messages at every turn.

These cultural norms encourage family members to rebuke the child's attempts at individuation instead of helping the child to become a healthy adult. Ultimately a damaged self emerges; it is far from the self-actualized person one could be if freed from the effects of familial repression. The Recovery Movement claims that the net effect of such a damaging socialization is that the child grows up emotionally injured. Especially harmful are the messages about self that the child learns: The wounded person . . . tends to think "I *am* a mistake," rather than "I have made a mistake." Internalizing such negative messages creates feelings of shame, guilt, and abandonment, which in turn poison relationships and damage people's search for actualization. The miracle of healing begins when a person can recognize those feelings, understand that they were externally imposed on the child, and free oneself from their negative effects.

EMOTIONAL SCARS RUN DEEP

The third belief of the Recovery Movement affirms that if individuals do not confront the effects of their pernicious socialization, they will remain stuck in abusive relationships, never really knowing why they are harming themselves over and over again. Their warped psychic heritage stunts individuals; they carry those wounds into adulthood. Diana was one such wounded person who appeared on the "Montel Williams Show." Her family was in turmoil; her 15-year-old daughter, Katrina, had attempted to kill her younger sister by throwing a butcher knife at her back; Katrina also has started assaulting Diana; and the younger daughter, Rachel, has begun to burn herself with cigarette lighters in order to get attention. Mom had written Montel, asking for help for Katrina. For a while, it seemed that the girls were the ones in need of healing, after all the show was entitled "Violent Teen-age Girls." But as the program continued, Montel's expert, a psychologist, had the opportunity to question the girls' mother. Their exchange identified other, long-lasting wounds, that go a long way, it was claimed, in explaining this family's violent history:

Dr. Farrell: OK. I understand that—that this is not—this is not something that is just kind of confined to your daughter, that you had some past history, right? . . . Of what?

Diana: Of abuse.

Dr. Farrell: Of abuse. You abused somebody or you were abused?

Diana: I was abused. . . .

Montel Williams: Did you—did you ever participate in any—any abusing of your own? Did you ever hit your mother?

Diana: Yes. I have slapped my mother.

Montel Williams: When—you were how old when you slapped your mother?

Diana: Fourteen. . . .

Montel Williams: Did—did you ever hit your sister?

Diana: Yeah.

Montel Williams: How old were you when you did that?

Diana: Twenty-one. . . .

Montel Williams: . . . What we're trying to do today is we're trying to see if these two girls, that are your daughters and you can have good relationship, one that's not the same kind of relationship that you had when you were growing up . . . one that you remember so well that in some ways, whether you want to admit it or not, Mom, you may have planted the seeds of what's happening now with them by watching all the violence that has been in your life.

According to the Recovery Movement, one's past, left unexamined, traps the individual in unhealthy patterns. In Diana's case, a new generation is repeating the same old mistakes. The unspoken assumption is that there had to be reasons for Diana's violence to her mother and sibling— reasons that came before (and probably in fact explained) her two violent marriages. Montel and the psychologist seem to take the worst possible interpretation of a highly ambiguous passage. They appear to suggest that Diana's violence was severe and ongoing rather than exactly what Diana said it was—one incident years ago, followed by second incident of violence against her sister seven years later. The religion of recovery interprets *any* act of physical aggression as abuse, and therefore a sign the victimizer needs healing. To try to explain or justify why one acted abusively is to be in denial about one's own wounded past.

HEALING TAKES HELP

But being able to connect the wounds inflicted within the family of origin to one's adult problems is only the beginning of the journey into recovery. Montel Williams and his expert seem to believe that they have helped

Diana make that first tenuous step. But there is more work to be done by the family, as Montel Williams tried to point out:

> What I'm trying to do is make mom stop for a minute and realize—what you need to do—these girls are wide open, and they're ready. She is more ready to—to communicate with you than you even know. I'm telling you, she is ready, she's begging, she wants it. You need to be in some serious counseling, continual counseling . . . you do.

The family never returned to the air, but the audience was left hoping that Diana, Katrina, and Rachel will eventually be able to stop the generational pattern of abuse. That help will come in the form of some sort of therapeutic intervention. Although it may begin with private counseling sessions for each family member, then perhaps family counseling, at some point it is logical to assume that each individual in this "sick family" would be encouraged to become a member of some sort of therapeutic group to aid in her recovery. The fourth belief of the Recovery Movement is that healing from one's past is a journey not to be taken alone. Facing the deep-seated injuries left by being abandoned and abused by one's parents and siblings takes the support and encouragement of others who have "been there."

Healing becomes communal. The belief that recovery takes help becomes rooted in member's consciousness through perhaps the most famous practice of the Recovery Movement, attendance at group meetings. The individual who is sick but no longer in denial must find like-minded others who are willing to "work the program." Although no one is responsible for another's recovery, recovery discourse claims that the mutual support found at daily or weekly meetings profoundly assists members. But just what do these recovery groups discuss? Clearly the movement believes that it is about wounded people bolstering each other in order to feel and act better. It claims that the primary injury occurs within the family unit; its toxic methods of socialization do extensive harm to the child's sense of self. Secondary harm accrues when these emotionally crippled individuals interact. And new victims are created when they pass the illness onto their children. Members go to discover their deepest wounds, face them, and begin to mend. But what is this disease that has devastated so many Americans and from which they need to recover?

HOOKED ON BEING HOOKED

It has many labels. Some call it dysfunctionality, others call it the disease of the wounded self, but most refer to it as addiction. A growing number of Americans confess to being powerless to resist an ever-expanding list of addictions. Money, food (too much or too little), sex, "putting oneself down," the Internet, people, gambling, alcohol and other drugs, exercise, "loving too much"—these are but a few of the things for which one can find a support group. But such a list is perplexing at first; some items are potentially harmful substances one could consume, but most are behaviors that become troublesome. The former behaviors neatly fit the conventional definition of addiction, but the latter do not. This points to the fifth and last belief—the Recovery Movement has significantly revised what the term *addiction* connotes. Recovery discourse now contends that there are two kinds of addiction, ingestive and process. The latter addresses an addiction to a way (or the process) of acquiring the addictive substance. The function of an addiction is to keep us out of touch with our feelings, morality, awareness. An addiction, in short, is any substance or process we feel we have to lie about. The revision of the term to include process addiction broadens the potential pool of addicts in need of recovery considerably; in fact it has created its own disease. Codependency is the new recovery buzzword; it is the disease *du jour*. Codependents are products of dysfunctional families, who in turn are the products of our culture's sick socialization process. Children learn to follow externally imposed rules, to "dance to their parents' drummer" instead of their own. Children are taught to obey rather than to become their own selves. This sickness results in children who feel abandoned and abused, emotionally if not physically. This is a significant revision of the term abuse; now it means any behavior that does not foster the self-actualized child. The effects are devastating to overcome. A codependent pleases others excessively and gets her identity from others, she has no self-esteem or self-worth, and is isolated from her feelings. The codependent has few, or rather few healthy, boundaries between self and others. The codependent obeys the wishes of others without question, never thinking of her or himself. Indeed, untreated codependents often do not even admit to having needs; they are frequently able to define themselves only through obligations to others. Codependency then, by its very nature, is antithetical to the Recovery Movement's goal of each person becoming one's true self. The illness eats away at the very core of the person until it profoundly deforms the individual. Worse, recovery religion promotes the belief that the illness of codependency is contagious. Until one begins to recover, each encounter with others will infect them as well. Codependents damage each and every relationship they participate in until they are willing to admit they have a problem and seek salvation.

CONCLUSIONS

The religion of the Recovery Movement is comprehensive. It has redefined sin to be anything that suffocates the self in the making. Parents and society are chief among the sinners, for they teach stifling rules that need to be followed for order to be maintained, first within the family and then the nation. In this new religion, salvation is attained through works; members must attend meetings and follow the twelve steps learned there. But the journey of faith that the religion of recovery calls for is an eminently solitary one, for it focuses not on healing the world, but solely on healing yourself. And so, the language of therapeutic relationship seems to undercut the possibility of other than self-interested relationships. Taking care of and being true to oneself are its highest moral values.

VII
Social Problems and Troubled People

Introduction to Section VII

One way in which successful claims change the world is through the *troubled persons' industry*. This is a very general term for all the organizations, programs, and groups designed to do something for victims, potential victims, villains, and potential villains involved in social problems. Places in the troubled persons' industry range from prisons and reformatories to rape crisis hotlines, pregnancy education programs, counseling and support groups for all types of people constructed as troubled and in need of help, rehabilitation, and/or punishment. These places are the consequences of successful social problems claims.

Successful claims produce images of troubled people who need assistance of the particular sorts constructed in prognostic claims about what should be done. While we most often think of social activists as claimsmakers, scientists and physicians also can construct claims about troubled people in need of their assistance. Dorothy Pawluch considers "Medicalizing Childhood." She begins with a problem facing pediatricians (children's doctors) in the 1950s: They were running out of clients. Because many childhood diseases had been conquered, the number of children needing pediatric care was diminishing. Pediatricians resolved this crisis in two ways. First, they redefined "childhood" to include adolescents and even young adults. This redefinition expanded the age range—and therefore the number—of people constructed as needing pediatric care. Second, they medicalized a range of childhood troubles by defining behaviors such as temper tantrums, sibling rivalry, bedwetting, fears and phobias, shyness, and running away from home as medical problems they could resolve. In this case, social problems claims-making served to increase the number of people judged troubled and needing the care of pediatricians. The component of the troubled persons' industry called pediatric medicine was enlarged.

The category of "gifted children" offers a very different example of how categories of people come to be defined as troubled and in need of services. These children are constructed as different from other children

215

because they have been identified by their teachers as children with greater learning capabilities. Yet *educators* constructed gifted children as troubled: These children were in classrooms with others who were not so gifted, they were not being properly stimulated, so their capacities were not being nurtured. Hence, Leslie Margolin, in "Teaching Gifted Children," argues that programs were organized to give these children superior learning experiences so that they could develop their perceived superior abilities. On the surface, this seems very beneficial because these children's abilities are nurtured. Yet his examination raises perplexing questions: While we might applaud the special programs for these children, it remains that they have learning experiences *not* available to other children. And, although gifted children education works—these children typically grow to be talented adults—we can ask how much of their adult talent is a result of their perceived high intelligence and how much is the result of their superior education? What would be the result of giving children who are *not* categorized as "gifted" these superior learning experiences? Would these experiences also lead them to excel? We don't know because entry to these gifted children's programs requires labeling a child as gifted.

Workers in the troubled persons' industry—be they highly educated or uneducated, highly trained or untrained, paid or volunteer, do the important work of deciding which people requesting service will become clients. For this task they sometimes rely on their professional training but they always rely on their practical experiences and popular wisdom. Workers also rely on their understandings of the *local culture*, the set of understandings about what the organization or group wants to accomplish, the characteristics of typical clients, the preferred routes to service provision, and so on. Local cultures differ. The local culture in some places offering family therapy, for example, emphasizes the importance of maintaining parental authority over children, while other places emphasize the importance of communication between parents and children in order to reduce parental authority. Some places who have clients labeled "delinquent" (villains or potential villains) have a local culture stressing treating these young people with respect, others have local cultures emphasizing the importance of encouraging these people to respect authority.

James A. Holstein considers the topic of "Constructing Insanity in Involuntary Commitment Hearings." This is a very important site in the troubled persons' industry because court workers can decide to commit people to mental hospitals in spite of their objections. He finds a local culture that presumes mental illness in the people appearing before the court, one where workers at times will "trick" a person into voluntary commitment or into acting in ways leading to involuntary commitment. From the outside, this appears a grave violation of rights, but workers in this place—

attorneys and judges—understand their work to be in the best interests of the people committed to mental hospitals.

Workers in the troubled persons' industry therefore do the work of evaluating and classifying people: Which people should be evaluated and classified as mentally ill? Or as child abusers? These evaluations are powerful in shaping people's lives: To be evaluated and classified as learning disabled, for example, leads to special programs and assistance; to be evaluated and classified as a criminal leads to jail or prison, and so on. Within local cultures, using professional knowledge, practical experience and popular wisdom, workers evaluate and classify people and those evaluations and classifications lead to help or punishment.

Workers in the troubled persons' industry also do another kind of social problems work: They attempt to change their clients' behaviors, attitudes, and/or understandings about their selves. Young, pregnant teens can be taught how to be good mothers and how to think of themselves as mothers, while children seemingly headed for delinquency can be taught how to think of themselves as other than criminals. The attempts to transform clients' behaviors, attitudes, or self-evaluations often revolve around talk. Whether this is between one worker and one client or among members of support groups, this talk can be understood as attempts to bring clients' own understandings of their experiences, their lives, and their selves into line with whatever local culture operates in that place. So, for example, Donileen R. Loseke examines "Formula Stories and Support Groups for Battered Women." In this instance, the local culture of support groups promotes the formula story of wife abuse and the character of the battered woman. Women coming into these groups tell many types of stories about their lives and their selves: Some women believe the violence is bad but not intolerable, some believe they cause the violence they experience, and some believe their partners are good people with problems rather than an evil, wife abuser type of person. The work in these groups is to encourage women to understand themselves as instances of battered women. The groups consider themselves successful to the extent that individual women change their own understandings and identify with this character in the social problems formula story.

It is not possible to offer one overall evaluation of the success of organizations and groups in the social problems industry. At times, organizations and groups in the troubled persons' industry are *successful*: Their clients evaluate their services as beneficial, even life-saving; the places seem to do what they set out to do, so all is well. At other times these places are obviously *unsuccessful*. It is not too much of a stretch, for example, to claim that prisons tend to produce people who are dangerous outsiders. Granted, people do things to be sent to prisons, but the experience of living in a prison nonetheless tends to encourage behaviors and attitudes that are the opposite of what is needed to be successful outside prisons. Likewise, most of the large mental hospitals so popular until the 1950s now have been closed because claims successfully portrayed these places as encouraging their clients to be "mentally ill." What we can say, however, is that the organizations, places, and groups in the troubled persons' industry are a consequence of successful social problems claims-making. Categories of people are singled out and evaluated as victims or potential victims in need of help and/or rehabilitation, just as categories of people are singled out and evaluated as villains or potential villains in need of rehabilitation or punishment. Social problems claims-makers construct images of categories of people; the troubled persons' industry attempts to help, rehabilitate, or punish the real people whom workers evaluate as instances of these types of people.

25

Medicalizing Childhood

DOROTHY PAWLUCH

Over the last several decades the practice of pediatrics has changed radically—so much so that pediatricians often describe their specialty today as the "new pediatrics," or refer to the problems they treat as the "new morbidity" in pediatrics. What makes these new pediatrics "new" is its shift away from the physical problems of children, which once dominated pediatrics, to problems of a nonphysical nature. While in the past pediatricians were primarily concerned with treating and preventing life-threatening infectious diseases, those practicing the specialty in most of North America today deal with problems such as temper tantrums, sibling rivalry, bedwetting, eating and sleeping disorders, fears and phobias, shyness, nightmares, thumb-sucking, nervous tics, nail-biting, glue-sniffing, stealing, fire-setting, running away, using obscene language, overdependent relationships with parents, school difficulties, reactions to chronic illness, adoption, and traumatic experiences such as child abuse.

This is only a partial list of the wide range of difficulties that now fall under the pediatric purview. The "new pediatrics" oversees not only children's physical growth and development, but their emotional, psychological, social, and even, as some pediatricians have interpreted it, their spiritual well-being.

Another feature of the new pediatrics is its concern with adolescents. Until the 1950s, pediatricians primarily treated children under the age of 12. Today, many pediatricians follow their patients through their teens, and, in some cases, into young adulthood. Adolescent health care has its

This chapter is excerpted from Pawluch, Dorothy (1996). *The New Pediatrics: A Profession in Transition* (Chapters 1, 7). Hawthorne, NY: Aldine de Gruyter.

own distinctive problems: acne, sports injuries, and the gynecological needs of young women.

But since adolescence is the healthiest stage in the life cycle in physical terms, providing health care for teenagers really means attending to behavioral and psychosocial concerns such as sexual activity and birth control, gender preference, peer relationships, relationships to authority figures, truancy and school dropouts, as well as drug abuse.

As dramatic as these changes have been for pediatricians, their impact has not been limited to the practitioners of the profession. The new pediatrics is linked to a shift in the way that we as a society think about children, teenagers, and their difficulties. In redefining pediatrics and extending the limits of their professional responsibilities, pediatricians have, in effect, redefined and medicalized many behaviors that they now treat. Behaviors that were once unnamed or unnoticed, those that we once thought we could do nothing about, or that we might have been prepared to overlook or to accept as a normal part of growing up, now evoke concern. Conditions that were once attributed to random variation in character, aptitude, appetite, and energy level, or to "normal" teenage rebelliousness, we now understand within a medical frame of reference as symptoms of an underlying condition. Behaviors that we once punished are now referred to pediatricians and other doctors or experts. Labels such as "hyperkinesis" or "hyperactivity," "minimal brain dysfunction," "attention deficit disorder," "learning disability," have replaced labels such as "naughty," "mischievous," "rambunctious," "lazy, " "shy," "stupid," "wild," and "delinquent." Deviance has become a disease and medical treatment has replaced discipline as the appropriate way to deal with many troublesome behaviors.

Many people, especially parents, have welcomed and even pushed for greater involvement of pediatricians in children's lives, with its promise of more effective management, if not a total "cure," for their nonphysical difficulties and a less troubled, disrupted, and conflict-ridden passage for them into adulthood. But there have been critics as well, charging that the medicalization of childhood misbehaviors is no more than a massive and insidious program of child control and a justification for using medical techniques, including drug therapy, to bring into line those behaviors in children that adults find objectionable, annoying, or bothersome. Some observers have argued that medical labels and treatment for childhood deviance became popular with the advent of the children's rights movement of the 1960s and the general liberalization of attitudes that made overtly coercive means of maintaining order unpopular, if not illegal. Disease labels met the political and social necessities of an age searching for an explanation to the classic problems of deviance. These disease labels continue to be popular, especially among the middle class because they are less stigmatizing than moral labels such as "delinquent," and they absolve parents of blame for their children's misbehaviors. Other critics describe Ritalin, an amphetamine prescribed for hyperkinesis, as a way of regimenting and restraining spirited kids. Others suggest that medical labels for childhood misbehaviors are often thin disguises for the difficulties that children experience in adjusting to specific social, family, or scholastic situations.

In practicing a medical specialty devoted to children, pediatricians have been in a position to arbitrate questions dealing with the health and illness of children. By incorporating problematic behaviors into the boundaries of proper pediatric care and providing services in these areas, pediatricians have implicitly legitimized and given official approval to the medical definitions of children's nonphysical problems. If we are now more likely to see children's behavior as a health care concern, it is largely because pediatricians have endorsed this view. Why have pediatricians been willing to assume responsibility for the problematic behaviors of children and teenagers, and to provide services that they never previously considered part of their specialty?

THE RISE OF THE NEW PEDIATRICS

The new pediatrics was an outcome of a series of crises that shook the specialty after 1950. Over the first half of the twentieth century, the infectious diseases of childhood came under control and the health of children improved. Pediatrics began to experience difficulties. The rates of infant and childhood death (mortality) and illness (morbidity) fell. This did not directly affect the university-based professors of pediatrics who continued to teach and do research on the physical problems of children. Nor did the change affect the small group of consulting pediatric subspecialists who concentrated on studying and treating the serious, though relatively rare, medical conditions that still struck children. The group hardest hit by the improvements in children's health were the thousands of general pediatricians in private, primary care practice.

The problem was not that these pediatricians had fewer patients to treat. On the contrary, the growing popularity of pediatricians as doctors of choice for children and the postwar baby boom combined to create an overwhelming demand for pediatric services. The problem for primary care pediatricians lay in the kind of medicine they found themselves practicing. Their practices increasingly consisted of preventive work—weighing and measuring babies and otherwise supervising the normal growth and development of their young patients—and the treatment of minor illnesses that were easily handled or disappeared on their own without any treatment at all. The growing frustration and boredom with such practice generated a crisis of purpose for the specialty. The crisis, which pediatricians themselves referred to as the "dissatisfied (or disgruntled) pediatrician syndrome" was a pervasive sense of malaise among primary care pediatricians who doubted whether their specialized, disease-oriented skills were serving any real purpose in child health care. It was in the context of the dissatisfied pediatrician syndrome that some within the specialty began to suggest that primary care pediatrics could be revitalized if pediatricians addressed themselves to children's unmet needs, particularly those that were not strictly medical. Pediatricians were encouraged to be creative in their exploration of new areas of care.

Key segments within the profession resisted the expansion of pediatrics into nonphysical areas. But the specialty's ambitions in these new areas were fortified during the 1970s when a new crisis hit—a supply crisis. Pediatricians found themselves competing for a dwindling child population with new groups of health care practitioners eager to provide their services to children, pediatric nurse practitioners, and the budding specialty of family practice. This supply crisis pushed the specialty further toward the new pediatrics. The new pediatrics became more than just a way to make the practice of primary care pediatrics rewarding and fulfilling. It was now the linchpin in pediatricians' assertions that they were the professional group best equipped to deal with children's total health care concerns.

Pediatricians, then, were not seeking to gain a greater measure of control over children's lives. What they were seeking to do was to preserve a place for themselves in primary child health care at a time when their role in the area was threatened. By redefining what proper pediatric care involves to include the new pediatrics, they hoped to secure a future for themselves as primary care practitioners. But in the process, they altered fundamentally our view of children, their problems, and their lives.

GOAL TRANSFORMATIONS AND SOCIAL PROBLEMS

There are parallels between pediatricians who transformed the mission of pediatrics and organizations and social movements that have transformed themselves. The Foundation for Infantile Paralysis (FIP), for example, was established to raise funds to support research into infantile paralysis (poliomyelitis) and to assist victims of the disease. Once Jonas Salk developed the vaccine for polio, the FIP became redundant. Rather than disappearing, however, it changed its name to the March of Dimes and found a new objective in fighting arthritis and birth defects. Other examples of movement change include the Red Cross, whose initial concerns revolved around wars and other national emergencies, but after World War I it became involved in public health. Also, a movement to stem the dangerous and unethical marketing practices of companies supplying infant food formulas to third world countries—the Infant Formula Action Coalition (INFACT)—was formed in 1977 and initiated a national campaign aimed at changing the practices of American companies and the Swiss giant, Nestle. INFACT led a seven-year boycott of Nestlé products and eventually forced the company to alter and restrict its marketing tactics. In the aftermath of its victory, INFACT broadened its objectives to include international campaigns to stop abuses of transnational corporations that endanger the health and survival of people all over the world.

These professions, organizations, and movements share with pediatricians the experience of having to reinvent themselves to survive. But in doing so, most promote new views of the behaviors and/or conditions they take on as goals. The March of Dimes, the Red Cross, and groups such as INFACT have drawn public attention to a broad range of previously unnoticed health issues. And pediatricians have fundamentally altered children's "misbehaviors" and adolescents' "growing pains."

CHILDREN, PEDIATRICIANS, AND MEDICALIZATION

Certain groups have been particularly vulnerable to the medical labeling of their behaviors and circumstances. Women are one such group; children are another. The relative powerlessness of women and children and their limited ability to resist medicalization have made them prime targets. Several studies examine claims-making efforts related specifically to children. While some of these focus on children's problematic behaviors—for example, studies on hyperactivity and learning disabilities and juvenile delinquency—others have examined issues that are, in other ways, child-related, including child abuse, missing children, sudden infant death syndrome, child custody and child support laws, and accidental poisoning.

Many of these studies touch on the role played by the medical profession and its tacit approval of, if not active involvement in, the campaigns that turned these issues into public concerns. Once certain forms of childhood deviance were labeled as "hyperkinesis" or "hyperactivity," the medical profession assumed the responsibility for managing and controlling them. Some studies single out pediatricians as key players. Pediatricians were the first to draw attention to poisoning as an alarming danger to children and were at the forefront of the poison control movement. In fact, the first poison control center, established in 1953, was organized in Chicago under the sponsorship of the Illinois chapter of the American Academy of Pediatrics. A paper in the *Journal of the American Medical Association*, reviewing the development of poison control over five years after the first center was established, noted: "Probably the most noteworthy of these developments is the realization by the medical profession, especially by pediatricians, that poison accidents constitute a major health problem."

But none of the studies examines the forces that propelled pediatricians to involve themselves in the medicalization of so many childhood issues. Pediatricians' involvement in the seemingly relentless medicalization of children's lives was linked to the crises that the specialty faced over the past half century and their efforts to adapt to the changing circumstances around them. The new pediatrics was rooted not in any naturally expansionary or imperialistic tendencies of the medical profession to extend its privileges and prerogatives—a conclusion that some analysts come to about medicalization—but in the concerns of a primary care specialty struggling to survive. An understanding of the dilemmas that pediatricians faced and the professional concerns that have preoccupied them since the 1950s is critical to understanding their involvement in the medicalization of children's deviant behaviors and other problems in their lives.

SOCIAL PROBLEMS AND PROFESSIONS

The new pediatrics raises questions about the forms that professional claims-making can take. If the discovery of new medical diseases and the creation of medical diagnoses is claims-making, another, more obvious, form that claims-making takes is social or political activism in relation to issues that a profession feels strongly about and that it often claims it is uniquely equipped to solve. Pediatricians, individually and collectively, have engaged in both types of claims-making. They have been among the "discoverers" of specific new behavioral conditions in children and have participated in the political campaigns that have brought such issues as child abuse, seatbelt use, and accidental poisoning to light as social problems.

But the incorporation of so many childhood and adolescent difficulties within a medical frame of reference was more subtly the consequence of a redrawing of the boundaries of pediatric practice. In changing and expanding their definition of their political task, pediatricians cleared the way for the production of specific disease labels and for political activism on the part of pediatricians as well as others. This suggests that forms that professional claims-making can take, and how various forms relate to each other, need to be more clearly specified. We need a better understanding not only of why professions become involved in the social problems process, but also in what ways they do so.

26

Teaching Gifted Children

LESLIE MARGOLIN

To imagine how perception of the superior depends on perception of the inferior, we might look at the contrasts by which Jodie Foster displayed the gifted boy in her film, *Little Man Tate*. She made us believe in Tate's giftedness not only by portraying his sensitivity and intellect, but also by constantly treating us to images of the nongifted's stupidity, brutality, coarseness: Here an ordinary child is picking his nose; here another is hitting a child over the head; we see two boys fighting with pencils; still others are teasing and calling names. While Tate examines a Van Gogh still life, the nongifted students are sitting impassively, rocking, tapping, staring blankly. Against such backdrops, Tate's alertness and sophistication are striking. Conversely, in comparison to Tate, the nongifted appear as a lower life form.

The most general consequence of this linkage between giftedness and nongiftedness is that we always have nongiftedness at the same time as—and precisely because—we have giftedness. Going further, we may even say that the more intense the belief in giftedness, the more intense will be the belief in nongiftedness: "An age of saints . . . will also necessarily be an age of Satans or demons and vice versa" (Douglas 1970:4). And just as individuals strive for goodness to the same degree they strive against evil, so we can expect gifted child advocates to hold ordinariness in contempt in direct proportion to their admiration of giftedness. The most positive affirmations of giftedness always occur alongside the most negative characterizations of the nongifted.

This chapter is excerpted from Margolin, Leslie (1994). *Goodness Personified. The Emergence of Gifted Children* (Chapter 7). Hawthorne, NY: Aldine de Gruyter.

ASSEMBLING ORDINARINESS

According to gifted child scholarship's rhetoric of inclusion, the gifted are not more special or unique than anyone else. They are not worth more. They do not deserve more. Gifted education does not foster and support social hierarchies. Gifted child scholars deny that gifted-child discourse assumes a two-tiered caste system with the gifted representing the good and deserving, and the "not-gifted" representing the negative. They claim that the distinction is formed as one of degree, not kind.

Among gifted child scholars, explicit contrasts between the gifted and nongifted are *not* common. Texts on giftedness routinely describe these children without direct reference to the nongifted. Because the purpose of this discourse is not the lowering of the nongifted but the elevation of the gifted, the nongifted rarely assume center stage in gifted-child texts and research studies. Consider, for example, that among the 32 papers examining samples of gifted children published in the *Gifted Child Quarterly* from 1988 through 1991, only seven used samples of nongifted children to empirically assess contrasts.

The favored method for displaying the nongifted does not consist of direct description of their failures and inadequacies. Rather, the portrait of the inferior group is most commonly elaborated implicitly and indirectly through description of the gifted's superiority. In this regard, every expression used to describe gifted students has an implicit reverse meaning for the nongifted. To illustrate, consider an assertion: The gifted are more disposed to fair play, sympathy, kindliness, and honesty than are children at large. This claim also means that the nongifted are *less* disposed to fair play, sympathy, kindliness, and honesty. To take another example, a claim that the composite impression of the gifted are of a group valuing independence, and prizing integrity and independent judgment creates a composite impression of another group—the nongifted—who value conformity and do not prize integrity or independent judgment.

Consider the phrases most commonly associated with giftedness: Has keen powers of observation, shows a passionate desire to learn, asks endless questions, is interested in everything, is ambitious to excel, has a fine command of language, has fine reasoning powers, answers always to the point, has a keen sense of humor, is more dependable than other children his age, conscientious to a fault, such a lovely child, and so on. These phrases only make sense alongside the belief that the nongifted do *not* have keen powers of observation, do *not* show a passionate desire to learn, do *not* have a fine command of language, fine reasoning powers or a keen sense of humor. Thus, the phrase "such a lovely child" can only be called a gifted child descriptor if we treat it as exceptional for the nongifted.

Any description or understanding of the one silently defines the other. It is in this regard that all talk about the gifted necessarily elaborates a sense and appearance of nongiftedness. In other words, when we speak of the gifted's superiority, when we say, for example, "the gifted think better," we see an outline of the nongifted's inferiority, but they are otherwise undifferentiated.

Accordingly, through positive discourse on giftedness, the feeble-minded, the dull, and the average are lumped into a single colorless, undifferentiated mass. They are so joined not in order to suppress or malign them. Rather, the purpose is to recognize the gifted who themselves are portrayed as the suppressed population because their superior ability often is not recognized.

Differentiating the gifted from the nongifted is thus explained as a rescue operation organized by caring people with good intentions. This is not a plot for the elite to take over the world, it simply is an attempt by parents and educators to create a better learning environment for the gifted. Far from an effort to deny resources or recognition to the nongifted, this pedagogy seeks to provide superior children the recognition and resources due all children. Far from being elitist, this pedagogy is formed as a truly democratic way of treating gifted children. Programs for the gifted provide them with opportunities to exercise their potential that are lacking in classrooms for ordinary children.

What goes unsaid, however, is that the belief that one group has extraordinary potential is based on the presumption that a contrast group has a conspicuously different sort of potential. Nowhere is this clearer than in the discussion of the gifted's leadership training. For the gifted to lead, the nongifted must follow. Consider claims made in a 1981 article titled "Training Extraordinary Leaders": the gifted leader "figures out what is wrong," "shows others how to solve problems," "handles abstract ideas and sees a broad perspective," and "plans and follows through." If this is so then the nongifted are those who are told what is wrong and are taught how to solve problems; they are the ones who have the narrow perspective and need to have someone make plans for them.

We can see that, although gifted child scholars repeatedly claim that "giftedness" occurs on a continuum, they always end up treating giftedness as a dichotomous variable representing a difference in kind rather than degree. And we also can see that whatever is treated as the opposite of giftedness is reconstituted as negative by virtue of this comparison. The nongifted may be called by different names—the mass, the mediocre, the dull, the average, the normal or ordinary—but they always have the same negative valence when their existence is invoked in comparison to the gifted. Apparently, the child who thinks, speaks, and acts "better" is seen as fundamentally different. What remains to be considered is how the ceaseless elaboration of a two-tiered caste system harms those on the lower level.

THE EFFECTS OF ORDINARINESS

Does the continual contrast between "gifted" and "nongifted" have adverse effects on the "nongifted"? Dewey Cornell (1983) did a study on gifted children's family experiences. Using a sample of 42 families with children ages 6 to 11, 22 of whom have children attending gifted programs, Cornell found that having a gifted child is associated with greater feelings of pride and closeness by parents. The gifted child is the focus of this pride and has the highest status in the family. By contrast, the nongifted siblings of gifted children are significantly less well adjusted than are children who do not have gifted siblings. Cornell describes the nongifted siblings of gifted children as less outgoing, more easily upset, and more shy and restrained. They also were more excitable and impatient and more tense and frustrated.

Other researchers have noted that parents appear more accepting of their gifted child's unusual requests and behavior: Parents believed that their gifted children were "entitled" to be given more opportunities, more allowances. Requests for "secret places," "hundreds of rocks in the playroom," "yards of string to make a magic web," and to "paint his room black," were understandable once the child was labeled gifted.

In my own observations of gifted children in family therapy, I was struck by how listless and detached the nongifted were in comparison to their gifted siblings. Whether this difference is a result of giftedness or represents a reaction to what goes on at home or is simply a reaction to family therapy at the clinic for gifted children, I cannot say. However, I did note that the nongifted were rarely addressed or noticed during the family therapy sessions. They were treated as entirely peripheral to what was going on. Reflecting their secondry role, a few of the nongifted dozed during the sessions. Others attempted to get some attention for themselves by protesting their secondary status but in the end were passed over or ignored in favor of the gifted sibling.

Because the large majority of gifted students spend all but two or three hours per week in regular classrooms, comparison or differentiation between members of the gifted and nongifted populations is a common event. If the curriculum for gifted children is one enabling them to exhibit the characteristics that define them as gifted, then ordinary children can be expected to routinely bear witness to these displays of giftedness. In fact, without ordinary children serving as audience and contrast group, the exhibition of giftedness would not be possible. Weiler's (1978:185) study of gifted and nongifted students' interactions in regular classrooms illustrate:

> A teacher of second grade assembled her six MGM [mentally gifted minors] children at a table to build a gingerbread house from graham crackers, candy and icing. The rest of the children, who were seated in the same room and had been assigned math workbook exercises, watched the fun the MGMs were having. (The work-book exercises were not remedial; some of the non-MGMs were, in fact, achieving far better in math than some of the ginger-bread builders). Later the principal explained that the gingerbread house was a culminating activity for the MGMs' "qualitatively different" study of geometric shapes; to use his words, "They couldn't all make a gingerbread house!"

Other examples include the time the gifted from the second through sixth grades went to a computer center and played video games: "The children also named favorite colors, friends, pets, and pastimes; using this information, the computer printed out a personalized story for each child. When they returned to school, the children shared the excitement of their trip with classmates who had not been able to go" (Weiler 1978:185).

According to Weiler, the nongifted participate in gifted activities, too, but as the audience: A movie made by the gifted (a soap opera entitled "As the Stomach Turns") was presented at a school open house ostensibly so that all could get some benefit from gifted children's activities. Similarly, the gifted interested in space travel built and launched model rockets with funds set aside for the gifted program. Again, the role of the nongifted was that of observers: "The launchings were performed during P. E. class so that all children could watch what gifted children . . . do" (Weiler 1978:185).

Although gifted children are mixed with ordinary children in regular classes partly to make their special education less conspicuous and to avoid the appearance of elitism, the gifted are routinely pulled from these classes so that they can receive their "qualitatively different" educational experience. Indeed, some of the field trips they are pulled out for are quite costly, appear inexplicably like vacations or rewards, and are clearly appealing to both the gifted and nongifted: "MGMs flew from Northern California to Palm Springs for two days to study the terrain. Another trip was a flight to San Diego for a two-day boat trip out of La Jolla. I understand that the purpose of this trip was to study whales and marine ecology. (I have since been told that MGMs from another junior high enjoyed a three-day trip to Yosemite to study biology and geology)" (Weiler 1978:185–86).

No one says that gifted children are more deserving. And no one argues for a first-class education for the gifted and a second-class education for everybody else. Yet, if ordinary children do not get to build gingerbread houses, make films, visit computer centers, launch rockets, go on boat trips, and study whales when they would enjoy and prefer to participate, they can only conclude they are undeserving. If ordinary children are not provided a clear rationale for their exclusion, their exclusion feels unjust.

Similarly, in every instance, gifted children appear more likely to benefit from gifted-child programs than do their nongifted peers. This is because when scholars assess gifted-child programs, they frame the inquiry in such way that only one verdict is possible. For example, when scholars test whether a gifted-child program works, they examine the program's effects on the gifted students who participate . What they do not do is examine the benefit that might be derived from using the same or equivalent resources with the nongifted. Because they do not ask whether program benefits given the gifted are important or worthwhile relative to the needs of the nongifted, the nongifted are seen as having only a phantom existence.

To illustrate, when assessing the efficacy of an enrichment program for gifted learning disabled children, Susan Baum noted an improvement in the gifted subjects' self-esteem. She concluded that the major reason this program was successful was that these students had been singled out for their special abilities . All of this was well intentioned, but is it any surprise that a group of children—any group of children—would respond positively to large doses of positive attention and support? By limiting the inquiry to the gifted, however, a program that could reasonably benefit *all* children was treated as if it was only suitable to the gifted. The conclusion that "gifted learning disabled children require a supportive environment which values and appreciates all individual abilities" (Baum 1988:230) appears justified based on the way the question was framed. But if we now believe that "gifted learning disabled students must become aware of their strengths and weaknesses and be helped to cope with the wide discrepancy between them" (Baum 1988:230), then, implicitly, nongifted learning-disabled students do not have to become aware of their strengths and weaknesses. What is conspicuously vital for the gifted is conspicuously less vital for the nongifted.

From 1985 through 1992, I located 13 studies in *Gifted Child Quarterly and the Journal for the Education of the Gifted* that assessed the efficacy of various programs on gifted children. Because only one of these studies compared the effects of such programs on both the gifted and the ordinary, we are left with the impression that gifted education is irrelevant to the ordinary, that it has no effects on them. We are left with the impression that excluding the nongifted is normal, reasonable, justifiable. And because we have these beliefs, the resources that go into gifted education are not seen as resources pulled from general education but are only considered a net gain for the gifted.

REFERENCES

Baum, Susan. 1988. "An Enrichment Program for Gifted Learning Disabled Students." *Gifted Child Quarterly* 32:226–30.

Cornell, Dewey. 1983. "Gifted Children: The Impact of Positive Labeling on the Family System." *American Journal of Orthopsychiatry* 53:322–335.

Douglas, Jack D. 1970. "Deviance and Respectability: The Social Construction of Moral Meanings." Pp. 3–30 in *Deviance and Respectability* edited by Jack D. Douglas. New York: Basic Books.

Weiler, Dorothy. 1978. "The Alpha Children: California's Brave New World for the Gifted." *Phi Delta Kappan* 60:185–87.

27

Constructing Insanity in Involuntary Commitment Hearings

JAMES A. HOLSTEIN

While commitment proceedings provide a measure of due process and advocacy, they hardly resemble criminal or civil proceedings where legal adversaries single-mindedly contest case outcomes. Several interpretive concerns shape the proceedings, moderating adversarial relations, relaxing judicial and legal procedures, and influencing the ways that participants formulate commitment arguments and decisions.

MENTAL ILLNESS ASSUMPTIONS

Nearly everyone involved with the involuntary commitment proceedings I observed believes that people whose commitment is under consideration are mentally ill. This is a working assumption that other studies of contemporary commitment proceedings also have noted. Courtroom personnel—including judges and patients' attorneys—anticipate that people brought before the court will be severely disturbed. In part, this reflects their experience that anyone advancing to a commitment hearing already has been thoroughly screened by the mental health system. Moreover, because commitment cannot even be considered without evidence of profound mental disturbance, the psychiatric testimony at commitment hearings invariably certifies people sought to be committed as mentally ill.

This chapter is excerpted from Holstein, James A. (1993). *Court Ordered Insanity: Interpretive Practice and Involuntary Commitment* (Chapter 3). Hawthorne, NY: Aldine de Gruyter.

These diagnoses are very rarely challenged by defense attorneys or patients.

According to courtroom personnel, direct experience with patients confirms the psychiatric testimony. One Metropolitan Court judge, for example, indicated that "I know all of these people—every one of them—have problems. That's why they're here. Most are very, very sick." A judge from another jurisdiction somewhat less tactfully suggested that "Everyone of them that comes through here is crazy in one way or another." Informally, nearly all courtroom personnel use terms like *crazy, loony, nuts, unbalanced, or ready for the nuthouse* to characterize proposed patients. This is even true (perhaps especially true) of representatives of the PD's (Public Defender) office, who ostensibly are arguing for the release of the very people they refer to as *weirdos, nut cases, insane,* and the like.

Nearly everyone also assumes that patients' psychological afflictions are chronic; they view their lives as ongoing "careers" in mental illness. The general feeling is that there is little hope for cure or recovery. Symptoms episodically arise and abate in a cycle of acute disturbance, remission, then relapse. While such prognoses are not optimistic, the personnel involved in commitment proceedings generally believe that psychiatric treatment and therapies are beneficial, if only in containing symptoms of psychological distress. They are aware, however, of the shortcomings and side effects of most conventional treatments, so one seldom hears anyone connected with commitment proceedings arguing that commitment or psychiatric treatment of any sort might effectively cure psychiatric problems, or even contain them for an extended period. In short, court personnel and others involved in commitment proceedings tend to assess patients and the psychiatric services being offered to them in ways reminiscent of members of the psychiatric community themselves. Their commonsense model of craziness or insanity resembles the medical model of psychiatric disturbance, but they talk about it in more familiar, less technical terms. Commitment proceedings, then, are very much concerned with the issues of insanity or craziness, as practical descriptive categories that must mesh with the legal categories to which proceedings orient.

Despite the skeptical (some would say realistic) view of patients' conditions and chances for recovery, some type of psychiatric intervention is nearly always preferred to inaction or benign neglect. In particular, court personnel generally feel that psychotropic medications can be used to stabilize the behavior of people in the midst of acute episodes and to prolong periods of remission. Finally, while judges and others involved in commitment proceedings believe that mental illness causes people to behave strangely or irrationally, they nonetheless acknowledge that patients—no matter how "sick"—are periodically capable of lucid, reasonable behavior. "You can get them up there on the stand and they are just as reasonable as you and me," noted one judge. "It doesn't last, but they can pull it together from time to time." In addition, most feel that mental illness does not completely incapacitate its victims, even the chronically afflicted; it may affect only certain behavioral or cognitive realms, impairing some faculties only slightly or sporadically. Nevertheless, when patients behave in a reasonable, competent manner, others involved in commitment proceedings are likely to regard this "normalcy" as a charade—a hoax perpetrated by a crazy person in order to secure one more chance at freedom.

While past research has been concerned with establishing candidate patients' psychiatric condition independently from the assessments used in actual commitment proceedings, my analysis focuses on members' practical, working definitions. I treat mental illness as something that participants in commitment hearings believe is real; they construe its presence as an objective feature of the people whose commitment is under consideration. My analysis will explore the ways that the "practical reality" of mental illness influences the commitment process.

ORGANIZATIONAL ORIENTATIONS

A variety of people are involved in producing commitment decisions, though some of them seldom appear in court. The people whose commitment is under consideration generally come to commitment hearings via the mental health care system, frequently with long histories of both out- and inpatient care in a variety of psychiatric settings. Physicians, psychiatrists, psychologists, social workers, and other psychiatric and social service personnel and agencies invariably have been involved in screening, treating, and caring for patients as part of the legally mandated procedures for involuntary detention and treatment. Patients are also likely to have encountered law enforcement personnel, often during episodes that lead to the commitment proceedings. These actors constitute an interorganizational network within which commitment decisions are made.

In most jurisdictions, the legal, psychiatric, and social service personnel routinely work with each other, developing working relationships that transcend any particular case. While this clearly contributes to the shared assumptions, definitions, and descriptions of mental illness, it also creates a common orientation to the task at hand. Commitment proceedings therefore take place in a rather "closed community," where the patient is something of an outsider, both in terms of organizational station and by virtue of his or her presumed mental illness. This has two important and related consequences. First, a sense of local professional or bureaucratic community develops, built on cooperation between members. The result is a routine way of processing cases that keeps the business of the courts and related agencies flowing relatively smoothly. A mood of "we all work together here" sets the tone for dealings in Metropolitan Court; similar cooperative outlooks prevail in other commitment settings as well.

Second, commitment hearing personnel are aware of the interorganizational matrix within which commitment proceedings take place. They share a set of presumptions about what has already been done to and for the patient, as well as what options remain open. They recognize policies and practices of the various actors in the mental health care and legal systems, and anticipate the repercussions of commitment decisions for both patients and the agencies patients might encounter, depending upon the court's decision. This results in a shared sense of the available possibilities for any particular case.

Like other social control agents, court personnel employ a justificatory decision logic regarding coercive responses to the mentally ill that frames civil commitment as a remedy of "last resort." Judges appear keenly aware of this, assuming that the court is, in a sense, insulated by several layers of organizational procedures to which apparently disturbed people are subjected before involuntary commitment is sought. These people's troubles come to be understood by reference to remedial efforts that are presumed to have been tried. Commitment is seen as a viable option *only* if the patient is severely ill, this illness has been repeatedly confirmed elsewhere, and a number of other less coercive and restrictive interventions have been tried and have failed. Consequently, court personnel, like others in the mental health care system, typically look for less intrusive options that might be tried before commitment must be sought.

These concerns combine in a way that often leaves participants in commitment hearings in something short of adversarial positions regarding hearing outcomes. Most participants rely upon the smooth operation of the system to permit them to do their jobs efficiently and effectively. Adversary confrontation over issues about which they generally agree would serve only to complicate their work. And, despite a seeming insensitivity to the psychological distress plaguing most patients, most court personnel do care about what happens to the patients. Indeed, on some occasions they appear more concerned with securing patients' well-being and "best interests" than they are with providing uncompromised legal advocacy or aggressive "prosecution." In a sense, this is a further manifestation of "working together" in commitment proceedings to accomplish a common goal.

PROMOTING PATIENTS' "BEST INTERESTS"

The mental illness assumption provides an interpretive background against which an "interventionist" orientation to mental health problems was maintained in the courts I studied. Courtroom personnel generally preferred resolutions that attempted to do something for the patient, to contain or remedy the problems at hand. Any decision rendered—even decisions to release—were apt to be characterized as measures taken on the patient's behalf. Judges invariably argued that "sick" or "crazy" people needed help, noting that "we have to do whatever is best for these troubled people," and "we have to do something, anything, to help the poor souls, or they'll just get worse."

Generally, hospitalization was framed as a remedy that, in the words of a Metropolitan Court judge, provides the opportunity "to get people back on the right track, straighten them out, get them stabilized, and get them under control. Then they can go out and stay out for a little bit longer." Hospital stays were depicted as integral parts of mental illness careers, and although repeated admissions stood as evidence of hospitalization's ineffectiveness in curing mental illness, the notion persisted that severe disturbances would proliferate and endure without it. One Northern Court judge summarized this position: "They never get well, but if they don't get help—someone always looking after them, medication, therapy, trips to the hospital—they will always fall back."

Arranging the most desirable outcome for everyone concerned often involves negotiations vaguely resembling the plea bargaining that takes place in criminal courts. In all of the jurisdictions studied, even the PDs, who ostensibly represented patients' interest in *avoiding* commitment, were just as anxious to see some of their clients hospitalized, as were the DAs and psychiatrists who opposed them in court. To this end, PDs often employed a variety of informal practices to arrange treatment and custody while circumventing actual commitment decisions. While several studies have implied that candidate patients are often coerced into such arrangements, I never encountered evidence that patients were forced to forfeit their rights to court hearings. Nonetheless, it was clear in all the jurisdictions I studied that avoiding involuntary commitments was a high priority for nearly everyone involved.

For example, staff members at psychiatric facilities often tried vigorously to persuade patients who were confined on emergency admissions to sign "voluntary" admission papers in order to facilitate treatment, but also to avoid the administrative difficulties associated with actual legal commitment proceedings. Their persuasive tactics might include implying that criminal charges could be filed and imprisonment might result from disturbances associated with the emergency hospitalizations. In other instances, patients might be told that they could "check out" anytime they wanted if they agreed to a voluntary admission, but that an involuntary commitment could result in long-term confinement. In one jurisdiction, staff in the state psychiatric facility housing many involuntary patients suggested that patients would receive better treatment, with extended freedom and privileges, if they were voluntarily admitted.

As cases moved toward formal commitment proceedings, court personnel often took up the challenge of reaching a "reasonable disposition" of a case that would keep a patient under supervision and treatment without resorting to formal involuntary commitment. Even PDs often believed that arguing strongly on behalf of a client's desire for release was not always in the client's best interest. Often their contact with delusional or nonresponsive clients convinced PDs that further hospitalization and treatment was clearly in order. In most such instances, they tried to convince their clients that further hospitalization and treatment was the best course to pursue, and occasionally they went to great lengths to prevent their clients from going forward with formal hearings.

For instance, one PD in Metropolitan Court capitalized on her client's "delusional" state of mind to extract an agreement to stay in the hospital and voluntarily drop his request for a hearing. The client, Patrick Claire (all names are pseudonyms), a white male perhaps forty years old, was seated in the hallway outside the courtroom when he beckoned Joan Kingman, a PD who apparently was trying to find a client she was supposed to represent later that day. Mr. Claire very politely and directly asked Ms. Kingman if she was a lawyer, or "one of those shrinks." Kingman asked Mr. Claire who he was, and was only slightly taken aback when he replied "You mean you don't recognize the President of the United States?" Kingman apologized and excused herself momentarily. After glancing at one of the files she was carrying, she turned back and asked, "You wouldn't be Patrick Claire, would you?" "They keep saying so, but I'll not hear of it," replied Mr. Claire. The PD then returned to the man's original question, telling Mr. Claire that she was a lawyer, in fact, the attorney appointed to represent him in his commitment hearing that afternoon. Mr. Claire, clearly pleased, drew her close and, in a conspiratorial tone, offered her a proposition.

> You know that as President, I can do your career quite a favor. You get me out of this [hospitalization], and I'll fix you up. Jack Kennedy gets his way around Washington, you know. You work something out, and I'll name you attorney general. Bobby [Kennedy] wants to run for senator, so I'll need someone to take over. You show me you're a good lawyer and you've got the job.

The conversation continued for several minutes, with the client repeatedly asserting that he was President Kennedy, even as the PD reminded him that Kennedy had died twenty years before. Several times Ms. Kingman suggested to Mr. Claire that perhaps "it would be best in the long run if you took a little more time off" in the hospital. She finally excused herself, sought out a representative of the DA's office, and told him that she had a "difficult" case on her hands. She inquired about the argument the DA was going to make, and was told that the testifying psychiatrist was adamant that Mr. Claire was actively schizophrenic, with severe delusions and other symptoms. The DA was going to argue that Mr. Claire was gravely disabled, and he felt confident that the judge would deny the writ and continue the hospitalization "unless you [the PD] throw a wrench in the gears."

The PD assured the DA that she had no intention of doing anything but letting "President Kennedy" testify on his own behalf. She then returned to Mr. Claire and asked him once more if he wouldn't reconsider dropping his petition for a court hearing. Finally, with somewhat exaggerated concern in her voice, Kingman pleaded:

> Mr. President, if you go through with this hearing, it will end your political career. Just think what people would think—the President in court to see if he needs to be locked in a mental asylum. Even if I get you out, you're finished politically. Think about it. But if you take a few more days in the hospital, a week or two maybe, you can say it's just for a rest, you know, recuperation from the stresses of the presidency. No one needs to find out.

Mr. Claire paused for a moment, then conceded: "OK, let's do it, but let's keep this whole thing quiet." The PD hurried off to find the psychiatrist from the facility treating Mr. Claire to ask him to get Claire back to the ward as quickly as possible, while she informed the court that the writ had been dropped.

While not a typical case, nor a typical way of representing a client, this illustrates the commonly spoken preference of court personnel—Public Defenders included—for working out "reasonable" dispositions rather than insisting on adversarial hearings and judicial decisions. Indeed, several PDs and three of the judges studied explicitly noted that they thought they should make every effort to avoid commitment proceedings. As one PD suggested, "I'm here to provide legal counsel and representation, but I also think I should be doing all I can to prevent these hearings."

The prevailing sentiment articulated by court personnel, then, combined a concern with judicial oversight with a desire to see troubled people get the care they were thought to need. PDs, DAs, and judges frequently cooperated to get patients into treatment, actively negotiating resolutions that they believed were best for the patients involved. Of course, this often meant that patients' opinions and desires were viewed skeptically, if not disregarded. Instances like this display both the general concern for patients' best interest (regardless of what the patient might say), and court personnel's desire to work together to accomplish the court's goals and conduct business as efficiently as possible. While this means that patients' expressed wishes were often ignored or manipulated, many hearings and involuntary commitments were avoided.

The desire to see that patients received needed treatment was evident in several related ways. In one jurisdiction, PDs who felt their clients needed extended treatment would ask that their cases be "continued in order to properly prepare." This was a legitimate legal maneuver, and routinely produced delays of up to ten days that could be used to provide treatment that might stabilize patients. Indeed, this length of time closely corresponded to the time local psychiatrists believed was necessary to "saturate" patients with psychoactive medications, then begin to reduce dosages in order to find a manageable maintenance dosage.

In what they perceived as extreme cases, PDs—often in a sort of collusion with the judge and DA—could all but ensure a decision to commit by allowing a client to present his or her case for release in such a way as to display mental disturbance and interactional inappropriateness, tacitly corroborating the testimony from their clients that would prove damaging to their pleas for release. For example, clients might be asked questions that provided the occasion for displays of "delusions" or other "unreasonable" claims, stories, and descriptions. Or PDs might underscore the implausibility of their clients' claims by ironically summarizing problematic statements as if they were unimpeachable arguments for release.

While instances like these are common, they do not mean that PDs abandon their role as their clients' advocates; patients' legal rights and representation were not consistently or completely compromised. To the contrary, on most occasions PDs listened patiently to their clients' stories, discerned their desires, familiarized themselves with the psychiatric and social details of the case, and presented arguments for release professionally and convincingly. Given the size of their caseloads, the extremely limited time they had to meet with clients and concerned others, and the sorts of problems that typically arise when dealing with clients facing commitment hearings, PDs capably managed the extremely tenuous and difficult position by trying to use their legal expertise and position to serve their clients in ways they believed were both humane and respectful of clients' legal rights. Literally thousands of cases were formally processed through the court during the years of this study, and about half of all commitment hearings across all jurisdictions studied resulted in release. But aggressive advocacy and adversarial zeal were sometimes subordinated to what court personnel argued were more important and humane goals.

28

Formula Stories and Support Groups for Battered Women

Donileen R. Loseke

Thirty years ago "wife abuse" didn't exist; there were no "battered women" or "abusive men." Of course, that doesn't mean that men were not being violent toward women. Rather, it means that the *social problem* of "wife abuse" was not yet in public consciousness; the "battered woman" and the "abusive man" were not publicly recognizable identities. This problem and these identities appeared on the social scene only as the result of successful social problems claims-making.

Part of establishing the social problem of "wife abuse" was creating new formula stories that placed "battered women" and "abusive men" at the center of depictions of domestic violence. Formula stories are narratives about types of experiences (such as "wife abuse") involving distinctive types of characters (such as the "battered woman" and the "abusive man."). As such, stories become widely acknowledged ways of interpreting and conveying experience, they can become virtual templates for how lived experience may be defined. As formula stories pervade a culture, people increasingly can use them to make sense of their lives and experiences.

Lived experience, however, isn't easily categorized. While formula stories can help make sense of such troubles, in the process such stories tend to leave the complexity of lived experience in the background, glossing over this in favor of lurid accounts of heinous behavior, depraved perpetrators, and helpless victims. Hence, the relationship between formula

This chapter is excerpted from Loseke, Donileen R. (2001). "Lived Realities and Formula Stories of 'Battered Women.'" Pp. 107–26 in *Institutional Selves: Troubled Identities in a Postmodern World*, edited by Jaber F. Gubrium and James A. Holstein. New York: Oxford University Press.

stories and lived experience can be quite ambiguous; we can't merely assume that formula stories offer an actual recipe for making sense of everyday experiences.

Here I explore how formula stories shape the experiences of women who participate in support groups for those who have experienced violence at the hands of their male partners. In addition to providing compassion and understanding for their members, support groups are designed to promote particular ways of understanding experiences. In the process, they work to transform women's identities. In a sense, support groups are storytelling groups that provide members with "better" stories, populated with familiar institutional identities.

But the institutional mediation of the battered woman identity is not a straightforward or deterministic process. Support groups do not simply assert identities. Members undertake considerable narrative identity work in order to articulate the battered woman image with the lived experiences of group members. Moreover, women often find alternative ways of conveying their experiences.

My data come from four support groups held in a shelter for battered women as well as from ten consecutive weekly meetings sponsored by an outreach group for such women.

THE NARRATIVE PLOT OF VIOLENCE: "TELL US WHAT HE DID TO YOU"

Support group facilitators most often started the hour-long meetings with questions such as "I don't know everyone here. Just so I can get an idea of where everyone is, would you each tell me a little about yourself and why you're here?" Such instructions asked women to tell a particular type of story: why you're *here*, with "here" being a support group for battered women.

Not surprisingly, because the experience of abuse is the central plot of the formula story of wife abuse, group members often would competently narrate the violence in their lives. Consider the first two sentences offered by one woman (pseudonyms throughout) in response to the facilitator's question:

> I'm Patti. My husband was physically and emotionally abusive. I always put up with his crap because I didn't think I had any other options.

While women often competently narrated the experience of extreme violence as the reason why they were "here," sometimes their initial stories didn't offer the formulaic depiction of violence. Indeed, at times, women failed to include the *necessary* element of violence. Consider the following example that starts when a facilitator asks Megan, a new group member, to "tell us a little about why you're here." Megan replied:

> I'm Megan. I got my divorce, I have my boys. Things are really going good. I'm on probation because of him. I beat up his girlfriend and slashed the tires on her car. That's why I'm on probation. I still don't know why he left me for her. He had everything, I worked, he never did. The kids are doing good. They were always used to him being gone a lot anyway. He pays his child support.

Megan first constructs her self as a woman for whom "things are really going good." Her story does not contain an element of the violence she experienced—it includes only a component of her violence toward her partner's new "girlfriend." She also doesn't characterize her former partner as an abusive man. Others learn only that he was irresponsible (never worked) but that he paid child support. Nothing in her first comments characterize her experiences as those of wife abuse. Another group member, Jessie, specifically asks Megan to enlarge her story to include violence:

Jessie: Was he physically abusive?

Megan: You name it, he did it. But I wouldn't have left. In fact, I tried to reconcile for months after he left. I guess I just couldn't handle the fact that he left me for her.

Facilitator: Emotional abuse can certainly be as damaging as physical abuse. Most people don't recognize that. [Group continues to discuss the problems of emotional abuse]

While Megan answers Jessie's question about abuse by saying "you name it, he did it," she does not elaborate but immediately returns to her preferred theme of the unfairness of being left for another woman. The facilitator then transforms these themes of infidelity into the preferred theme of abuse.

Furthermore, desired stories have violence as the *central organizing theme*. Consider the following story offered by a new member, Margarite. Notice how violence *is* embedded in her story (we argued and he got violent) but how it does *not* seem to be the major story theme.

Margarite: I don't know if I should be in a group like this. I thought my life was pretty normal. I just got sick of doing it all and not being respected. I never worked outside the home; my husband has a good job and I didn't have to work. I always did everything at home [elaborates]. I've been doing everything I could to make a wonderful home for us. Cooking his dinner late because he worked late and it turns out he wasn't working late—he was with another woman! I found out and confronted

him. We argued and he got violent. That's the first time he ever touched
me but I filed for a divorce and I found out when he got served he broke
down and cried. He sent me flowers for Valentine's Day. She didn't get
flowers, only me.

Megan: I give you a lot of credit. My husband was always running around
but I kept trying to get him back [two minutes elaborating on the
unfaithfulness of her own partner].

Facilitator: So, Margarite, you say he got violent. Can you tell me exactly
what he did to you?

While Margarite's story reasonably might be read as one of an "unappreciated wife" and "marital infidelity," and while Megan makes such
links between her own story and Margarite's story, the group facilitator
ignores Megan's talk and the substance of Margarite's story. Margarite is
not a betrayed wife or an unappreciated wife, she is a victim of violence,
of what her husband *did to her*.

In brief, these women knew they were attending support groups for
women experiencing wife abuse, yet they did not invariably tell stories
that fit a discursive environment privileging stories featuring the centrality of violence. Redirections and questions from facilitators or other group
members encouraged this type of story.

THE NARRATIVE PLOT OF RESPONSIBILITY AND CONTROL: "HE'S CONTROLLING YOU"

While violence forms the core of the story of "what he did to you," the
plot of the formula story of wife abuse assigns responsibility for the violence to men and it assigns a motive for this violence: Men do violence in
order to control women. This plot simultaneously develops the characters
of the battered woman and the abusive man.

Consider the following exchange where a group member, who had just
told a story of extreme violence, continues by narrating her understanding
of its cause (*I used his credit card*), and immediate relational context (*we'd
been arguing*). She concludes by raising an explicit question about her
own implication in the abuse:

Peg: I went to bingo and used his credit card for cash advances. The night
I ended up in the emergency room, I didn't expect it. He found out
about the credit card a few days before and we'd been arguing ever
since. Maybe I shouldn't have used his credit card?

Facilitator: How much did you spend?

Peg: Over $2,000. I really don't know exactly how much.

Facilitator: What he did to you was wrong. Financial control is one of the ways men deny women power in relationships.

In this instance, although the facilitator was inquisitive about the amount of money Peg spent, her response was unequivocal: What *he did to you* was wrong. The second sentence of the facilitator's response, "financial control is one of the ways men deny women power in relationships," depicts Peg's husband's behavior as indicating his desire for "financial control." It transforms Peg's husband into an instance of a category of people: men. It constructs a motive for men's financial control: to deny women power.

At another support group meeting for shelter residents the conversation for some minutes had drifted around the general topic of problems of transportation. This was a very real, immediate, and practical problem because this shelter was geographically isolated; there was no decent public transportation to it. Notice in the following exchange how the facilitator transforms a woman's statement about a current and personal condition (*I feel* isolated) to a prior and general condition (how *many* of you *felt* isolated). This transformation from current and personal to prior and general obviously was heard by other women as sensible: Sara responded that isolation is what "they" do, which constructs the character of the abusive man, Randi offers a specific example from her past experiences.

Cathy: I really need a car, I feel isolated.
Facilitator: How many of you felt isolated?
Sara: Oh yes, they isolate you.
Randi: He would take me to the door and scream at me and the neighbors heard and they wouldn't talk to me.

The wife abuse formula story is about violence not created by women; it is a story in which men control women. The plots of responsibility and control simultaneously construct the characters of the battered woman and abusive man; she is a victim who is not the author of her experience; he is a villain who knowingly seeks and actively maintains control over her.

INTERPRETIVE COMPLEXITY AND IDENTITY

Clearly, while support groups promote the wife abuse formula story as a template for understanding and narrating participants' experiences, the complications of lived experience hinder the formula's uniform application. Women can experience their lives in ways that contradict or collide with the formula story, and this leads to stories that vary significantly from the institutionally preferred narrative. While group meetings rely upon both the plot and the characters of the wife abuse formula story, they cannot unilaterally impose these identities upon the lives of women in the groups.

While there are multiple ways to make sense of the lived experience of violence, the wife abuse narrative offers much to women who embrace it as their own story. Clearly, the "long-suffering wife" story that promotes the goodness of saving marriages can be very dangerous for women who are in life-threatening relationships. Also, consider that within our cultural understandings, victims deserve sympathy and support and the battered woman character clearly is such a victim.

Yet while the wife abuse story often benefits women, it is not a story embraced by all women experiencing something potentially tellable as a story of wife abuse. Why do some women fail to use this narrative although it has so much to offer? Social workers and shelter workers often answer this question by asking: what is wrong with *women* who do not want to understand themselves as a character in the wife abuse story? As an alternative, I ask what is it about the *formula story* of wife abuse that might encourage women to reject it as their own story?

One reason to reject the wife abuse story might be that this narrative does not easily encompass the messiness of the lived experiences of troubles in general or of marital troubles in particular. The wife abuse narrative focuses exclusively on the experience of abuse; it leaves little space to include the complexities, indeterminacies, and situated nature of marital troubles. Furthermore, unless the abuse is experienced as extreme, there are questions about whether or not it is an example of morally intolerable "abuse" or of the more common—and less pejorative—cultural category of "normal violence." Still further, unless the partner can be constructed as a man with no redeeming qualities, it might be difficult to cast him as an abuser who is nothing but evil.

At the level of practical experience, women might find it difficult to see themselves as an example of the battered woman. The lived experience of women can be one where love and hate, caring and violence are perceived as simultaneously coexisting, where the violence is difficult to classify given folk understandings of "normal violence," where designating pure victims and pure villains ignores perceived relational cores of troubles. Perhaps the formula story is just too neat, with too many pat answers and not enough ambiguity.

In conclusion, *clearly, most certainly, and without a doubt*, I do not want these remarks to be interpreted as meaning that the wife abuse formula story should be discarded because it is not useful. Countless women *do* see themselves in this narrative and for those women the wife abuse formula story can be nothing less than lifesaving. Yet it remains that other women whose stories are potentially tellable as those of wife abuse resist this narrative as a way to understand their lives and their selves. Rather than simply assuming that some form of individual psychopathology underlies these women's resistance, it seems beneficial to examine characteristics of the narrative itself as it relates to their particular circumstances.

VIII
Evaluating Constructionist Perspectives on Social Problems

Introduction to Section VIII

In comparison to *objectivist* approaches that examine social problems as objective conditions in the environment, *constructionist* approaches explore how meaning is created by people who say things and do things to convince others that a problem is at hand and that something must be done. Clearly, objectivist and constructionist approaches differ. Objectivist approaches are concerned with how the world *is*, constructionist approaches focus on what people *think* the world is. Objectivist approaches lead to questions such as: What causes social problems? What should be done to eliminate these conditions? Constructionist approaches lead to questions such as: Why do we worry about some things and not about others that are, objectively speaking, just as harmful? How do successful constructions shape the objective world? How do they influence the ways we evaluate and categorize our experiences, our selves, and those around us?

From the perspective of most people, it makes the most sense to study social problems as objective conditions: Social problems create very real harm so it makes sense to want to understand what causes them and what can be done to eliminate them. Therefore a primary question about constructionist approaches is about their usefulness. We live in a world with seemingly endless amounts of pain and suffering created by social problems so why should we bother with understanding how people define this pain and suffering? Does constructionism divert our attention from more important questions about social problems? The articles in this section demonstrate some of the very practical lessons about social problems that we can learn from constructionist analysis.

The first example, "'Crack Babies' and the Politics of Mothering," by Jacquelyn Litt and Maureen McNeil, demonstrates how social constructionism can expose race and social class biases in constructions of social problems. Especially in the mid-1980s, but continuing to this day, there is public concern about "crack babies," who are babies born to women who have used crack-cocaine during their pregnancies. Litt and McNeil first question the objective reality behind public perceptions that these babies are *necessarily doomed* from birth. Scientific evidence indicates that while some of these babies do fit this typification, others do not. They argue that the incredible public concern about these babies is less rooted in scientific or medical findings than in powerful social concerns about poverty and motherhood. Poor, black, inner-city women are constructed as dangerous, evil women. The prognostic claims accompanying this construction focus on punishing such women. This particular construction leaves much in a shadowy background. For example, while the typification of the "crack mother" is of a poor black woman who lives in an inner city, not all pregnant women who use crack have these characteristics. In addition, women who *are* poor and black receive much more attention from police and child protective service workers than do women with other characteristics because police and child protective service workers are prone to assume such women are dangerous. And, while places in the troubled persons' industry that punish these women receive funding, there are not enough places for these women to receive medical care, and far too few drug treatment programs. Constructionist analysis can show us how public perceptions of social problems—what we worry about—are influenced by racial and social class biases.

Constructionist analysis also can show us how specific conditions can receive considerable attention because they are symbolic of other conditions. Philip Jenkins considers "The Symbolic Meanings of 'Pedophile Priests.'" He begins by noting that there is no way to know whether, objectively speaking, a greater percentage of priests are "pedophile," than are, say, ministers or soccer coaches. Yet public attention has targeted priests. Why? Jenkins argues that the pedophile priest problem is symbolic of claims about problems in the Catholic Church. Feminists, for example, long have argued that the priesthood should be open to women, many lay Catholics long have argued that priests should be able to marry, and the Catholic Church continues to be a primary opponent of rights for gays and lesbians. Although the hierarchy in the Catholic Church has not been responsive to claims made by feminists, homosexuals, or lay Catholics about needs for modernization, it might well be responsive to the widespread public outcry about "pedophile priests." Constructionist analysis can ask: What lies under the surface of claims about particular social problems?

Third, constructionist analysis can demonstrate how audience members can be persuaded to evaluate claims as important by appealing to emotion rather than to logic. In "Horror Stories and the Construction of Child Abuse," John M. Johnson examines the appeal of the social problems formula story of child abuse that evokes feelings of horror from audience members. By dramatizing extreme violence and extreme consequences, this formula story encourages audience members to evaluate the condition as intolerable. While such formula stories are effective in gaining audience support, Johnson argues that the proliferation of such stories leads to a "psychological numbing"—we can feel emotionally overwhelmed. In addition, social problems formula stories appealing to emotions might well move us to support a cause, but are emotions enough to sustain the long-term commitment we need to actually resolve social problems? Constructionist examinations can lead us to ask questions about sources of the appeal of claims, they can alert us to how audience members might be emotionally manipulated.

At first glance, social constructionist questions about how people construct the meaning of our world might not seem as important as questions about what causes social problems and what should be done to eliminate these conditions. Why, for example, should we be concerned with how the Nazis constructed the "Jewish problem?" Ronald J. Berger looks at the process of "Constructing the 'Jewish Problem' in Nazi Germany." He argues that Hitler appealed to deep-seated German beliefs about a type of person, "the Jew." The Final Solution—the mass extermination of people categorized as Jews—was, in part, possible because "the Jew" was constructed as a type of person whose killing did not pose a moral dilemma. We look back on this time in history now with horror and ask, how could it happen? Berger argues that at the time it was a "most ordinary thing to do." Social constructionist analysis can remind us that when types of people are constructed as dangerous outsiders, they will be treated as such. The words we use, the typifications we construct, are very real in their consequences. That is the power of social constructionism.

29

"Crack Babies" and the Politics of Mothering

JACQUELYN LITT AND MAUREEN MCNEIL

The term "crack baby" acquired currency and resonance during recent years in the United States. The term refers to infants and children who were exposed to crack cocaine during their mothers' pregnancies. Yet, the term "crack baby" also stands as a metaphor for a range of medical, social, and political difficulties in contemporary society—physically disabled and socially disadvantaged children, increasing numbers of women taking "street drugs," and the seemingly endless cycle of poverty in urban centers. The mass media creates these associations in their accounts of "crack babies," linking pregnant women's crack cocaine use to these most pressing social problems.

Increased prosecutions against pregnant women using illegal drugs reflect a new concern that women's drug use threatens not only the woman herself but also her child and ultimately her community's future. Federally funded research also reflects a new emphasis on curtailing pregnant women's drug use. From all of these quarters—legal, medical, and political—we have the makings of a moral crusade to save the "crack baby" from the "pregnant addict." In the wake of this surge of concern, social critiques and scientific reappraisals of the fears associated with "crack babies" have begun to emerge. Hence, it is appropriate to explore

This chapter is excerpted from Litt, Jacquelyn and Maureen McNeil (1994). "'Crack Babies' and the Politics of Reproduction and Nurturance." Pp. 93–116 in *Troubling Children: Studies of Children and Social Problems*, edited by Joel Best. Hawthorne, NY: Aldine de Gruyter.

the imagery associated with this term and to consider what has been at stake in the labeling and associated panic around the "crack baby."

The term "crack baby" itself is striking. It is terse and deterministic; the fate of these children is attributed to one factor—their mothers' use of crack cocaine. They become essentially designated by this single aspect of their formation and environment. Juxtaposing maternal corruption with childhood innocence evokes horror and condemnation. And as we will see, the fate of these babies appears fixed from birth, indeed, prior to birth.

What animates the so-called problem of the "crack baby"? We argue that the problem of "crack babies"—the very idea of the category "crack babies"—emerges from a particular packaging of contemporary social problems rather than from a discretely identifiable medical condition. We see in the fashionable construction of the "crack baby" a simultaneous creation of the "crack mother" and argue that fears about these children are being mobilized on the basis of suspicions about their mothers.

IDENTIFYING THE PROBLEM

The range of potential "signs" of damage associated with crack cocaine use during pregnancy is extensive. Early research attributed respiratory and urinary tract difficulties and even sudden infant death syndrome (SIDS) to cocaine exposure in the womb. Studies of prenatal cocaine exposure have linked it to a range of adverse maternal, fetal, and natal outcomes that include an increased incidence of spontaneous abortion, fetal death, prematurity, congenital malformations, decreased fetal growth, "small-for-gestational-age births," and adverse neurological development. The reported problems of "crack babies" are multidimensional and go beyond the medical domain. They include the burden so-called crack children place on adoptive parents, biological grandparents, school teachers, and hospital staff, as well as on society in general. A number of reports point to the increased demand on public expenditures that "crack babies" will require as they enter and go through the public school and social service systems.

Behind this imagery and the broad range of signs used to measure the putative impact of crack cocaine on babies, the medical profile of these problems is contested and now shows signs of optimism. There is "an absence of credible scientific data regarding the sequelae of prenatal exposure beyond the newborn period" (Zuckerman and Frank 1992:337). Even the evidence from this newborn period has been described as too inadequate and inconsistent to allow any clear predictions about the effects of prenatal exposure to cocaine on children's development and behavior.

Questions also have been raised about bias in the representation of research findings, about the inconsistency in those findings, and about the difficulty of isolating the effects of crack cocaine use from those caused by the use of other drugs and environmental factors.

Revisions in medical discourses indicate that fears about "crack babies" and the significance of the label itself are rooted less in consistent medical findings than in a moral panic around children and mothers in the inner city. This panic is linked to a series of interrelated and powerful social concerns around poverty and motherhood. An adversarial relationship between a putatively dangerous mother and an innocent, vulnerable fetus or child structures the discourse on "crack babies," as it does a number of related controversies regarding reproduction: abortion, reproductive technologies, genetic counseling, and fetal protection policies. It is poor, black, inner-city mothers who appear as the characteristic villains in this particular drama around crack cocaine. Correspondingly, although illegal drug use cuts across all class and race lines, women of color and poor women are more likely to be arrested and prosecuted for allegedly harming their fetus. The particular packaging and treatment of the problem minimize any claim these mothers might make for social resources for themselves and their children.

A NEW BIO-UNDERCLASS?

The early, albeit contested, emphasis on the neurological damage that "crack babies" suffer may signal a new political landscape, where public resentment might well shift away from the so-called "welfare queen" to a new "bio-underclass." What we once thought of as a cultural problem—the transmission of welfare dependency from one generation to the next—now becomes a biological matter. The attention given to another newly identified medical condition, fetal alcohol syndrome (FAS), could be seen as part of this trend.

The term "crack baby" symbolizes biological determinism and is compatible with a more general trend to see identities and life trajectories as set from birth. The contemporary obsession with genetic determinations and the ubiquitous search for "causal genes" for alcoholism, homosexuality, and so on are part of this wider pattern. In the context of increasing attribution of features of our individual being to genetic traits, the fears associated with "crack babies" are very much of these times.

The enthusiasm for genetic explanations runs parallel to a more diffused concern for identifying groups associated with biological vulnerability, and "crack babies" are seen as one such group. The media attention given to "crack babies" is dominated by expectations of permanent neurological damage (medical findings notwithstanding) that may create generations of impaired, dependent people. We would add that targeting socially and economically disadvantaged groups (specifically black and Latino urban communities in relation to "crack babies" and Native-American communities in relation to FAS) through biomedical designations is also a way of sidestepping thorny social and political issues. People can be blamed for their social disadvantage by designating them through medical labels.

The failure to suspend moral censure may in fact be related to the association between this putatively new "bio-underclass" and the wider panic about the so-called urban underclass, a topic that has received enormous attention in the academic and popular press. The alleged "bio-underclass" of "crack babies" biologizes the scenarios of urban poverty elaborated by scholars of the urban underclass; permanent and concentrated pockets of poverty and social isolation are created and recreated here through biological damage.

This biological version of the urban underclass rests on a gendered construction of the transmission of poverty; it rests, in fact, on the identification of women as the "vectors of transmission;" literally reproducing poverty from one generation to the next. Blaming mothers, particularly black mothers, for the reproduction of poverty has a long history in U.S. public policy, social science, and media reporting.

Moreover, recent representations of black mothers register some of the new circumstances of their lives, including their increasing involvement in the drug scene and their participation in street cultures. Although the assumption of a "culture of poverty" continues to underlie assumptions about irresponsible black mothers, it is now their biological legacy that is targeted for much of the blame. Of course, what remains with this change of imagery is the continuing pathologization of black women and the mobilization of fears about their threats to social order.

We see this mobilization of fears about biological damage in the celebration of middle-class biological motherhood embedded in the new reproductive technologies. The development and extended use of new reproductive technologies, including genetic counseling, genetic engineering, and fetal surgery, can be seen as part of this more general trend to think about children as products whose quality can be controlled. Because these developments involve major economic and social investments in biological improvements, they are predominantly used by more privileged parents and would-be parents seeking to control and improve their heritage.

Juxtaposed with these developments, the panics over "crack babies" and FAS are about controlling biological heritage, albeit in a different way.

They focus on the lower end of the social spectrum. The predominant images of "crack babies" in both popular articles and the medical press concern the urban poor, often black women. Hence, the bifurcation of the biological damage to the "crack baby" and the biological perfectibility of the highly medically monitored baby expresses social expectations about reproduction in contemporary society. Privileged consumers use more of their own resources and draw on social resources to facilitate their reproduction. Meanwhile, the panic around "crack babies" expresses strong fears about, and moral indignation toward, reproduction among the urban poor. In stark terms, the reproduction of the relatively privileged becomes identified with scientific achievement, whereas the reproduction of the underprivileged is linked to biological degeneration.

THE POLITICS OF NURTURANCE

The possibilities offered to more and more women to control their reproduction have rendered traditional categories of biological inevitability unstable. Pregnancy—and thus biological motherhood—are now seen as achievements, albeit contested ones, rather than "natural" outcomes of a biological process. Measuring mothers by their capacity to provide (both biologically and socially) for the child is precisely what underlies the discourse around "crack babies." What are these mothers providing for their children? Are the provisions adequate or, indeed, dangerous? And if not the mother, who shall provide for these children? The problem of provision is linked to "family values": abstinence, morality, and discipline, all "values" that crack mothers allegedly lack.

In their elaborations of the harms inflicted on "crack babies" in their own homes, medical, media, and academic accounts show remarkable continuity, outlining a trajectory of maternal neglect during early child-rearing, leading toward the production of another generation of crack users. Paralleling the reproduction scenario embedded in the constructions of a bio-underclass, the discourse categorizes children as an at-risk category and their mothers as ultimately failing to provide the necessary elements for growth and development.

A series in the *New York Times*, "Children of the Shadows" (1993), features the lives of ten young people (primarily teenagers), all of whom live in urban neighborhoods dominated by "temptations," "chaos," and "danger." The plots in these newspaper narratives center around the pressing question of whether children can be motivated to leave behind or stand above the degeneracy of the urban ghetto and on the question of who will save the children from these dangers. Fathers are virtually absent; mothers are present but, although occasionally angelic, most often are constructed as negligent. According to these accounts, the children's prospects depend on how their families function; and although many children find safety and acquire middle-class motives from church or school personnel, it is around the family—and its ability to secure these connections to school and church—that the child's life depends.

What is striking about this collection of narratives is the unitary portrayal of children at risk in profound, life-threatening danger. Urban settings appear as uniformly dangerous and chaotic, and only rarely are children portrayed as finding protection in their own homes. Unlike the conventional ideal where the home serves as a "haven in a heartless world," the private domain of maternal activity is represented here as steeped in the chaos and dangers of public life. Most often it is the drug-addicted mother who appears as the dangerous figure.

Against this backdrop of the nonnurturant, neglectful mother is the implicit standard of the good, providing mother. Indeed, representations of the negligent "crack mother" depend on a familiar, accessible image of the normative mother, and it is this latter image that constructs all others as marginal and deviant.

What worries us about this and similar representations is that women's social and economic difficulties are denied. The conclusion readers are encouraged to draw from such studies is that the solution to the crack problem is to curtail the freedom of women involved with drugs and possibly to curtail women's freedom more generally in the urban environment—and to do so in the name of children.

CONCLUSION

What guides the discussions of "crack babies" is a presumption of child saving, a presumption embedded in media, social science, medical, and social service involvements in the problem of crack cocaine. Various experts effectively speak for "crack babies," forcefully silencing their biological mothers.

It is out of this authority and the oppositional model of mother and child that some experts create what we see as a particularly punitive response to pregnant women using crack cocaine. This dynamic emerges most clearly in the push toward criminal sanctions against crack-addicted mothers rather than toward establishing economic, health, and rehabilitation support for these women and their children.

There is a severe shortage of prenatal and drug rehabilitation care for pregnant drug addicts. According to a survey undertaken by the House

Select Committee on Children, Youth, and Families, two-thirds of all hospitals studied had no drug treatment programs available for pregnant patients, and none of the hospitals reported special programs providing both drug treatment and prenatal care. Instead of rehabilitation and support, women receive attention from the criminal justice system, which effectively separates these children from their biological mothers. "Crack mothers" attract a kind of police and prosecutory brutality that differs little from the physical beatings that have received wide public attention and scorn. Aggressive prosecutors have brought fetal endangerment charges against women, mainly against women of color.

These child-saving efforts are organized around identifying certain categories of women as reproductive and maternal risks. In an interesting analysis of the American welfare system, Deborah A. Stone sketched the increasing importance of identifying groups "at risk" and the cultivation of individual responsibility as ways of restricting the expansion of welfare provision. Stone (1989:630) outlines the historical trajectory of American welfare provision that has led in this direction: "In the context of cost-containment and efficiency goals, the at-risk status is converted into a form of dangerousness, not just to self but to others." Media coverage designates crack mothers as "at risk" and embodying this "dangerousness." The reference to "crack babies," and by implication "crack mothers," as potentially increasing the burden on society as a whole is a familiar element in reporting on crack cocaine. As the American public groans under the burden of health care costs, as welfare provisions are cut back and refashioned, and as minimalist taxation is in public favor, the imperative to restrict claims on the public purse is powerful. Within what Stone calls "the context of cost containment and efficiency goals," coverage of the "crack baby" problem maximizes attention to the burdens that these women create for a starved federal budget and minimizes any claim on social resources they might make on behalf of their children.

REFERENCES

Stone, D. 1989. "At Risk in the Welfare State." *Social Research* 56:591–633.
Zuckerman, B., and D. A. Frank. 1992. "Crack Kids?: 'Not Broken'." *Pediatrics* 82 February:337–39.

30

The Symbolic Meanings of "Pedophile Priests"

PHILIP JENKINS

In the last decade, the issue of sexual abuse of minors by priests and ministers has come to be seen as a widespread social problem requiring urgent remedies. The issue itself is by no means new; the stereotype of the pedophile priest has existed in anticlerical rhetoric for centuries. In fact, sexual imagery and speculation formed a major component of the virulent anti-Catholicism that was so central to American politics during the nineteenth century. However, such overt manifestations of religious conflict had subsided greatly during recent years, and it is remarkable to observe the vigor and alleged scale of the current clergy sex abuse problem.

"Clergy abuse" has been reported within most major Christian denominations, and the issue has been discussed in Jewish circles, though by far the largest number of stories have involved the Roman Catholic church. This is a critical point that rarely receives notice in the literature, either scholarly or popular, for "clergy abuse" has become synonymous with the issue of "pedophile priests," a convenient alliteration that appears to blame Catholic clergy as opposed to pastors, preachers, ministers, or rabbis. There is no central organization that tabulates reports of abusive clergy or ministers but the major body providing liability insurance for religious institutions reports that in the past decade, there were several hundred known cases of clerical child abuse involving non-Catholic clergy. The centrality of Catholic priests in the construction of the problem will thus require explanation.

This chapter is excerpted from Jenkins, Philip (1995). "Clergy Sexual Abuse: The Symbolic Politics of a Social Problem." Pp. 105–30 in *Images of Issues, Typifying Contemporary Social Problems*, 2nd edition, edited by Joel Best. Hawthorne, NY: Aldine de Gruyter.

THE MEDIA AND CLERGY SEX ABUSE

Clergy sex abuse is a model example of a social problem that appears to undergo mushroom growth, receiving virtually no attention from media or policymakers before about 1984, yet becoming a major focus of popular concern within a few years. To explain the rapid growth of interest, we must appreciate changes in the mass media during these years. At mid-century, the mass media exercised considerable restraint in investigating or reporting news stories involving scandals in mainstream churches. Before the 1970s, the cinema seldom portrayed a priest in anything other than a heroic or saintly guise. Partly, this may have reflected concern about criticizing such powerful interests, and films with a religious content went to great lengths to avoid commercially disastrous condemnation by Church authorities.

The recent interest in clergy abuse represents a reversal of this trend, and reflects a fundamental shift in news values during the 1970s and 1980s. There was an unquestionable shift toward sensationalist coverage in the news media, toward tabloid television news shows, sensationalistic talk shows, and "true crime" documentaries, which often blurred the line between fact and fiction. The preponderance of speakers on these programs were from groups very critical of the clergy and the Church hierarchy. All suggested that the prevalence of abusive behavior was extremely high, and that the Church had for years systematically engaged in cover-ups. Although it would be inconceivable to present a "balanced view" of the issue by having a speaker defend pederasty, programs effectively presented no speaker who argued that the Church had ever responded correctly or honestly to the problem.

Changes in media attitudes are critically important because they increased the likelihood that individual abuse cases would become widely known, which in turn increased public awareness of the prevalence of the offense, and fostered future reporting. The media also provided a wider arena in which interest groups could present and establish claims about the nature and severity of the problem.

PROFESSIONAL INTEREST GROUPS

Apart from the mass media, certain professional interest groups have played an important claims-making role in defining and shaping the clergy abuse problem. The legal profession is an obvious example. During the 1980s, numerous legal cases established child sexual abuse as a major area of litigation, in which large sums of money could be won from defendants or their insurers. In practical terms, this had the effect of encouraging those who believed they had been victimized to pursue their grievances, and nursery schools had been heavily hit by a series of liability claims. Successful lawsuits proliferated from 1985 onward. Between 1985 and 1994, between $400 million and $1 billion is reported to have been paid in settlements and legal costs.

The ensuing scandals can be seen as having a snowball effect, encouraging past victims, real or imaginary, to come forward and register their complaints. Moreover, the media criticized church attempts to defend such suits, and the CNN program "Fall from Grace" complained that Sunday donations were finding their way to the defense of pedophile priests.

Like lawyers, therapists have a clear vested interest in the promotion of distinctive views of the clergy abuse problem. The earlier recognition of the child sexual abuse phenomenon had greatly enhanced the authority and visibility of therapists and psychologists as experts in dealing with this problem. Throughout the 1980s, a series of court battles and legal controversies established and expanded the expertise of therapists, and it was natural that the therapeutic community would be closely involved in the new clergy abuse problem.

Therapists and their ideas were important in several ways in propagating certain views of the abuse problem. Also vital were the victims' self-help groups, which drew on the familiar rhetoric of the "survivors" movements that had earlier mobilized victims of rape, abuse, or incest. "Survivors" of clergy abuse formed well-organized pressure groups such as SNAP (Survivors' Network of those Abused by Priests). These were extremely successful in keeping the issue in the news by a variety of tactics, such as demonstrating at gatherings of the episcopal hierarchy, and providing articulate spokespersons for news programs and documentaries.

THE POLITICAL CONTEXT

Political factors account for the extremely critical picture presented of the churches in general and the Catholic church in particular. The abuse crisis would not have erupted so quickly without a preexisting public demand or expectation about the likely truth of such charges. The atmosphere of belief and acceptance was to some extent created by the more general concern over child abuse during the previous decade, but specific concerns about the churches were enhanced by the apparently growing gulf between traditional religious values and changing social patterns. Since the 1960s, changes in American society had resulted in a general weakening of traditional family structures and an increasingly independent role for women. Within the religious communities, some churches accommodated women's demands for greater visibility and power. However, the Catholic church remained obdurate to calls for changes in attitudes in matters such as divorce, abortion, and contraception, as well as to women's ordination and an end to priestly celibacy. The church thus seemed increasingly visible as a bastion of "patriarchal" values, and even of hostility to women's claims to social equality. In addition, the Catholic church emerged as a primary opponent of gay rights, either within the clergy or in society at large. In the moral and social issues that were central to American politics during the 1980s, the Catholic church had become a prominent and powerful force on the side of conservatism and traditional values. This was all the more important because of the church's status in communities (above all urban ethnic groups), which were likely to be strong supporters of many liberal and Democratic causes.

There was some outright criticism of the church's political positions, but in political and media terms, this was quite risky for the groups involved. However, the abuse issue placed Church critics in a very different position because its consequences could be presented in terms of sharp contrasts and contradictions: while the Church affected to speak for traditional values and sexual restraint, its clergy were heavily involved in sexual excess and exploitation; while the Church denounced homosexuality between consenting adults, its clergy committed homosexual acts against vulnerable children; and while the Church's "pro-life" stance asserted the absolute value of human life and the defense of small children, the institution made strenuous efforts to protect clergy who assaulted and raped the young.

The clergy abuse issue also had wide appeal in feminist circles, and a broadly feminist analysis has been very influential in mainstream media reporting of the problem. It is scarcely coincidental that one of the phrases most commonly employed in such reports is some variation of "the sins of the fathers." Since 1990 there have been lengthy and repeated discussions of clergy abuse in magazines directed chiefly at a women's audience including *Vanity Fair*, *Redbook*, and *Ms*. All emphasize the same themes: the frequency of the offense, its roots in patriarchal values and beliefs, and the structural inability of the church to eradicate the problem without abandoning traditional gender roles. Generally speaking, such accounts focus on the abuse involved when clergy have sexual relations with women, rather than the more publicized exploitation of minors, but the articles subsume both into a common pattern of deviance.

Feminists thus found in the abuse issue potent ideological ammunition for an attack on the institution of the Catholic church. However, it would not be correct to see this critique as solely an external assault upon the institution, as the same feminist arguments also appeared within radical or dissident sections of the church itself. Clergy abuse thus served as a focus for debates and controversies that had been simmering within the church for decades, battles over the privileged position of the clergy, and the role of women. Among Catholics, since the 1960s there had been demands for a greatly enhanced role for the laity and a change in the strongly hierarchical nature of the church. In the 1980s, dissent was manifested in issues such as the right of Catholic clergy and theologians to support moral and political positions contrary to official teaching, and the question of women's ordination. Critics of the policy on celibacy charged that a substantial number of priests might be ignoring the church's regulations by illicitly engaging in sexual relationships with women.

As the clergy abuse issue emerged, then, there was a large constituency within the Catholic church predisposed to affirm the rights and powers of the laity against those of the clergy, and of the lower clergy against the Church hierarchy. This also meant criticizing the hierarchy for its entrenched bureaucratic positions and its tendency to deal with clerical failings through secretive internal procedures.

The significance of the abuse issue for feminist and other dissidents within the Church can be best appreciated in the context of the remedies suggested for the problem, as these included essentially all the major changes advocated by liberal Catholic reformers for decades, though now with the added force supplied by the pedophile theme. Demands included an end to mandatory celibacy, the ordination of women to the priesthood, and limitations on the sanctity of the confessional. Reformers argued that each would in its way contribute to the protection of the young.

CONCLUSION

Sexual relations between adults and minors can occur in almost any social or institutional setting, and some individuals are likely to commit such acts on a frequent or habitual basis. The issue is therefore not so much to understand what makes an individual become a "pedophile priest," but how these discrete cases become constructed as part of a generalized social problem, and the moral or political dimensions that such a problem will attain. In typifying the "clergy abuse problem," it is possible to imagine interpretations that might have blamed (for example) the changing sexual standards of the wider society, the prevalence of pornography, or the aberrations of the individual priests involved. Yet these alternative interpretations did not occur, and both the emphasis and the stigma have clearly been on the institution of the Catholic church. That the problem developed in this direction is richly informative both about the underlying hostility that the Church and its hierarchy had attracted in the previous two decades, and the resulting political agendas that emerge forcefully in media coverage and expert interpretation of the issue.

The clergy abuse affair says much about values, in the sense of those things that are most prized in a given society, and the extent to which these values now are in flux. At least rhetorically, contemporary American society has come to place a very high premium on certain concepts of childhood, and these cultural values must be protected even at the cost of sacrificing what were once considered profoundly important religious and cultural beliefs, such as the sanctity of the priesthood, the secrecy of the confessional and so on. In addition, the increased social status of women has made suspect any institution that explicitly asserts masculine and patriarchal authority.

For activists, the clergy abuse issue reinforces valuable lessons about the best means of making and establishing claims, and the best grounds of authority on which a problem can be built. In contrast to earlier centuries, it would be quite unsound today to base an argument on traditional religious criteria ("The Bible says . . . ," "The Church has always believed . . ."), or indeed on traditional authority of any kind. Far more successful is any approach that links the issue in question either to defending and promoting the status of women, or to any threat that can be postulated against children. For example, pornography is depicted as evil not because it violates the Seventh Commandment, but because it leads both to child pornography and sexual violence against women. Drugs appear to represent consensual victimless crimes, but drug-taking leads to the innocent suffering of "crack babies." A celibate clergy is wrong not because it is antiscriptural, but because it creates a situation in which priests molest children. The rhetoric of contemporary social problems thus illustrates the fundamental importance of placing the interests of women and children in the forefront of any feasible issue, to take advantage of new sensibilities.

31

Horror Stories and the
Construction of Child Abuse

JOHN M. JOHNSON

Everyone recognizes that the mass media's power extends beyond the mere transmittal of information. Their power (and some of their mystery) also derives from their ability to elicit emotions. Eliciting emotions often paves the way for action. We recognize the importance of this process at a common sense level. The civil rights movement of the 1960s, for example, gained much support and momentum from the publication of emotionally provocative photographs and accounts of the brutalities at Selma and Montgomery, Alabama. Press coverage helped shape public action, leading to subsequent civil rights reforms. The Vietnam War—the first mass media war—offers another good example. The pervasive newspaper stories and television accounts of daily battle scenes were important influences at all stages of the war, for both its supporters and detractors.

Sociologists recognize the relevance and importance of emotionally provocative mass media accounts for creating new social problems. Sensationalized mass coverage often is an important aspect of social problems claims-making. This chapter analyzes mass media's use of child abuse horror stories, emotionally provocative stories about violence to children. Such horror stories have played an important role in the political, social, and institutional success of the child maltreatment movement in the United States.

Child abuse began as a relatively esoteric concern of a few medical researchers, but a dramatic article published in a medical journal in 1962

This chapter is excerpted from Johnson, John M. (1995). "Horror Stories and the Construction of Child Abuse." Pp. 17–31 in *Images of Issues: Typifying Contemporary Social Problems*, 2nd edition, edited by Joel Best. Hawthorne, NY: Aldine de Gruyter.

attracted the mass media's attention. Professional and mass media publications offered complementary coverage, which was critical to the early agenda-setting and political successes of the social movement. Initially, the emphasis was on physical abuse or "battering," but as the movement achieved legitimacy, the scope of both media and movement concern expanded to other areas, including child neglect, emotional abuse, and, eventually, incest and sexual abuse of children The publication of child abuse horror stories has played a prominent role in the social, political, and institutional successes of the child maltreatment movement during the last 25 years. These horror stories are mass media reports of individual cases that involve dramatic or unusual injuries to children and that evoke an emotional response about the problem of child abuse or neglect.

My data are from a larger study of all newspaper stories on child abuse and neglect that appeared for 32 years in the *Arizona Republic* and the *Phoenix Gazette*, the two major newspapers in Arizona. During the 1948-80 period, a total of 623 news stories about child abuse and neglect appeared in these newspapers. In addition, I collected clippings from many other newspapers, magazines, and other media over a period of more than 10 years. Much of this coverage featured child abuse horror stories. I analyzed these reports to identify the formal properties of child abuse horror stories. The focus here is on how these stories evoke negative emotionality.

EVOKING NEGATIVE EMOTIONALITY

Ideally, parents love and protect children. Families are the source of intimacy and selfhood, and, even though parents have more power than their children, parents presumably use this power in the child's best interests. Family experience is, for most people, largely favorable and rewarding. For some, it is not, but few view their family experience with emotional neutrality. Thus, stories about violence within the family have a great potential to elicit an emotional response from their audience.

Mass media accounts of domestic violence play upon our common family experience, whether actual or desired, to elicit emotions. The term *child abuse horror story* obviously suggests that such stories evoke feelings of horror, but I use the concept more broadly, referring to stories that elicit strong negative feelings. Whether the specific feelings evoked are horror, shock, revulsion, sadness, anger, tragedy, or some other is less important than the fact that the feelings are strong ones for most individuals. Stories about horrible injuries or gruesome circumstances may produce emotional reaction:

> The Baltimore Police found Patty Saunders, 9, in the 23 × 52 inch closet where she had been locked for half her life. She weighed only 20 pounds, and stood

less than three feet tall. Smeared with filth, scared from parental beatings, Patty had become irreparably mentally retarded. (*Newsweek*, October 10, 1977:31)

The preceding story evokes negative feelings, not only by portraying inhuman treatment, but by specifying the terrible, life-long consequences. Another example:

Alyssa Dawn Wilson died at the age of six weeks in a Beauford, South Carolina clinic. An autopsy disclosed that the infant had a ruptured liver and spleen and eye injuries, a fractured knee, 14 broken ribs, bite marks on her cheeks, bruises on her stomach and back and alcohol in her bloodstream. Her father was arrested for murder. (*Newsweek*, October 10, 1977:32)

In both examples, the injuries are such that the reader can clearly see that they could not have been either unintentional or accidental. At a comonsense level, we impute moral responsibility or culpability for intentional or willful injuries. We commonly do not hold people blameworthy if it can be shown that their actions were unintentional or accidental. But only the foolhardy could believe that the injuries in these examples could have resulted "from an accident." It is the fact that they are intentionally inflicted, rather than their consequences, that makes these injuries so horrifying.

Negative emotions may be aroused by detailing the gruesome acts of the injury, or the consequences of the abuse, or even the circumstances surrounding the investigation:

The body of a missing two-month-old boy was found in a pile of rubble Tuesday, hours after the infant's parents were charged in connection with his death. The nude body was found under some dirt, leaves, and cement in the foundation of a torn down house, about four blocks from the parents' home. "The location was given to us by the father," said Detective Larry Connors. Thus far, police do not know if the death was the result of child abuse that went too far, or the result of a deliberate slaying. (*Fort Wayne Journal Gazette*, December 27, 1978:3)

Child abuse horror stories use two journalistic conventions to elicit an emotional response from the reader: ironic contrast and structural incongruity. They are related and similar in some respects, but nevertheless distinct. The press prefers certain kinds of stories because they allow for a better display of the intrinsic properties of the medium. Newspaper reporters have a strong preference for "man bites dog" stories, for example, because the print medium and the linear display allow for a greater exploitation of ironic contrast. Presenting the story in print maximizes its ironic possibilities.

For example, one story concerns Herbert Smith, Jr., who faced five years to life in prison for the fatal beating of his stepdaughter, whose death he tried to prevent through a lawsuit. Smith, from Wichita, pleaded no contest to a charge of second-degree murder. His daughter fell into a coma, and Smith filed a civil suit to prevent doctors and the child's mother from unhooking the child's respirator. Smith claimed in the suit that he could face more serious charges if the machine were unhooked. The injunction was denied, and the respirator was unhooked. In this case, the irony comes from the fact that the person responsible for the injuries became the litigant to "save the child's life."

Structural incongruity need not involve a formal irony, but it usually does include some feature that strikes the reader as bizarre, strange, unusual, or "out of place." One well-known example is the now infamous case of the 1984 arrest of the grandmotherly (and 77-year-old) Virginia McMartin, founder and director of the McMartin Preschool in Manhattan Beach, California. Along with six relatives and coworkers, she was charged with nearly 30 counts of sexual abuse and molestation of the children in their care. A second example:

> A nine-year-old girl was sexually molested by her father and uncle, an aunt and her brother's boyfriend over a seven year period without any of the suspects knowing the others were involved. "You should have seen the look on their faces," said Detective Don Gultz. It was "You too?!" The four adults were charged with 53 felony counts." (Overland, Missouri, United Press International, August 16, 1985)

THE ROLE OF HORROR STORIES IN THE CONSTRUCTION
OF CHILD ABUSE AS A SOCIAL PROBLEM

Publishing child abuse horror stories serves a wide range of uses. One of the most obvious is that it fits the organizational needs and interests of news organizations. But more than just news organizations are involved. The publication of child abuse stories also helps many professional and occupational groups, social science and medical researchers, and various private and nonprofit agencies. These agencies establish agendas for the child abuse movement. They are invariably tied to requests for more resources and more public funds.

It would be a mistake to see child abuse as merely a creation of the media. News organizations played a creative role in the process; some would argue a major role. But, just as important, news organizations *responded* to a sense of urgency created by other groups, agencies, and sectors of the public. The press occasionally stimulated government action and legislative initiative, sometimes on their own, but more commonly at the bidding of other parties. Either way, the mass media reports of child abuse and neglect seem to have played a strong role in legitimizing this problem, serving at all phases to present the official conception and definition of child abuse, as well as promoting existing or planned official interventions, policies, programs, and budgetary requests. It is easy to see that the mass media perspective on child abuse is that promulgated by official agencies and their professional supporters. Insofar as the press criticizes official definitions or agencies, its criticism is coupled to the plea that officials do not have the resources they need to do a better job.

It is very important to understand that there is a larger cultural and historical context within which child abuse horror stories have appeared. Many of our contemporary social welfare and criminal justice institutions originated in the Progressive Era of the 1880s to the 1920s, a time of great optimism for institutional solutions to social problems. Today, we seem to have entered a New Progressive Era, characterized by significant cultural optimism about the capabilities of the welfare state to resolve social problems. The mass media organizations that have disseminated child abuse horror stories have, in addition, published many stories on incest, sexual abuse of children, child prostitution, drugs, crime of all sorts, pornography, drunk driving and so on. Such coverage has proliferated to the extent that the term of "psychological numbing" has been coined to refer to the feeling of being overwhelmed or inundated by such problems, even to the point of apathy or cynicism on the part of many citizens.

Educated people who follow press coverage will experience the "psychological numbing," and so we can understand the existence of apathy and cynicism. Such feelings, however understandable, are transitory and situational for most people and do not reflect the long-range commitment to solving social problems. It is important to have a realistic and informed basis of knowledge about modern mass media, definitions of social problems, and welfare state operations to make the best choices we can for a better future.

32

Constructing the "Jewish Problem" in Nazi Germany

Ronald J. Berger

The "Jewish problem" in Nazi Germany had deep-seated roots. The Nazis built upon what came before, upon a longstanding collective representation of "the Jew." Following Émile Durkheim, collective representations refer to culturally shared symbols, systems of meaning, or categorizing systems used by individuals to make sense of themselves and the society in which they live. When applied to a group of people, collective representations work somewhat like stereotypes by providing simplifying schemes of interpretation that enable individuals to view a heterogeneous group of people as constituting a homogeneous category whose members are "all alike." In this way, collective representations can be used to construct or typify particular kinds of individuals (such as Jews) as problems that warrant particular kinds of treatment.

TYPIFYING THE JEW

Studies of contemporary social problems often emphasize the ways in which particular types of persons have been constructed as victims who are morally deserving of public sympathy and whose suffering justifies remedial social action. I consider an obverse type of construction that was applied to an entire ethnic group: In Nazi Germany, Jews were typified as persons who victimized others, who were morally unworthy of sympathy,

This chapter is excerpted from Berger, Ronald J. (2002). *Fathoming the Holocaust: A Social Problems Approach* (chapter 3 and pp 8–9). Hawthorne, NY: Aldine de Gruyter.

and whose continued presence constituted a problem that needed solution. The Jew as a social type was not merely an unsympathetic character but a despised and less-than-human being. A dehumanized group like the Jews can be constructed and then isolated and even exterminated through social processes that are in themselves quite ordinary or banal.

Christian Claims and European Discontents

Arguably the "Jewish problem" has one of the longest histories known to humankind and one that has been diffused across a wide range of geographical contexts. The Nazis drew upon a centuries-old tradition of anti-Semitism rooted in religious hostility and combined it with German nationalism and pseudoscientific racial theory to articulate a powerful collective representation of the Jew. This representation defined Jews and Germans in "complementary opposition," as groups whose motives, interests, and essential nature were diametrically opposed to each other.

The general features of an oppositional collective representation of the Jew did not originate in Germany. Historical accounts suggest that since the dawn of Christianity, Jews and Christians were each other's "disconfirming other," for genuine belief in the veracity of one religion required belief in the falsity of the other. Although Jews were a powerless minority in Christian-dominated Europe, their continued presence constituted a permanent challenge to the certainty of Christian belief.

Social problems claims-making typically entails the assignment of responsibility or attribution of blame for problems. In Christian culture the collective representation of the Jew was constituted through claims about Jewish responsibility for a host of horrific acts. In addition to holding the Jewish people almost exclusively responsible for Christ's death, Jews were accused of engaging in "blood libel" (the murdering of Christian children for religious purposes), desecrating the body of Christ (despoiling the Christian sacraments of bread and wine), poisoning wells, and spreading plagues and famines.

As a discriminated minority group, Jews were often forbidden from agricultural land ownership and hence excluded from a common source of livelihood. They thus sought their economic survival in areas that complemented the majority population. In a world where commerce was poorly developed, people lacked literacy skills, and usury was discouraged by Christian Scripture, Jews found a niche as merchants, traders, artisans, physicians, and moneylenders. However, their very success in these areas bred resentment. Importantly, Jews were perceived as unlike any other minority group, for the threat they posed did not emanate from local conditions of friction or conflict with the dominant population. Rather, the Jewish threat was ubiquitous, vague, and diffuse; and hostility toward Jews could be found among people who had never seen them, and in countries where Jews had not lived for centuries.

By the eighteenth century the Enlightenment, or Age of Reason, opened up new possibilities for European Jews. Enlightenment philosophy promoted the belief that humanity could rely on rational thought rather than on religious authority to govern its affairs. Historically the monarchical states of Europe had used one brand of Christianity or another to delineate the boundaries of national identity. But the Enlightenment, which promoted democratic ideals and the separation of religion from politics, fostered Jewish emancipation. Jews achieved greater formal political equality and moved forward on a path of assimilation. At the same time, traditionalists such as church officials and royalists who favored religious-based monarchies over secular, democratic governments blamed Jews for fostering unwanted social change. Modernists, on the other hand, expected Jews to relinquish their religious "superstitions" in order to become full citizens of the nation.

The architects of the Enlightenment were themselves divided on the "Jewish question." Some of the most influential Enlightenment thinkers such as Voltaire were intensely anti-Semitic. However, this prejudice was derived not from the Christian tradition but from secular notions (which can be traced to Greco-Roman pagans) that viewed Jews as a people who were inherently deceitful, greedy, intolerant, and arrogant. It was a racist view that predated nineteenth-century biological racism. Thus Jews remained a lightning rod for the social strains and discontents of modern Europe.

The more sympathetic Enlightenment thinkers thought that this inferior Jewish character was due not to the nature of Jews but to their circumstances or environment. Others thought that the way to solve the "Jewish problem" was for the Jew himself to become "enlightened" and detach himself from his religion. In practice, this often meant conversion to Christianity, for to remain un-Christian was to remain a perpetual and potentially disloyal outsider.

German Nationalism and Nazi Claims

Cross-national diffusion of social problems requires the adopters of claims to define conditions in their own society as similar to those that are the source of those claims. Clearly, the diffusion of Christianity established the basis for the diffusion of anti-Semitic constructions of the Jew. Still, each individual society puts its own stamp on this construction. In Germany, the sixteenth-century theologian Martin Luther (1483–1546) is often credited with Germanizing the Christian critique of Judaism and establishing anti-Semitism as a key element of German culture and national identity. Luther denounced Jews as Germany's particular "misfortune," "plague," and "pestilence."

In the late nineteenth and early twentieth centuries, this religious-based collective representation of the Jew was given a new foundation through anti-Semitic interpretations of modern biological and anthropological research. This transformation of anti-Semitism from a religious ideology to a "scientific" theory of race elevated the social credibility (and eventual legal legitimacy) of Nazi claims about the "Jewish problem."

The British biologist Charles Darwin (1809–82) postulated that life had evolved through a process of natural selection or survival of the fittest among diverse species, including humans. Social Darwinists in both Europe and the United States applied this theory to the social realm, assuming that some races had natural qualities that made them more fit members of society than others. In addition, Sir Francis Galton (1822–1911), Darwin's cousin, had pioneered the eugenics movement. *Eugenics,* which means "well born" or "good genes," was a philosophy that advocated social intervention to regulate the genetic composition of the population by encouraging the breeding of parents with good genes and discouraging the breeding of parents with bad genes. The United States was, in fact, the first country to pass laws calling for compulsory sterilization in the name of racial purification. In 1923 a prominent German medical director wrote to the Ministry of the Interior: "[W]hat we racial hygienists promote is not all new or unheard of. In a cultured nation of the first order, in the United States of America, that which we strive toward was introduced and tested long ago" (cited in Rubenstein and Roth 1987:141).

In Germany the belief that there were distinctive Jewish and German characters or types led anti-Semites to conclude that Jews were an inferior race and Germans were a superior race. In Aryan racial theory, Caucasians were seen as superior, with the so-called Nordic race (Germanic people of northern Europe, especially Scandinavians) characterized by tall stature, light hair, and blue eyes viewed as the original Caucasian stock. German eugenicists favored social policies that would promote the purity of this race. Thus in Nazi doctrine race was viewed as the basic element of human society.

While some historians doubt whether Hitler really believed the scientific basis of Nazi racial theory, he was nonetheless committed to translating these ideas into action, to finally and once and for all doing something about the Jews. As Hitler is reported to have said:

> I know perfectly well . . . that in the scientific sense there is not such a thing as race . . . [But] I as a politician need a conception which enables the order which has hitherto existed on historic basis to be abolished and an entirely

new and antihistoric order enforced and given an intellectual basis. (quoted in Yahil 1990:37)

APPEALING TO AUDIENCES AND GARNERING SUPPORT

Social problems claims-making involves the construction of collective representations of types of persons who constitute problems. Successful claims-making, however, ultimately requires public endorsement if it is to achieve legitimacy. Social movements are often the vehicles for advancing claims about social problems and translating these claims into publicly supported actions. Social movements use an ideological "frame" or scheme of interpretation that provides members with a coherent explanation of a rather diverse and ambiguous set of facts and circumstances. This frame promotes solidarity among adherents and mobilizes them to work on the movement's behalf. It is also used to make appeals to new audiences that might support the movement in various ways—as rank-and-file activists, financial supporters, or voters, for example. A social movement has a greater chance of success when its frame is aligned with sentiments in the larger culture. As we have seen, there was much sentiment in German culture that was congruent with Nazi claims about Jews. As Hitler observed in 1922:

> I scanned the revolutionary events of history and . . . [asked] myself: against which racial element in Germany can I unleash my propaganda of hate with the greatest prospect of success? . . . I came to the conclusion that a campaign against the Jews would be as popular as it would be successful. (quoted in Rose 1990:379)

It was not always (or even usually) anti-Semitism that was the Nazis' most effective theme in garnering popular support. At various times and with different audiences the appeal to nationalism, complaints about the Versailles Treaty, opposition to communism, and proposed solutions to economic problems were more attractive issues. Nevertheless, the Nazi's vehement anti-Semitism was well-known, and supporters were not bothered by this stance, at best.

ORDINARY GERMANS AND THE BANALITY OF EVIL

While Hitler's central role is undeniable, so is the broader range of responsibility for the Holocaust. And this responsibility goes beyond a small inner circle of dedicated Nazi ideologues. Here historians have made us aware of the widespread complicity and active participation of ordinary Germans who voted for Hitler and the Nazi party, provided the state with voluntary denunciations of Jews and anti-Nazi resisters, staffed the bureaucracy of destruction, and directly killed innocent men, women, and children.

As she watched Adolph Eichmann (1906–62) being tried by the Israeli government for war crimes and crimes against humanity, Hannah Arendt (1963) arrived at the view that evil was accomplished in large part by ordinary people acting in ordinary contexts. A former traveling salesman, Eichmann was the leading Nazi expert on Jewish affairs and a key engineer of the Final Solution—the mass extermination of Jews. Psychiatrists at his trial remarked that he seemed clinically well adjusted and has positive relationships with family and friends. Eichmann denied that he held any ill-feeling toward Jews and claimed that he joined the Nazi party to further his career, not to pursue an ideological objective. At the trial he represented himself as an "ordinary bureaucrat" who was carrying out the duties of his office.

As a criminal defense, the "I was only following orders" claim is self-serving and unconvincing, for Eichmann exhibited considerable initiative, zeal, and persistence in helping to plan and carry out the Final Solution. Nonetheless, the banality-of-evil concept helps us see that one did not have to be a madman or monster to perpetuate extraordinary evil. Rather, many individuals did their job (of killing) as if it were the most ordinary thing to do. That they did so, however, should also lead us to ask: Could they have acted otherwise? Why was following orders so commonplace that too few disobeyed? Was anti-Semitism so taken for granted, so much a "natural attitude," that too few thought to question what they were doing?

REFERENCES

Arndt, Hannah (1963). *Eichmann in Jerusalem: A Report on the Banality of Evil*. New York: Viking.

Rose, Paul L. (1990). *Revolutionary Anti-Semitism in Germany: From Kant to Wagner*. Princeton, NJ: Princeton University Press.

Rubenstein, Richard L. and John K. Roth (1987). *Approaches to Auschwitz: The Holocaust and Its Legacy*. Atlanta: John Knox.

Yahill, Leni (1990). *The Holocaust: The Fate of European Jewry*. New York: Oxford University Press.

CPSIA information can be obtained at www.ICGtesting.com
Printed in the USA
LVOW12s0103030715

444797LV00017B/432/P

9 780202 307039